Power, Politics, and Organizations

Power, Politics, and Organizations

A Behavioural Science View

Edited by
ANDREW KAKABADSE
and
CHRISTOPHER PARKER
Crainfield School of Management

JOHN WILEY & SONS
Chichester · New York · Brisbane · Toronto · Singapore

79930

Library of Congress Cataloging in Publication Data:

Kakabadse, Andrew.
    Power, politics, and organizations.

    Includes index.
    1. Organization—Addresses, essays, lectures.
I. Parker, Christopher. II. Title.
HD38.K268 1983   658.4'02   83–14523
ISBN 0 471 90278 0

British Library Cataloguing in Publication Data:

Kakabadse, Andrew
    Power, politics, and organizations.
    1. Power (Social sciences)
    2. Organizations
    I. Title   II. Parker, Christopher
    302.3'5   HM131

    ISBN 0 471 90278 0

Typeset by Input Typesetting Ltd, London SW19 8DR
and printed by the Pitman Press Ltd., Bath, Avon.

Contents

List of Contributors

MARY S. CAVANAUGH, Ph.D *Consultant, Training Service Associates, 2961 North Lakeridge Trail, Boulder, Colorado 80302, USA.*

JOEL R. DELUCA, Ph.D *Human Resources Consultant, The Office of Organization and Management Effectiveness The Sun Company, 100 Matsonford Road, Radnor, Pennsylvannia 19087, USA*

HARRY L. GRAY, Ph.D *Principal Lecturer in Education Management, Faculty of Education, The Polytechnic, Holly Bank Road, Huddersfield*

WILLIAM E. HALAL, Ph.D *Associate Professor of Management, Department of Management Sciences, School of Government and Business Administration, George Washington University, Washington DC, USA*

RONALD G. HARRISON *Lecturer in Administration, Strathclyde Business School, 130 Rotten Row, Glasgow G4 0GE*

ANDREW KAKABADSE, Ph.D *Professor of Management Development, Cranfield School of Management, Cranfield Institute of Technology, Cranfield, Bedford MK43 0AL*

ADRIAN McLEAN *Lecturer in Organization Behaviour, University of Bath, Claverton Down, Bath, BA2 7AY*

CHRISTOPHER PARKER *Director of In-Company Programmes, Cranfield School of Management, Cranfield Institute of Technology, Cranfield, Bedford MK43 0AL*

DOUGLAS C. PITT, Ph.D *Senior Lecturer in Administration, Strathclyde Business School, 130 Rotten Row, Glasgow G4 0GE*

PETER REASON, Ph.D *Lecturer in Organisation Behaviour, Centre for the Study of Organizational Change and Development, University of Bath, Claverton Down, Bath BA2 7AY*

MARGARET RYAN, Ph.D *Lecturer in Business Studies, Bristol Polytechnic, Frenchay, Bristol BS16 1QY*

Introduction

I

The idea for this book and the stimulus to develop it arose from a feeling of dissatisfaction; a dissatisfaction with the behavioural sciences as applied to organizations. Whether examining organizations from a total perspective—organization strategy, organization culture—or from a particular viewpoint—small group behaviour, individual motivation, job design—it is noticeable that numerous writers and researchers have laid great emphasis on exploration and identifying the forces active in a situation, but relatively little on the application of the knowledge they have uncovered. Further, those who write on approaches to the application of behavioural science knowledge in organizations seem to have generated an espoused philosophy of sharing, trust, and care for the others. Such a philosophy is most noticeable amongst the Organization Development (OD) writers and practitioners, but by no means exclusive to them. The writers and researchers examining motivation, job design, and group behaviour equally conclude with similar sentiments—that unless caring, sharing, trusting behaviours are entered into, little of value will emerge from the situation.

As an academic, but also as a practising consultant, I have observed people behaving in non-caring/sharing ways, with no intention of altering their behaviour, not taking much notice of the substantial volume of behavioural science theory generated. In fact, I have noticed people discussing and paying substantial attention to what can be loosely described as 'power and politics in the organization'.

From those occupying roles at the very bottom of the organization hierarchy—cleaners, maintenance operatives—to those at the top, in their boardroom surrounded by the outward trappings of success, possibly the one common element they share is their interest in the power bids and political interactions entered into by various persons in the organization.

Further, from my experience as a consultant, I conclude that few share a common definition of the concepts of power and politics. In fact, irrespective of a person's position in the organization, few even bother to attempt to define power and politics and care even less as to the lack of specificity. It is the emotive element that is of concern. The subjects of power and politics do seem to be able to generate volatile emotions in individuals. It has also surprised me to find that success, achievement, well-conducted tasks at whatever level in the organization seemed to stimulate less excitement and exhilaration than some form of interaction between particular individuals or groups that could be labelled political. From the cleaners who sweep the floors to the directors of the organization, the one topic over which they are most fluent is that of the power/political interactions that they see taking place between people in the organization.

With such experiences in mind, I turned to examine the literature on power and politics in organizations. It is extensive, as can be seen from some of the contributions in this book. Yet many authors feel the need to state that power and politics in organizations is an insufficiently developed, emerging discipline in the behavioural sciences. They are right. Although much has been written, it is still a developing subject area. However, my view is that for any consultant, interventionist, or line manager, the literature is of only limited value. Although some of the definitions of concepts and analyses of case-studies are undoubtedly beneficial, the style of writing is apologetic. It is as if writers and researchers wished they had never entered into the subject area, recognize power and politics to be a valuable area of exploration, but apologise for it being the darker, tainted, underhand side of interpersonal interactions.

The simple response is that power and politics in organizations are not the corrupting and unpleasant side of human nature; they are, as concepts, representing life itself. People, at times, can afford to be open and sharing with each other and at other times find it impossible to adopt such behaviours. Hence, they may search for alternative concepts to help them make sense of their situation or for alternative ways of achieving their particular objectives. The point is that to behave in an open or more calculative way, both extreme forms of behaviour are concerned with involvement; involvement is concerned with influence—influencing others to accept, or at least accommodate, one's own point of view. Hence, for me, behaving in a manner labelled as political is nothing more than a process of influence. On this basis, most aspects of life in organizations can be identified as political.

Bearing in mind my own interpretation of political behaviour in organizations and my view as to its importance concerning life in organizations, Chris Parker and I asked a number of writers to prepare a chapter on power and politics in organizations from their perspective. The contributions were many and varied. Of those finally selected, two broad categories emerged— attempts to understand the nature of power and politics in organizations and attempts to identify strategies for more effective political action and change. Hence we decided that the book should be split into two: Part I, 'Overview of the Concepts', and Part II, 'Applications, Cases, Tales, and Myths'. The chapters themselves are self-contained and best read in that way, without any attempts by us to summarize them.

Finally, it may seem rather odd for the reader to find an introduction in two parts. However, we, the editors, although sharing a common interest, do have clearly identified differences of personal values. In respect to each other, the introduction is written in two halves, with each editor presenting his own values, viewpoint, and reasons for involvement in this project.

ANDREW KAKABADSE

II

Awareness and perception of 'Political Activity' in organizations is increasing, for a number of reasons. In modern, complex organizations, task-related job content appears to be inversely related to hierarchical position. The growing increase in specialisms means that as people move into management or administrative roles further removed from task centres, they tend to engage in goal-directed behaviour, removed from the primary organizational goal. For example, it may become more important for a personnel department to create over-accurate records than to maintain the morale of the workforce.

As people move away from task-oriented centres, there is more emphasis on the social relations content of jobs as opposed to the task content and that means people tend to be negotiating their existence more. As this occurs, there is a great latitude for individuals to determine their own roles and apply their own personal values and beliefs to the way they operate.

As social relations activity increases, tribes and subcultures develop based on different value systems and beliefs about the *raison d'être* of organizations and departments. These subcultures in turn reinforce individuals to maintain or amplify personal-oriented behaviour as opposed to the primary task required by the organization.

The degree to which this becomes 'pathological' is dependent on the context in which it occurs. Various forms of 'mass pathology' have been described. Parkinson's Law described how people make their work expand to full the time available. Offee (1977) argued that within any organization there is the potential for different departments or individuals to be involved in 'task-continuous' and 'task-discontinuous' activities.

Thompson (1961) described the outgrowth of 'task discontinuous' behaviour as 'bureaupathic' with individuals driven more by 'the image of efficiency' rather than by actual effectiveness in the market place.

Macobby (1976) takes this further and contrasts 'craftsmen-type' executives near to the task and concerned with functional job content with the 'gamesmen' who exhibit little interest in functional job content and are more concerned with winning internal battles than with being externally competitive.

As power and influence fluctuates, it is often difficult to separate organizational from non-organizational goals. Whether the latter are illegitimate is debatable. Some current non-organizational goals can be emergent organizational goals, such as future policy in the making.

As complexity increases and degrees of change accelerate, people in organizations find themselves managing more differences than commonalities. People tend to be negotiating their existence and coping with divergent values, goals, and objectives.

It is hardly surprising that the sexiest area in organization psychology is 'politicopathy'. There are a lot of models being formulated, some of which take an individual perspective and others which are concerned with large-scale cultural issues. These models are helpful but it is difficult to find a model that captures the dynamism of 'politicopathy'. Politicopathy occurs in dynamic systems and often involves the manipulation of symbols, myths, and tribal cultures which are often not apparent at first sight.

Often the apologetic nature of some of the writings to which Andrew Kakabadse refers are a product of people external to the system taking snapshots of activity out of context or entering tribes with a hypothesis to prove or a set of beliefs so disparate from the tribe being studied, that 'default reasoning' produces apologetic writing.

'Default reasoning' occurs very simply; it is a powerful, often subconscious mechanism which simply says 'If I perceive something is black, it cannot be white'. 'If I perceive something is a car, it cannot be a wide range of other things.' 'Default reasoning' in organizational politics is simply 'if I am surprised (shocked) by some policy, procedure or another's motives or actions' conscious reasoning runs along the lines 'I don't understand, it must be political'. Then 'default reasoning' operates—'political, ignore', 'political, nasty', or 'politics, can't play, won't play'. It is this 'default reasoning' which is damaging. It leads to 'ostrich-like' behaviour—'bury your head in the sand only to have your rear end kicked by politicians'. Perhaps the most damaging aspect of this ostrich-like behaviour is that it mostly occurs as a response to imposed change or during lobbying and the build up to internal change.

The degree to which the number of non-task-discontinuous functions have increased in organizations means that the potential for value differences or belief clashes has increased and led to increased 'politico-pathology'. My interest and motivation in this area is the whole notion of 'politico-pathology' and the 'default reasoning' linked to it. My primary concern is that many competent, capable managers create unnecessary internal barriers to their development because they view too many organizational occurrences as political-pathological. This is especially true of those involved in task-continuous jobs. The 'default reasoning' of pathology linked with politics does not help individuals to cope effectively and to be externally competent.

A large number of individuals need to accept the process of political influence as a fact of modern organizational life. Often a problem for these people is that even the slightest divergence from task is pathological and 'default reasoning' operates—'I can't do anything about it' and the situation gets worse. These people need most of all to understand the processes of politics as opposed simply to reacting to its outcomes. In understanding these processes, I think models are important but I believe the most useful work in the area is descriptive, ethnomethodological, and ecologically based, that is to say detailed description of internal and external contexts.

Describing politics as it happens in tribes and cultures in a dynamic and changing environment is perhaps the most effective way of helping individuals to understand more about the process and how to manage it. This is because politics in organizations is more the manipulation of symbols and metaphors, myths and legends; the interpretation of facts rather than facts themselves. These features are best understood by accurate description, unhindered by 'default reasoning', and from this useful models can then be built.

Value-free research in the social sciences is impossible but there is currently a great deal of value-laden work in the area of organizational politics which does little to help people overcome their own 'default reasoning'. For me, the type of description in Part II of this book is more what is needed so that individuals can better understand political processes and maybe manage value and belief differences more effectively.

CHRISTOPHER PARKER

REFERENCES

Macobby, M. (1976). *The Gamesman*, New York: Simon & Schuster.
Offee, K. (1977). *Industry and Inequality: The Achievement Principle In Work and Social Status*, New York: St. Martins Press.
Thompson, V. A. (1961). *Modern Organisations*, New York: Alfred A Knopf.

PART I

Overview of the Concepts

Power, Politics, and Organizations: A Behavioural Science View
Edited by Andrew Kakabadse and Christopher Parker
© 1984 John Wiley & Sons Ltd

Chapter 1

A Typology of Social Power

MARY S. CAVANAUGH

INTRODUCTION

As physical power—energy—becomes a moving force of the 1980s, social power and its manifestation in both interpersonal and organizational sittings is emerging as a critical variable. The study of power and its role within social relationships has been hindered by a literature which is diffuse and an application which has been idosyncratic to individual needs. This chapter examines present and past research on the concept of power. In the course of this review several conceptual frameworks emerge and provide a vehicle for collapsing a variety of theoretical approaches into a more workable system. This typology addresses power in light of the following five categories: (1) power as a characteristic of the individual; (2) power as an interpersonal construct; (3) power as a commodity; (4) power as a causal construct; and (5) power as a philosophical construct. The purpose of this presentation is to bring refinement and clarity to the application of the variable of power within social science research.

In 1938 Bertrand Russell predicted that the concept of 'power' would emerge as a fundamental issue in the social sciences. Since that prediction, forty years of research and theorizing have not yet produced a single, uniform conceptualization of power. Statements such as 'power permeates all human action. . .' (Clark, 1974, p. 74), or 'power, in short, is a universal phenomenon in human activities and in all social relationships' (Bierstedt, 1950, p. 730) are commonly found throughout the power literature. Bierstedt (1950) used an appropriate analogy when he asserted, 'We may say about it (power) in general only what St. Augustine said about time, that we all know perfectly well what it is—until someone asks us' (p. 730). Like time, power is an overlearned concept deeply embedded in our culture. Individuals tend to define power in highly idiosyncratic terms. Many social science researchers operationalize the variable 'power' based on preconceived notions, individual intuition, or personal dogma (Nagel, 1975).

If it is acknowledged that social power is a concept embedded in our culture, its potency as an underlying force within many interpersonal and organizational relationships must also be acknowledged. However, the role of power within these interactions will be difficult to pinpoint without a more systematic means of operationalizing the concept. Unfortunately, scholars have been unable to bring clarity to the study of the phenomenon of power. The research remains 'scattered, heterogeneous, and even chaotic' (Cartwright, 1965, p. 3). A recent examination (Cavanaugh, 1979) of the power literature produced a typological framework which may be useful for facilitating clarification and delineation of the amorphous nature of the concept of power. It does not provide a single definition, but it collapses dozens of definitions into a workable system.

Cavanaugh's division of the power literature into various frameworks or typologies is not a new approach. Clark (1968), Schopler (1965), and Cartwright (1965) have organized the power literature into systematic categories. However, it has been twelve years since those studies and the scope and breadth of the information and research on power has grown enormously.

The magnitude of the current examination required the creation of a category system which could realistically encompass the depth of the accumulated literature on power. This category system initially grew out of the discovery of three trends in the literature. First, power was discussed in several individual and interpersonal contexts. Second, in order to facilitate the measurement of power, it was discussed in either an economic or a causal framework. Third, a significant number of authors chose to discuss power in strictly philosophical terms. As each of these three trends was refined, a total of five distinct conceptual frameworks emerged: (1) power as a characteristic of the individual; (2) power as an interpersonal construct; (3) power as a commodity; (4) power as a causal construct; and (5) power as a philosophical construct. Each framework illustrates unique dimensions of the concept of power. These dimensions allow the term to be defined more appropriately within the context in which it is being used. By increasing the specificity of the concept of power, it becomes a more interpretable variable.

POWER AS A CHARACTERISTIC OF THE INDIVIDUAL

Power as a highly personal attribute emerged as the first conceptual framework of this typology. Characteristic of this segment of the literature is a discussion of power as it is situated in a single actor, and includes the personal nature of power, the notion of power as a person-environment interaction, and the interpretation of power through the concept of power motive.

Several scholars suggested that the locus of power resides within the individual (Hillenbrand, 1949; Guardini, 1961; Votaw, 1966). The exercise of power is ascribed to individuals, not institutions. It has been described as a 'specifically human phenomenon' (Guardini, 1961, p. 3) and Chein (1978) went so far as to postulate that the desire for power is inherent to the nature of man. Without a personal intent, power could not exist. As Berle (1969) summarized, 'Power is an attribute of man. It does not exist without a holder' (p. 60).

The intensely personal nature of power brought with it a paradox. Both Sampson (1965) and Adler (1966) described the dilemma in terms of power as a compensatory mechanism. For Sampson, the individual search for power occurred 'not so much from a positive love of power, but from the fear that they [an individual] will be insecure or impotent without it' (p. 235). Adler expanded upon power as a compensatory mechanism. The objects of individual striving were attempts to overcome insecurity and weakness and the desire for personal power became 'one of the concretizations of the striving for perfection' (p. 170).

There were those, however, who took issue with Sampson's and Adler's positions. Ogletree (1971) argued for a more positive feeling about the desire for power. He maintained that the manifestation of power reflected an ability to 'mobilize your own life resources to levels of peak effectiveness' (p. 47). In this sense, personal power is linked to self-actualization of one's potential. May (1972) was also concerned with this 'power to be' (p. 140). He saw individuals using their power as one means of ensuring survival. Some investigations of the personal nature of power moved beyond the presence of a human factor. It became manifested in the interaction between an individual and his or her environment. Minton (1967) defined this power perspective as the 'ability to cause environmental changes so as to obtain an intended effect' (p. 229). Heider (1958), Kahm (1963), de Charms (1968), and Haley (1969) all equated degrees of individual power with a person's ability to manipulate his (or her) surroundings and establish himself as either a change agent (de Charmes, 1968) or 'as the one who is to determine what is going to happen' (Haley, 1969, p. 36).

Within an organizational environment a powerful individual is seen as one who has the 'ability to get things done' (Kanter, 1977, p. 166) and this ability comes from an understanding of the environment. Kotter (1979) characterized effective managers as those individuals who understood their organizational environment so perfectly that they were able to use different types of power appropriately to achieve the desired outcomes.

The third perspective associated with power as a personal characteristic focuses on the satisfaction of particular personal wants or desires of an individual, but does not necessarily link the manifestation of power to the manipulation of an external environment.

The concept of power motive has been approached from several different directions. Veroff (1957) and Kipnis (1974) described power motivations as either a 'need state' (Kipnis) or a 'disposition' (Veroff) which could be satisfied only through control or influence over another individual.

Several years later, Veroff moved away from an emphasis on control to a definition of the power motive as a 'stable affective orientation to power goals' (Veroff and Veroff, 1972, p. 280). This was similar to Minton's (1972) analysis of the power motive. However, Minton distinguished between an intrinsic and an extrinsic nature to the power motive. The intrinsic power motive was the seeking of power through self-initiated efforts where the reward was a feeling of self-determination. The extrinsic power motive saw power as being sought as a reward external to any self-initiated efforts.

The most definitive work done with the power motive has been by Winter (1973) and McClelland (1970, 1975). Winter described the power motive as 'a disposition to strive for certain kinds of goals, or to be affected by certain kinds of incentives'. Whereas Veroff (1957) and Kipnis (1974) required the control or influence of the behaviour of others, Winter did not place that limitation on his conceptualization. For Winter the power motive was found by examining the 'thoughts, images, and themes in the minds of people when power is aroused or made salient to them' (1973, p. 10). Results of his research indicated that the power motive could be distinguished as an approach to or 'hope of power' or an avoidance of or 'fear of power'.

Similarly, McClelland made the distinction between a personalized face of power and a socialized face of power. McClelland (1970) characterized the personalized face of power as the negative aspect where power struggles were seen as 'I win, you lose' situations. The socialized face of power was considered more positive, reflecting a concern for group goals and making members within a group sense their own levels of strength and competence. It was McClelland's belief that managers reflecting a socialized face of power would be more effective. Later research findings led him to conclude that personalized power was a less mature stage of power development than socialized power (1975).

McClelland's (1975) later research also broadened the conceptualization of the power motive. This new focus on the power motive went beyond the presence of control of others or the existence of specific goals for the powerholder to a discussion of power as a 'thought about someone *having* impact' (p. 7). This concern for impact could be manifested in three ways: (1) through strong, direct action involving control or influence; (2) through the production of actions which could produce an emotional response in another individual; and (3) as a concern for reputation.

Summary

The central theme of this first conceptual framework centres around the importance of the individual as a catalyst in the manifestation of power. According to these scholars, power has no reality unless there is human activation and involvement. Interaction with the *environment* rather than interaction with other *persons* becomes pivotal. Indeed, the emergence of a power motive moves the conceptualization of power beyond control of others to the importance of the individual perceiving himself as having an impact. The interpretation of power as an intensely personal characteristic may be responsible for the connection between power and charisma. It also may foster the belief that when an individual is perceived as powerful he or she will carry that sense of power into a variety of situations. In that sense, power gains a kind of mobility rather than being only situation-specific.

POWER AS AN INTERPERSONAL CONSTRUCT

This second conceptual framework enlarges the previous concept of power as a personality attribute to power as an attribute of social relationships. Typically these scholars believed the consideration of power as a personal attribute constituted a major flaw in power research (Emerson, 1962). Dornbusch and Scott (1975) maintained 'it is always a simplification to speak only of *A*'s power, and to do so is to court danger'. Schopler (1965), Clark (1968) and Bell (1975) all stipulated that a power act required the presence of at least two actors; and Koehler, Anatol, and Applbaum (1976) saw power as an 'inherent' (p. 102) quality within that interaction.

Examining power within a social matrix required that the role of the target of the power relation be considered. The target's role was characterized by two main approaches. The first approach came under the rubric of a field-theoretic conceptualization of power. Here the concern centred around how much change *A* could induce *B* over and above *B*'s resistance. *B*'s perceptions of *A* also played an important role. The second approach focused on the reciprocal nature of power and 'on the nature of the outcomes each participant can provide for the other' (Schopler, 1965, p. 190). This approach was concerned only secondarily with the amount of change or the resistance to that change by the target. This approach built upon Lewinian field theory in which psychological forces produced a tendency toward change in some property of the life space of an individual (Lewin, 1951). Power is seen to exist within a social matrix, and consideration would be given to the extent of change *A* could induce in *B* over and above *B*'s resistance. Lippitt, Polansky, and Rosen (1952) were the first to apply this theory to social power. Social power became an individual potential for producing forces in other persons which would facilitate those other persons to act in a certain way or to change in a given direction. Cartwright (1959) refined this position by presenting power as 'those psychological forces acting in P's life space which are activated by agents other than P' (p. 218). He placed six boundaries on the domain of a power relation. First, power was placed within a dyadic relation where the two agents were of central importance. Second, the concern about power became the maximum amount of influence an agent had over a target *at a given time and in a given direction*. Third, only those forces of the agent that could activate forces within the target were important. Fourth, since the agent's force must tap a motive base within the target, a part of the agent's power was determined by motivational states of the target. Fifth, the power which an agent may have over a target could constitute a threat for that target. Sixth, the actual exercise of power required the performance of certain acts. Wolfe (1959), Levinger (1959), and Tannenbaum (1962) supported these boundaries but also emphasized the importance of the agent being *perceived* as the source of power by the target.

In establishing their bases of social power, French and Raven (1959) also relied on a field-theoretic definition. They defined power in terms of influence. Influence, in turn, was defined as psychological change. Psychological change included not only overt behavioural changes in the target, but also changes in attitudes, opinions, goals, values, and needs. Unlike Cartwright and Wolfe, French and Raven made a specific point of asserting that their theory was concerned *only* with an agent's impact on the target—not with the target's own forces nor with forces on the target from sources other than the agent. Their position was that if these two forces interfered too strongly, it could be said that a power relationship did not exist.

French and Raven (1959) concluded there were five bases of social power: (1) reward; (2) coercive; (3) legitimate; (4) referent; and (5) expert. Later, Raven (1965) added information power as a sixth base. Three of these bases of power (reward, coercive, and informational power) focused on the powerholder and his or her ability to change the behaviour of the target despite resistance by the target. The other three bases (legitimate, referent, and expert) placed part of the success of the powerholder on the perceptions the target had about him or her.

The field-theoretic model is concerned with perceived resources and target resistance. It makes an implicit statement regarding the reciprocal nature of the power relationship. The second model directly acknowledges the reciprocity of a power relationship. Bannester (1969) linked the perception of power to the perceived importance of the powerholder's resources. He called that condition 'socio-motive power' (p. 374). This entity emerged as the 'disposal' of a 'scarce resource' where the resource did not necessarily have an 'objective reality so long as it is perceived as such' (p. 374). Bannester, like Cartwright, did require that this resource have relevancy and value to the target and access and control over such resources resulted in a manifestation of power.

Lehman (1969) also discussed various aspects of power in terms of the possession of resources. First, he spoke about the 'resource basis of power' which was the control of sufficient resources on the part of the powerholder to impose his will upon others. Second, he spoke of the 'symbolic bases of power' by which the target attributes the possession of such resources to the powerholder, thus giving him or her the ability or right to impose his or her will (p. 454). Martin (1971) acknowledged that *B*'s resistance must be considered, but felt this could lead to a narrow interpretation of the power relation. He felt 'that power relations may be relations of mutual convenience; power may be a resource facilitating the achievement of the goals of both A and B. . .' (p. 243). In other words, 'One cannot develop his own power if he thinks only in unilateral terms and is unwilling to give others an opportunity to influence him' (Gross, 1968, p. 84). Adams (1975) also viewed power as reciprocal. He believed that 'both members of the relationship act in terms of their own self-interest and, specifically, do so in terms of the controls that each has over matters of interest to the other' (p. 22).

Thibaut and Kelley (1959) placed 'matters of interest' into an outcome matrix. Power thus became 'A's ability to affect the quality of outcomes attained by B' (1959, p. 101). According to Thibaut and Kelley power is exercised through either 'fate control' or 'behavior control'. By invoking 'fate control', *A* could affect *B*'s outcomes no matter how *B* behaved in response. This was accomplished by *A* supplying desired rewards to *B* with the minimum of inhibitory or cost factors to *A* (p. 102). The use of 'behavior control' produced an interaction effect. This interaction resulted from *B*'s awareness of *A*'s influence attempt and *B*'s ability to interfere or facilitate the outcome of that attempt. As a result, *A* might have to modify his or her behaviour accordingly in order to achieve the intended outcome. The outcome of the entire power act thus became a product of the interaction between *A*'s behaviour choices and the behaviour choices of *B* (p. 103).

Michener and Suchner (1972) also were interested in the reciprocal nature of a power relation and the importance of the outcomes. Unlike the field-theoretic approach, the importance of the powerholder's rather than the target's ability to resist became an important consideration. Michener and Suchner saw power as something which combined a 'capacity to influence' others with a 'capacity to resist' influence of others. Power emerged as an ability to deny desired outcomes (p. 239). Their position was similar to Eskola's (1961) notion that, practically speaking, power was only relative. In other words, Eskola examined the power *A* had over *B in relation to* the power *B* had over *A*.

Emerson (1962, 1964) approached the reciprocal aspect of a power relation by defining a social relationship in general as 'ties of mutual dependence' (1962, p. 32) where the manifestation of power was implicit in that dependency relationship. This dependency was directly proportional to the amount of motivational investment a target had in the outcome or goals that were mediated by the powerholder, and was inversely proportional to how available these goals or outcomes were outside of the present relationship between the powerholder and the target. If the goals were not important to the target or were readily available from someone other than the powerholder, the power of that source would considerably diminish. Emerson's concept of dependency paralleled Lasswell's (1948) and Martin and Sims' (1956) much earlier descriptions of power. Lasswell (1948) described it as:

> Power is an interpersonal situation; those who hold power are empowered. They depend upon and continue only so long as there is a continuing stream of empowering responses. Even a casual inspection of human relations will convince any competent observer that power is not a brick that can be lugged from place to place, but a process that vanishes when the supporting responses cease. (p. 10)

Martin and Sims (1956) presented a similar conceptualization of power. They maintained that 'men can only exercise that power which they are allowed by other men. . .' (p. 25).

Summary

The placement of power within the boundaries of an interpersonal relationship produces dimensions of power not present in the first framework. First, the agent must see himself or herself as having the ability to move forces within another individual. In order to do this, the source must correctly sort out which resources he or she possesses are important to which targets in what types of situations. Second, the perceptions of the target about the resources available to an agent must be considered. The importance of the target's perceptions underscores the probability that a power relationship should be considered reciprocal. This reciprocity is generated by either the desire by both parties to achieve valued outcomes or the existence of a mutual dependency between the two parties. A 'give and take' sense about power is beginning to emerge and crystallizes in the next conceptual framework.

POWER AS A COMMODITY

The third category of this typology develops from the interpersonal construct framework. While both are social matrix models, the nature of the power relationship is considered transactional in the commodity framework, rather than interactional as in the interpersonal construct framework. Generally, power is discussed in economic terms and treated as something that must be expended in order for an individual to manifest power. Central to this framework is the 'cost' involved in maintaining power and how that affects the behaviour of the powerholder. Not only is the *possession* of resources important, but also the value of those resources to the powerholder has to be considered. Resources are often scarce and individuals cannot possess everything they want. As a result, people are forced into a choice situation where one valued resource must be given up or exchanged in order to obtain another. The manifestation of power is inherent in this exchange.

Harsanyi (1962) was one of the first to examine the costs of power. As an essential dimension of power relations, Harsanyi distinguished between the *costs* of A having power over B and the *strength* of A's power over B. The *cost* of A having power over B was simply what it took from A's resources to influence B's behaviour. The *strength* of A's power over B included what it would cost B to refuse to do what A wanted. This approach to an understanding of power was particularly useful in making comparisons of degrees of power. In other words, if one individual can accomplish something at far less cost and with less resistance than another individual, the former can be said to possess greater power than the latter.

Baldwin's (1971) cost analysis focused on the agent's ability to preserve an 'essential structure' (p. 154) during the exercise of power. He presented four techniques an agent could use to influence a target. First, the agent could provide either an unconditional reward or a punishment. In either event, whether the target complied or not, the agent had incurred the 'cost'. Second, the agent might only pass on information (or misinformation) to the target. Whether the target complied or not, the agent still incurred the 'cost' of the communication effort. Third, the agent might rely on his legitimate authority to exert power. In this instance obtaining that legitimate authority initially might have been costly to the agent. Finally, the agent's commitment to a reward or punishment could be conditional. This was the only technique where the cost to the agent was solely determined by the target's compliance or non-compliance.

Breed (1971) presented a similar position. He saw the application of power as involving three different levels of cost: 'of the assets "consumed" as power is generated; of the power itself as it is spent; and of symbolic gestures which, the more often they are used, tend to hasten the point of actual expenditure' (p. 126).

Access to and control of resources is central to this framework. Burt (1977) assumed 'that actors are purposive in that they use their control of resources in order to improve their individual well-being. . .' (p. 6). He felt that by defining influence as the possession of resources and the ability to constrain the allocation of those resources, one could make more accurate predictions about the ability of an actor to realize his or her own interests despite resistance from other actors. Control and access to resources, particularly information, were keys to individual power within an organization. Powerful managers acquired resources by establishing lines of supply, lines of information, and lines of support. The ability to acquire resources which enhanced the managers' and their departments' positions contributed to the overall perception of a particular manager as powerful (Kanter, 1979).

Homans' (1958) exchange theory concretizes the interpretation of power as a commodity. In other words: 'For a person engaged in exchange, what he gives may be a cost to him, just as what he gets may be a reward, and his behavior changes less as profit, that is, reward less cost, tends to a maximum' (p. 606). Conversely, the greater the amount of activity or behaviour change required in an exchange, the more the 'negative value' (p. 97) increases and the less likely it is that an individual will engage in that activity. Powerful individuals are able to use power with the least amount of negative value. Thibaut and Kelley (1959), Tedeschi, Schlenker, and Lindskold (1972), and Koehler, Anatol, and Applbaum (1976) employed Homans' theory in discussing the acquisition and use of power. Each one emphasized that the exercise of power is not 'free' and an agent must consider the impact his (or her) use of power may have on his position. Stated another way, 'having power is thus being in a position to get others to do what one wants them to without having to make unacceptable sacrifices. The more the behaviour of others can be shaped to one's wants, and the less one gives up to achieve this, the more power one has' (Champlin, 1971, p. 94).

Summary

The transactional nature of power as a commodity is reflected in several ways. First, the acquisition of power can be considered an investment by the source. Second, because investment is involved, the source must weigh the trade-offs and costs required in the use of power or the maintenance of a power position. Third, the higher the cost of manifesting power, the less likely it is that an individual will invoke its use. These first three conceptual frameworks have concentrated on power either as an individual attribute or as an attribute of social relationships. The next framework examines power as a causal agent within relationships.

POWER AS A CAUSAL CONSTRUCT

Power as a causal construct is primarily concerned with developing specificity in the operational aspects of power. Researchers felt that by placing power within a causal framework, it would become less of an abstract notion and would thus lend itself to operationalization and study by more traditional empirical techniques.

Unlike the field-theoretic conceptualization of power, the importance of the target's perceptions is minimized within the causal interpretation and the uni-directional aspects of power become a prime consideration. Although Simon (1957) warned of the problems of asymmetry and causality within the social sciences, there were those who operationalized power through its link with causality. March (1955) pointed out that in order to explain observed events, there had to be a unique and specific ordering to them. For March, this meant considering power as an asymmetric relation. Both Oppenheim (1961) and Baldus (1975) argued that power as a causal relationship was the most concrete level of examination.

Nagel (1975) also believed the only viable definition of power was to treat it as a type of causation. He based his position on four arguments. First, there were many similarities between causation and power. For example, both denoted relations between or among individuals and both were asymmetric. Second, when power was viewed as a causal concept rather than a value or a resource, tautologies could be avoided. Third, by treating power as a type of causation, a wider range of empirical methods and statistical procedures could be employed. Finally, a causal theory could still account for the potentiality of power. For example, 'he can cause' as potential power, 'he will cause' as predicted power, and 'he did cause' as actual power (p. 8). Based on this argument, Nagel defined an actual or potential power relation as 'an actual or potential causal relation between the preferences of an actor regarding an outcome and the outcome itself' (p. 29).

Riker (1964) was also interested in power as an asymmetric, causal phenomenon. He maintained that 'power is the ability to exercise influence while cause is the actual exercise of it' (p. 347). Riker attempted to reconcile several different definitions of power and concluded that these differences could be attributed to differences in notions of causality. He contended that the agent's interest in the ultimate outcome of the power situation was parallel to the type of causality operating within that situation.

Riker envisioned two specific power outcomes emerging from two distinct types of causality. One was 'other-oriented' and emphasized the disutility of some other *person*. In this instance the causal relationship involved a manipulated variable which was presumed to cause an intended outcome. If no manipulation occurred, then no causal relationship existed. The second outcome was 'ego-oriented' and the emphasis was on controlling the *interaction*, thus enhancing the agent's position. Necessary and sufficient causality provided the underpinnings of this power outcome. When necessary and sufficient condition causality operated, the attention was on a full explanation of the outcome. The effect itself became the focal point, not the manipulation of a variable to produce that effect.

Several scholars discussed the causal nature of power within a probability context. Power was thus defined as 'the ability of one person or group of persons to . . . change the probabilities that others will respond in certain ways to specified stimuli' (Kahn and Boulding, 1964, p. 12).

Simon (1957), Dahl (1957), and Oppenheim (1961) provided the earliest discussions of the probability aspect of power. They observed that if A's action did not increase the probability of B doing response X, then it could be said that A had no power over B for that action and that response.

Gamson (1974) and Schopler and Layton (1974) expanded the notion of subjective probability and the power relation. Gamson determined that the conceptualization of power as a change in probability was reflected in terms of how much and what kind of power an agent had over the domain of the target's decisions. He pointed out two different types of probability which formed a basis for measuring the exercise of power. The first type was the probability that a person would choose a given alternative *prior* to an alleged exercise of power. The second type was the probability that a person would choose a given alternative *after* an alleged exercise of power. Gamson concluded: 'Power has been successfully exercised if and only if there is a difference between time one and time two described above' (p. 21). He saw this notion of subjective probability as a potentially reliable, stable measure of power.

Schopler and Layton (1974) argued a position quite similar to Gamson. According to them, the 'maximum attributed power exists when B does something unpredictable which is perfectly predictable from A's intervention' (p. 40). Although Schopler and Layton had not directly tested their subjective probability concept of power empirically, they did apply it *ex post facto* to other power research and express 'guarded optimism' (p. 56) that it would be useful to future research on power.

Shapley and Shubik (1954) discussed power within a slightly different probabilistic context. They based their definition of power on the mathematical theory of games. They defined power of an individual as depending 'on the chance he has of being critical to the success of a winning coalition' (p. 787). All that was required to obtain an index of the power of an individual was to examine the number of times that individual was part of a group whose votes were *pivotal* to decisions made. Thus, a power index 'measures the number of times that the action of the individual actually changes the state of affairs' (p. 788). A member's vote was considered pivotal when he was the last member whose support was needed in order to assure passage of a given measure.

Summary

The notion of power as interactive or transactive disappears from this framework. By linking power with cause, specific behaviours of the source are interpreted to elicit certain responses from the target. The greater the probability of a source's ability to elicit specific responses from the target, the higher the degree of power which can be ascribed to that source. In this framework, quantities of power can now be determined. The last conceptual category of this typology moves the discussion of power out of the quantitative into the qualitative.

POWER AS A PHILOSOPHICAL CONSTRUCT

Much of the literature discussed power from a philosophical point of view. Within this fifth and final framework, several issues emerged. The first issue dealt with the morality or amorality of power. A second issue discussed power relative to values or value systems. A third issue focused on the relationship between power and responsibility. A final issue brought out the effect of social norms on public declarations about power.

With regard to the morality or amorality of power, Hobbes (1971) felt that '*the power of a man*, universally, is his present means to obtain some future apparent good. . .' (p. 75). In direct contract to that belief is Reich's (1970) contention that the fact power exists at all constitutes an evil. Generally power was seen as having an equal potential for good or evil. Either human intervention or circumstance would determine in which direction a power act would move (Rosinski, 1965; Sampson, 1965, Clark, 1974).

Votaw (1966), however, made an important distinction. He felt: 'A man who believes power to be essentially evil will approach the issues of power in a very different way from the man who sees power as a resource of human society, albeit subject to abuse' (p. 72).

A second issue which emerged from the philosophical components of the power literature is related to values and value systems. Kahn and Boulding (1964) postulated that different approaches to value systems would be reflected in different power patterns or the way an individual would choose to exercise power. One approach to values emphasized the individual's subjective feelings about them. A person with this approach would always be looking for 'what's in it for me' in a situation. He or she would want to arrange a power relation to be sure there would be 'something in it' for the target in order to make compliance enticing. A second approach completely depersonalized values. All choices made by an individual were governed by force. This individual would choose a coercive power mode and would try to legitimize power on the basis of an ideology rather than personal traits. A third approach to value systems presented by Kahn and Boulding reflected the middle ground to the previous extremes. In the relativist approach values became objective and grounded within the situation. An individual subscribing to this approach would choose to ground power in terms of expertise and would try to have others understand the situation as he or she did.

Berle (1969) also acknowledged the importance of a value system. He felt that power had to be considered in relation to a companion system of ideas and that the powerholder has to accept these formally and sincerely. Unfortunately this interdependency created an internal dilemma for an individual in a power position. The pragmatic exercise of power often was held to be in conflict with philosophical principles. Rubinoff (1968) saw this conflict as leading to the use and enjoyment of power for its own sake.

The value orientation of power for its own sake was, of course, not a new approach. The unyielding and purposive pursuit of power found its spokesperson in Machiavelli. Many individuals today embrace power as Machiavelli counselled several hundred years ago. . . 'that a wise prince must rely on what is in his power and not on what is in the power of others . . .' (1950, p. 63).

Closely related to the issues of values and value systems is the relationship between power and responsibility. Gross (1968) saw this relationship as paradoxical. He felt power could either be a corrupting force that would diminish responsibility, or power could serve to increase the amount of responsibility. In other words, by accepting great amounts of responsibility an individual also accepted the power that would be necessary to take the actions that went along with the responsibility. Rosinski (1965) best characterizes the paradox. He maintained that 'the counterpart of power is responsibility. Just as every individual has power, every individual has responsibility' (p. 197).

Berle (1969) envisioned the relationship between power and responsibility as crucial. According to Berle: 'Power is invariably confronted with, and acts on the presence of a field of responsibilty' (p. 115). He saw this 'field' developing between the powerholder and those that were affected by the power. Berle described this field of responsibility as a basic issue within democracy and as a 'high court of appeal' (p. 121) whose judgments provided checks and balances on the powerholders. The relationship between power and responsibility was directly proportional. 'The greater the power, the wider the field of responsibility. . .' (p. 121).

The fourth philosophical issue involved social norms which focused on either discussing power in general or publicly stating a desire for power.

Gross (1968) characterized the social attitude about power with an interesting analogy. As he put it: 'Power, like sex under the Victorians, has often been regarded as a subject not to be openly discussed but rather to be sought, thought about and used under the cover of darkness' (p. 77). McClelland (1975) declared that social norms have 'dampened and controlled' (p. 6) how an individual could express an interest in power activities. He contended that society would tend to regulate power-motivated behaviour because of its potential disruptive effect on society. He pointed out that an individual quickly learned that to act on behalf of others was legitimate, but to act on behalf of oneself was not. 'People are suspicious of a person who wants power, even if he wants it for sincere and altruistic reasons. He is often socially conditioned to be suspicious of himself' (1975, p. 256). This societal pressure leads individuals to talk about a desire for power in terms of wanting a challenge, or wanting to be a manager or other kind of leader, or as wanting something important to do (Hicks and Gullett, 1975).

Summary

This qualitative examination of power adds new dimensions. The role of individual or circumstantial intervention is presented as a determinant in the goodness or badness of a power outcome. Critical to that movement is the impact of value systems. This framework also illustrates the paradox of power and responsibility. The two are inextricably intertwined and each places a tremendous burden on the other. In addition to this paradox, the conflict between claiming power as a personal goal and social norms against such an expression becomes apparent. Although an individual may desire power, it is not always socially acceptable to admit such aspirations publicly.

Clearly, physical power—energy—has become a critical issue of the 1980s. It also appears that the study and discussion of social power is beginning to emerge from its Victorian age. As social scientists learn more about inter-personal and organization dynamics, the centrality of power to these dynamics and its manifestations within interpersonal and organizational interactions becomes more apparent. As Benson (1978) points out, power appears to be a 'basic explanatory variable' (p. 128) of all social relationships.

The typology presented here, however, illuminates the multifaceted nature of the concept of power. Each of the five frameworks represents a particular theoretical viewpoint about power. None of the frameworks are discrete. Theoretical components of one can be uncovered in any of the others. Yet the recognition of varying dimensions related to the concept of power will provide a means by which social scientists are able to focus on a particular aspect of power as it is relevant to a specific research question. Power can then be defined and applied as it relates to a given context, rather than on an *a priori* or idiosyncratic basis. This typology provides a system for approaching the analysis of social power without becoming overwhelmed by the magnitude of information available. As more is learned about the concept, scientists will be able to refine the use of the variable of power and apply it more precisely in their research.

REFERENCES

Adams, R. N. (1975). *Energy and Structure: A Theory of Social Power*, Austin, Texas: University of Texas Press.

Adler, A. (1966). The psychology of power, *Journal of Individual Psychology*, **22**, 166–172.

Baldus, B. (1975). The study of power: suggestions for an alternative, *Canadian Journal of Sociology*, **1**, 179–201.

Baldwin, D. A. (1971). The costs of power, *Journal of Conflict Resolution*, **15**, 145–155.

Bannester, E. M. (1969). Sociodynamics: an intergrative theorem of power, authority, influence and love, *American Sociological Review*, **34**, 374–393.

Bell, D. (1975). *Power, Influence and Authority*, New York: Oxford University Press.

Benson, D. E. (1978). Socio-psychological perspectives of power, *The Social Science Journal*, **15**, 122–128.

Berle, A. (1969). *Power*, New York: Harcourt, Brace & World.

Bierstadt, R. (1950). An analysis of social power, *American Sociological Review*, **15**, 730–738.

Breed, W. (1971), *The Self-guiding Society*, New York: The Free Press.

Burt, R. S. (1977). Power in a social topology, *Social Science Research*, **6**, 1–83.

Cartwright, D. (1959). A field theoretical conception of power in D. Cartwright (ed.), *Studies in Social Power*, Ann Arbor, Michigan: University of Michigan.

——(1965). Influence, leadership, control, in J. G. March (ed.), *Handbook of Organizations*, Chicago: Rand McNally & Company.

Cavanaugh, M. (1979). A formulative investigation of power orientations and preliminary validation of relationships between power orientations and communication behavior. Unpublished doctoral dissertation, University of Denver.

Champlin, J. (1971). On the study of power, *Politics and Society*, **1**, 91–111.

Chein, I. (1970). The concept of power, in F. F. Korten, S. W. Cook, and J. J. Lacey (eds.), *Psychology and the Problems of Society*, Washington: APA.

Clark, K. (1974). *Pathos of Power*, New York: Harper and Row.

Clark, T. N. (1968). The concept of power, in T. Clark (ed.), *Community Structure and Decision Making: Comparative Analysis*, San Francisco: Chandler Publishing.

Dahl, R. A. (1957). The concept of power, *Behavioral Science*, **2**, 201–215.

de Charms, R. (1968). *Personal Causation*, New York: Academic Press.

Dornbusch, S. and Scott, W. R. (1975). *Evaluation and Exercise of Authority*, San Francisco: Jossey-Bass.

Emerson, R. A. (1962). Power-dependence relations, *American Sociological Review*, **27**, 31–41.

——(1964). Power-dependence relations: two experiments, *Sociometry*, **27**, 282–298.

Eskola, A. (1961). *Social Influence and Power in Two-person Groups*. Transactions of the Westmarck Society, Vol. VI. Transl. by J. Railo, Munksgaard, Finland: Turun Saromalenti ja Kirjapaino Osakeyhtio.

French, Jr., J. R. B. and Raven, B. (1959). The bases of social power, in D. Cartwright (ed.), *Studies in Social Power*, Ann Arbor, Michigan: University of Michigan.

Gamson, W. (1974). Power and probability, in J. T. Tedeschi (ed.), *Perspectives on Social Power*, Chicago: Aldine.

Gross, G. M. (1968). *Organizations and their Managing*, New York: The Free Press.

Guardini, R. (1961). *Power and Responsibility: A Course of Action for the New Age*, Chicago: Henry Regnery.

Haley, J. (1969). *The Power Tactics of Jesus Christ and Other Essays*, New York: Grossman.

Harsanyi, J. E. (1962). Measurement of social power, opportunity costs, and the theory of two-person bargaining games, *Behavior Science*, **7**, 67–80.

Heider. F. (1958). *The Psychology of Interpersonal Relations*, New York: John Wiley.

Hicks, H. and Gullett, C. R. (1975). *Organizations: Theory and Behavior*, New York: McGraw-Hill.

Hillenbrand, J. J. (1949). *Power and Morals*, Chicago: Columbia University Press.

Hobbes, T. (1971). Of power, in J. R. Champlin (ed.), *Power*, New York: Atherton Press.

Homans, G. C. (1958). Social behavior as exchange, *American Journal of Sociology*, **63**, 597–606.

——(1961). *Social behavior: Its Elementary Forms*, New York: Harcourt, Brace & World.

Kahn, R. and Boulding, E. (1964). *Power and Conflict in Organizations*, New York: Basic Books.

Kanter, R. M. (1977). *Men and Women of the Corporation*, New York: Basic Books.

——(1979). Power failures in management circuits, *Harvard Business Review*, July–August, 65–75.

Kipnis, D. (1974). The powerholder, in J. T. Tedeschi (ed.), *Perspectives on Social Power*, Chicago: Aldine.

Koehler, C. W., Anatol, K. W. E., and Applbaum, R. L. (1976). *Organizational Communication: Behavioral Perspectives*, New York: Holt, Rinehart & Winston.

Kotter, J. R. (1979). Power, dependency and effective management, in *Harvard Business Review: On Human Relations*, New York: Harper & Row.

Kuhn, A. (1963). *The Study of Society*, Homewood, Ill.: The Dorsey Press.

Lasswell, H. D. (1948). *Power and Personality*, New York: W. W. Norton.

Lehman, E. W. (1969). Toward a macrosociology of power, *American Sociological Review*, **34**, 453–465.

Levinger, G. (1959). The development of perceptions and behavior in newly formed social power relationships, in D. Cartwright (ed.), *Studies in Social Power*, Ann Arbor, Mich.: University of Michigan.

Lewin, K. (1951). *Field Theory in Social Science*, New York: Harper & Brothers.

Lippitt, R., Polansky, N., and Rosen. S. (1952). The dynamics of power, *Human Relations*, **5**, 37–64.

Machiavelli, N. (1950). *The Prince and the Discourses*, New York: Random House.

March, J. G. (1955). An introduction to the theory and measurement of influence, *American Political Science Review*, **49**, 431–451.

Martin, N. H. and Sims, J. H. (1956). Thinking ahead: power tactics, *Harvard Business Review*, **34**, 25–36, 140.

Martin, R. (1971). The concept of power: a critical defense, *British Journal of Sociology*, **22**, 240–256.

May, R. (1972). *Power and Innocence*, New York: W. W. Norton.

McClelland, D. C. (1970). Two faces of power, *Journal of International Affairs,* **24**, 29–47.

——(1975). *Power: The Inner Experience*, New York: Irvington.

Michener, H. A. and Suchner, R. W. (1972). The tactical use of social power, in J. T. Tedeschi (ed.), *The Social Influence Processes*, Chicago: Aldine-Atherton.

Minton, H. L. (1967). Power as a personality construct, in B. A. Maher (ed.), *Progress in Experimental Personality Research,* Vol. 4, New York: Academic Press.

——(1972). Power and personality, in J. T. Tedeschi (ed.), *The Social Influence Processes*, Chicago: Aldine-Atherton.

Nagel, J. H. (1975). *The Descriptive Analysis of Power*, New Haven, Conn.: Yale University Press.

Ogletree, T. W. (1971). Power and human fulfillment, *Pastoral Psychology*, **22**, 42–53.

Oppenheim, F. E. (1961). *Dimensions of Freedom: An Analysis*, New York: St. Martin's Press.

Raven, B. H. (1965). Social influence and power, in I. D. Steiner and M. Fishbein, (eds.), *Current Studies in Social Psychology*, New York: Holt, Rinehart & Winston.

Reich, C. A. (1970). *The Greening of America: How the Youth Revolution is Trying to Make America Liveable*, New York: Random House.

Riker, W. H. (1964). Some ambiguities in the notion of power, *American Political Science Review*, **58**, 341–349.

Rosinski, H. (1965). *Power and Human Destiny*, New York: Frederick A. Praeger.

Rubinoff, L. (1968). *The Pornography of Power*, Chicago: Quadrangle Books.

Russell, B. (1938). *Power: A New Social Analysis*, New York: W. W. Norton.

Sampson, R. V. (1965). *The Psychology of Power*, New York: Random House.

Schopler, J. (1965). Social power, in L. Berkowitz (ed.), *Advances in Experimental Social Psychology*, vol 2, New York: Academic Press.

——and Layton, B. D. (1974). Attributions of interpersonal power, in J. T. Tedeschi (ed.), *Perspectives on Social Power*. Chicago: Aldine.

Shapley, L. and Shubik, M. (1954). A method for evaluating the distribution of power in a committee system, *American Political Science Review*, **48**, 787–792.

Simon, H. A. (1957). *Models of Man*, New York: John Wiley.

Tannenbaum, A. S. (1962). An event-structure approach to social power and to the problem of power comparability, *Behavioral Science*. **1**, 315–331.

Tedeschi, J. T., Schlenker, B. R., and Lindskold, S. (1972). The exercise of power and influence: the source of influence, in J. T. Tedeschi (ed.). *The Social Influence Processes*, Chicago: Aldine-Atherton.

Thibaut, J. W. and Kelley, H. (1959). *The Social Psychology of Groups*, New York: John Wiley.

Veroff, J. (1957). Development and validation of a projective measure of power motivation, *Journal of Abnormal & Social Psychology*, **54**, 1–8.

——and Veroff, J. P. B. (1972). Reconsideration of a measure of power motivation, *Psychological Bulletin*, **78**, 279–291.

Votaw, D. (1966). What do we believe about power? *California Management Review*, **8**, 71–88.

Winter, D. G. (1973). *The Power Motive*, New York: The Free Press.

Wolfe, D. M. (1959). Power and authority in the family, in D. Cartwright (ed.), *Studies in Social Power*, Ann Arbor, Michigan: University of Michigan.

Power, Politics, and Organizations: A Behavioural Science View
Edited by Andrew Kakabadse and Christopher Parker
© 1984 John Wiley & Sons Ltd.

Chapter 2

Theories of Power

MARGARET RYAN

1. INTRODUCTION

Power is one of those topics of universal interest about which analysis, description, interpretation, and evaluative comment can be found in a variety of literature, novels, plays, and poems, as well as in the social sciences. In this chapter on the theories of power I shall confine myself to the literature of the social sciences, where most of the issues have been raised, and attempt to draw together the main ideas about power which can be derived from that literature.

To start with an outline sketch, the approach of the various authors on power can be divided very broadly into three camps: (1) those who deal with the subject primarily in the context of society and the state—writers such as Weber (1948), Miliband (1969), Agger, Goldrich, and Swanson (1964) and Freire (1973) are examples; (2) those who are mainly interested in power in the organizational setting—for example, Crozier (1964), Pettigrew (1973), Strauss (1962), Bacharach and Lawler (1980); (3) those who are mainly interested in power at the level of the individual, either in considering power as an aspect of personality or the individual's responses to power, including the strategies and skills employed—Adler (1958), Winter (1973), Emerson (1962), Zaleznik (1970), and Mangham (1979) come into this category. I say these are very rough divisions because they overlap to some extent. For example, Freire has some comment to make about the individual's response to power, although his main interest is at the level of society as a whole. Zaleznik, although primarily concerned with the individual, focuses on the business manager and therefore to some extent overlaps with writers in the organizational group, who, while they refer to individuals and to society, are mainly interested in the way organizations work. Most writers in all categories have some discussion about what the concept of 'power' consists of. For some, the substantive issue is the concept of power itself, with society, or the individual, or the organization, being used as examples to illustrate their

21

view of the concept. (For example, see Lukes, 1974; Peters, 1959; Bachrach and Baratz, 1962; Wrong, 1979; French and Raven, 1959). The focus of attention of authors therefore ranges between the poles of macro and micro social science and empirical study and philosophical discourse.

It would appear that power is not a concept easy to grasp in all its aspects and levels at the same time, and when it comes to the question 'What do you mean by power?' the boundaries of the concept are not too clear. Bacharach and Lawler (1980) suggest that the vagueness of the concept of power is due to its being a 'primitive term', sensitizing in function, rather than fully clarifying the phenomenon to which it draws attention. On this basis, 'influence', 'authority', 'control' and so on, are types of power, being concepts which clarify the primitive term 'power'. This seems a useful starting point for this chapter. In the following sections I shall explore the various issues and ideas about this general concept of power, and except where otherwise stated I shall use the word 'power' in the way Bacharach and Lawler suggest. I shall look first at the ubiquitous '*A* getting *B* to do something' model of power, and then consider the relevance of structures and values to the concept. Rules, a particular combination of both structure and value, will then be given some special attention, before finally the consciousness of the actors in political processes is considered.

2. THE *A–B* MODEL OF POWER

The concept of power is often expressed in the literature by the words 'the ability to . . .', as in Salancik and Pfeffer (1977) 'the ability to bring about outcomes you desire'. (See also Crozier, 1964; Goldner, 1970; Strauss, 1962; Kaplan, 1964; Deutsch, 1963; Hall and Bates, 1970; Winter, 1973; Tushman, 1977). However, for most writers this is not an ability innate in the person, but is seen as an aspect of a relationship between individuals, groups, institutions, or classes, in which *A* gets *B* to do something, 'do' being broadly interpreted to include thoughts and feelings as well as actions. Particularly in the more philosophical literature, this dyadic model is used in order to consider the questions it raises in attempting to map out the concept of power. Most of these questions are noted by Lukes (1974), those most often debated being as follows.

First, does the action of *A* have to be deliberate? Does *A* have *knowingly* to attempt to get *B* to do something before one can talk of the power of *A*? Bates (1970) is sure that the action of *A* must be conscious, Winter (1973), French and Raven (1959) that it need not be. For Wrong (1979) the action must be both intended and effective.

Second, should one distinguish between power, control, influence, and authority? Lukes (1974), Peters (1959), Winch (1959), Hall (1972), Lasswell (1930/60), French and Raven (1959) and (Wrong, 1979) all wish to make the distinction between power and other forms of *A* getting *B* to do something, such as influence or authority. Influence can be seen as distinguished from power in that it is said to involve no coercion, and authority can be distinguished from power in that it is legitimized and implies acceptance of the *right* of *A* to get *B* to do whatever it is. Lasswell (1930/60) comments that coercion is the distinctive characteristic of what we call power: 'When coercion enters into the exchange (of resources) there is power'. Blau (1964) by contrast, distinguishes between power, which implies the possibility that *B* might choose punishment rather than compliance, and coercion which allows *B* no choice.

Handy (1976), on the other hand, calls the *activity* of *A* getting *B* to do something 'influence' and the *reason why B* will do what *A* wants, 'power' of *A*—some characteristic or situation of *A* which enables *A* to influence *B*. In this model, authority is seen as a type of power. One difficulty with this view is that it requires that some forms of 'influence' must be said to be coercive, and it makes less clear the distinction between coercion, and those instances of *A* getting *B* to do something where *B* is willing to comply—as in the example supplied by Winch (1959) of *A* teaching *B* how to play chess. In Bacharach and Lawler's (1980) scheme, 'authority' and 'influence', as types of power, play a different part from 'coercion' which is seen as one of four bases of power. Their scheme, too, shows 'coercion' as a basis for 'influence'.

Third, if *A* tries to get *B* to do something, and *B* as a result, acts in a way which is not precisely as *A* wishes, how are we to include this in the concept of power? One answer is to include the notion of control as a type of political interaction. Control is a topic with a literature of its own reaching out to the control of technical systems, and borrowing from these systems the notions of target-setting, monitoring and feedback, and corrective action. Social control and deviation at the level of the state, the group and the individual have also been widely discussed, see Lemert (1964). Seen from a political perspective, 'control' cannot exist in a social system without the implication that *A* is getting *B* to do something. Where *A* specifies a particular act to be performed by *B*—sets an objective or target—and *B* meets that objective as a result of *A*'s requirement, then one can say that *A* controls B. Olsen (1970) uses the idea of predictability to distinguish between control and influence. Where the outcome is predictable there is control, but where it is unpredictable, there is influence. French and Raven (1959) distinguish between positive and negative control, positive being where *B* does what *A* wants, and negative where *B* does the opposite, an idea which does not quite cover the situation where what *B* does is different rather than opposite. It should be said, however, that where 'control' is discussed in the literature, especially by authors writing in the mode of classical or systems theory, the notion of 'power' as a social system variable is not necessarily referred to (see Ouchi,

1977, for example). In other instances, for example Etzioni (1964), 'power' and 'control' are used as synonymous terms and Etzioni then distinguishes between 'coercive' and other forms of control (normative and utilitarian).

Notions of coercion and negative control suggest that resistance is related to the concept of power. Writers are divided on this point, however, French and Raven (1959) assuming that the resistance of *B* is necessarily involved, Weber (in Wallimann *et al.*'s 1980 translation) suggesting that it may or may not be involved.

Fourth, should all instances of *B* taking account of *A*'s wishes, even where these are not expressed by *A*, be regarded as the power of *A*? Social interaction is only possible at all because we make predictions about each other's behaviour and act accordingly. So if we answer 'yes' to this question we are saying that 'all behaviour at all levels and in all circumstances may be regarded as political' (Mangham, 1979). Some writers, however, want to make a distinction between political behaviour and other kinds. Lukes (1974) suggests that political behaviour should be distinguished from other kinds of interaction by saying that the term political should only be applied to 'significant events'. An insignificant event may show that *A* 'affects' *B* but this should not be called power. The problem with this idea is, of course, deciding what is 'significant'. French and Raven (1959) consider that the concept of power is 'useless' if every momentary social stimulus is viewed as actualising social power'. Blau (1964) also distinguishes political behaviour from other kinds. For him, political behaviour—'social exchange'—is goal-directed, and should be distinguished from 'expressive' behaviour, which is not. Although neither of these arguments is watertight, they do reflect everyday usage of the concept of power in which people tend to confine it to particular forms of behaviour and to be able to identify certain activities as 'political behaviour'. It is possible to summarize the ideas so far reviewed as shown in Figure 1. The brackets are in acknowledgement of the points made in the fourth argument above.

One can quickly become embroiled in arguments over such a scheme. For example, does it make sense to talk of a coercive act of *A* where the act of *B* is not specified? It might, if one admits the possibility that an act is coercive, not because *A* intends it as such, but because *B* sees it as coercive and is therefore coerced. Similarly *B* may see a specific act required, or see an event as significant, where *A* does not.

Few writers on power include *B*'s view of the situation as one of the factors which enables *A* to have power, but French and Raven (1959) show that *B*'s perception of *A*'s power is an important factor in the ability of *A* to influence *B*, and Mangham's (1979) Crocodile case-study provides an example of how 'coercion' over the use of Head Office systems existed very largely in the minds of the subsidiary company's managers, rather than in the direct intentions of Head Office. *B*'s perception may be based on experience of this

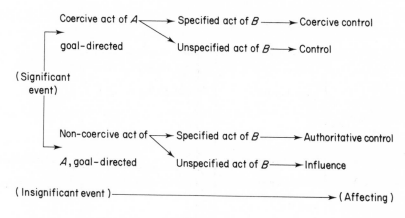

Figure 1

particular *A*'s past actions, or on *B*'s experience of interactions with others perceived as similar to *A*, and will also include *B*'s perception of the likelihood of *A*'s power being used.

Bacharach and Lawler (1980), in discussion of sanctions, which they see as *A*'s attempts to manipulate *B* by the use of rewards or punishments, point out that there are two probabilities which have to be weighed up by those involved: that the sanction will be applied and that it will have the required effect. They draw attention to the subjective nature of the process by which these probabilities are assessed and to the importance of the deterrence value of this assessment in any conflict. These various ideas about *A*'s capacity for power in relation to *B* and of *B*'s perception of the situation can be added to the previous diagram as shown in Figure 2.

Further characteristics of power which have a bearing on political interaction between *A* and *B* are discussed in the literature. Power has been identified as being distributed differentially, so that some people have more of it than others, and that theoretically its quantity can be measured. Power has been viewed as having magnitude, weight, scope, and domain (see Dahl, 1957; Perrow, 1970; Gamson, 1968; Tushman, 1977; Hickson *et al.*, 1971; Tannenbaum, 1973; and Zald, 1970). This nomenclature has the effect of reifying power, and leads also to arguments about whether power has absolute or relative magnitude (see Tannenbaum, 1973 and Dalton, Barnes, and Zaleznik, 1968). Other writers talk more of political acts—the exercise of power as action. For example Hall and Bates (1970) suggest that power involves directing activities of others, making rules for others, enforcing rules for others, setting goals and objectives for others, hiring and firing and making decisions. Decision-making, whether it be deciding to act or to do nothing, has been a central theme in the literature about power seen in its

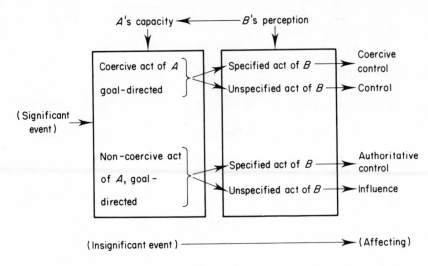

Figure 2

active sense (see for example Bachrach and Baratz, 1962; Pettigrew, 1973; Lukes, 1974). The symbolic interactionist view, on the other hand, focuses attention on the way in which in interactions people develop their definitions of the situation and engage in negotiations over these definitions, as well as over substantive issues (see for example Gamson, 1968; Hall, 1972; and Mangham, 1979).

The political processes resulting from the exercise of power are variously characterized in the literature as 'exchange', 'cons and deals', 'games', and 'demand and control' processes (see for example Blau, 1964; Bailey, 1977; Allison, 1971; Gamson, 1968). Behind many of these views is the idea of power as the outcome of dependence. Indeed, to Blau (1964) unless there is asymmetrical dependence between *A* and *B* there is no power relationship. Such views conclude that the more dependent *B* is on *A*, the more power *A* has over *B*. The strength of dependence is determined by the alternatives open to *B* and the relative value these alternatives have for *B*—see Bacharach and Lawler (1980), Blau (1964). Bacharach and Lawler also point out that although there may be objective conditions of dependence, the use of power is also based on the subjective judgments *A* and *B* make about these conditions (p. 22).

In general terms, the literature can be seen as expressing the need to see power in broadly two ways—as something one can identify as belonging to individuals or groups, so that it makes sense to say that *A* 'has' power, and as an activity between people, so that it makes sense to say that *A* 'exercises' power. Even if one rejects his labelling of the exercise of power as 'influence'

Handy's (1976) model reflects the need to distinguish the two aspects of power: *A* 'has' power and therefore can take action to get *B* to do something. Dalton, Barnes and Zaleznik (1968) cannot agree between them on this issue, Zaleznik wanting to see power as dependent on characteristics of *A*, and Dalton and Barnes as a relation between *A* and *B*. These differing views can be reconciled by making the distinction between power potential and power use, see Bacharach and Lawler (1980). There have been several classifications of potential power, or the bases of power. For example, it is suggested that power may derive from authority, or from control of resources, or from expertise, or from charisma. French and Raven (1959) and Wrong (1979) provide examples of such classifications, and their schemes are in some ways similar, except that Wrong uses the word 'authority' where French and Raven would use the word 'power'.

One further point must be made about the *A–B* model of power. Most of the literature in this vein tends to focus very largely on the activities of *A*, but there are some analyses of the responses of *B*. Emerson (1962) in particular looks at this side of the equation, pointing out that where there is a power imbalance, that is *B* is more dependent on *A* than *A* is on *B*, this represents a cost to *B*. *B* will try to reduce this cost, either by an alteration in values so that the issues involved become reduced in significance in the eyes of *B*, or by strategies for increasing the power of *B*. By such 'balancing' operations, the psychological cost of complying with *A* can be removed or reduced. Dalton, Barnes and Zaleznik (1968), in reviewing Emerson's work, suggest the following list of adjustments which can be made where dependency is unbalanced:

(1) Acceptance of dependency by those placed in the more dependent position.
(2) Reduced dependency or withdrawal by the more dependent party.
(3) Diffusion of dependency on to other objects by the more dependent party.
(4) Dependency increases initiated by the more powerful party.
(5) Blockage of alternate dependencies which the more powerful party might seek.

Some of these adjustments seem to require ego-defences, and several other writers have suggested defences by which *B* adapts to the power of *A*. *B* is said to increase communication with *A*, to distort the perceived differences between *B* and *A*, to over-identify with the views of *A*, to increase liking for *A*, and in general to decrease the psychological distance between *B* and *A*, provided that this distance is not too great to start with. These activities are seen variously in the literature as reducing the cost of *A*'s power, or as ways of striving to gain more power in relation to *A*, or as substitutes for such power (see Mulder, 1960; Hurwitz, Zander and Hymivitch, 1968; Horwitz, 1964). A line of argument found in the literature about the reactions of *B* to the power of *A* relates to item (1) on Dalton's list in suggesting that *B* 'accepts' the situation or regards it as 'legitimate', see French and Raven (1959).

Winch (1959), Blau (1964), and Mechanic (1962), for example, suggest that when a person joins an organization he or she is thereby indicating an acceptance of the authority of other persons. This raises the question of what 'acceptance' means in the context of working life. Dalton (1959) has pointed out that the executive may need to *dissemble* acceptance of the norms of the organization, while privately rejecting them. He was considering this question primarily from the point of view of *A*s—executives attempting to gain and maintain their power in relation to others—but *B*s on the receiving end of such attempts may dissemble just as much as *A*s. The practicalities of employment may include the absence of any alternative jobs and for this reason alone *B* may consider it advisable to *pretend* acceptance of the authority of *A*. Moreover, although *B* may accept the authority of *A* on first joining the organization, experience of working in it may bring a change of heart, and subsequent rejection of this authority. And what if *B*'s orientation to work is entirely instrumental? (Goldthorp, 1966). In this case the issues which in other circumstances might have involved a power struggle between *A* and *B* might be regarded as trivial or of no personal interest to *B*. The 'struggle for power' view of organization tends to make the assumption that all the actors are personally involved and interested in the various issues arising from the organization's mission and activities, but motivation theory indicates that this is not to be counted on. There is a difference between *B*'s complying with *A*'s wishes through necessity, identification, or fear, and *B*'s complying because the issue is of no importance to *B*, however important to *A*. Zald (1970) mentions as a fundamental problem of social systems, along with internal and external power relations, the motivational basis of individual commitment to the enterprise. One can look at the *A–B* paradigm and ask why *A* is keen to exercise power in relation to *B* in an organizational setting, but also what it is about *B*'s motivation which affects the outcome of *A*'s attempt. The fundamental problems cited by Zald are closely related to each other in that commitment can be said to affect political behaviour. Dalton, Barnes and Zaleznik (1968) support this view by suggesting that, in order to exercise power, a person must first internalize the authority structure of the organization, and that this internalization is a function of the individual's decision to participate in the work of the enterprise.

The 'acceptance' by *B* of the power of *A* can be considered at different levels. *B*'s overt behaviour may consist of doing what *A* wishes, but it should not be assumed that *B* accept's *A*'s power at a psychological level. *B* may deem it advisable to comply with the demands of *A*, but not internalize the norms which give *A* power. Etzioni's (1961) distinction between alienative, calculative, and moral involvement in the compliance relationship between *A* and *B* provides a framework for refining the notion of *B*'s 'acceptance'.

In his criticism of Luke's (1974) analysis of power. Bradshaw (1976) has pointed out that the 'A getting B to do something' model of power, though useful in the analysis of the concept, presents a picture of an interaction between two people devoid of any context, and is therefore misleading. It also assumes a clarity in the activities of *A* and *B* which is often absent in real life. The nuances of the history of *A* and *B* and their relationship, their motivation, the presence in the situation of other actors, and the surrounding circumstances, are not represented in this model. Useful though the philosophical writings of people such as Lukes (1974) are, for the greater subtleties and complexities of power one must turn to the empirical studies of writers such as Crozier (1964), Goldner (1970), and Pettigrew (1973).

3. STRUCTURE

One theme which emerges from the empirical studies and from authors mostly concerned with power at the group or organization level (for example Miliband, 1969) is the relatively permanent distribution of power—its structural aspect. Bacharach and Lawler (1980) see authority as a structurally derived type of power providing stability, and influence as derived from personality, expertise, and opportunity and providing change. In their analysis, power derives from the group, rather than from the individual. Hawley (1963) (quoted in Gamson, 1968) seems to be taking an extreme structuralist view when he says that although individuals appear to have power, this is an illusion, since their power derives only from their position in the system and it is therefore the system which has power, not the individual. Dalton, Barnes, and Zalenik (1968) consider that a distinction should be made between structures based on authority and the interaction between *A* and *B* which they call influence. Kanter (1972) criticizes the interactionist view of power for paying too little attention to structures and assuming too great a freedom for negotiation between individuals in decision-making processes, largely as a result of a predisposition for micro-analysis. Macro-analysis, on the other hand, tends to over-emphasize the structural limits on behaviour, but Kanter suggests that organizations do have collective as well as individual goals and takes the view that systems as well as individuals have power. Some of these views seem to be treating the abstraction 'structure' as though it were a person, and also to be confining the concept of structure to formal authority relationships, and hence limiting its usefulness in the analysis of organizational power. An alternative would be to see structure as the relatively stable differentiation of roles and groups and the relationships between these. When French and Raven (1959) say that 'Power is a useful concept for describing social structure only if it has a certain stability over time' they are implying a rather broader view of structure than just authority relationships.

The interaction between the political activities of *A* and *B* and the power structure which forms part of their context is demonstrated in the organization literature. Crozier (1964) for example, shows how the power struggle between individuals can be confined by the power structure represented by the hierarchy. Pettigrew's (1973) study shows how an individual was able to adopt certain political tactics in interaction with other people, because of the place he held in a power structure which provided him with access to decision-making committees and denied it to others.

The political structure of an organization can be seen as arising out of the division of labour (see for example Goldner, 1970). This differentiates the organization, setting up boundaries of demarcation between groups, which have an inclusive and exclusive effect. The creation of groups provides the individual with experiences of belonging and of being an outsider, and facilitates the divergence of norms of behaviour and objectives between groups. The greater the divergence between one group and another, the greater the chance of communication failure and the development of conflict. The differentiation of the organization makes co-ordination methods necessary—the hierarchy, bureaucratic procedures, committees, liaison departments, and roles—but just as differentiation provides the conditions under which groups begin to compete with one another, so the co-ordinating mechanisms become pressed into the service of organizational politics. The rational attempt to create organizational predictability provides the conditions and the weapons for undermining it. Bailey (1977) for example, shows how committees can be used by organization members for political purposes, Roy (1955) how a bureaucratic control system was made to serve the purposes of those subjected to it.

A structure of distributed power is seen in the literature as resulting from the interdependence between individuals and groups which in turn arises from the division of labour. To quote Tushman (1977) for example:

> If there is no need for joint decision-making (i.e. no interdependence) and there is no resource scarcity, then the sub-units can make independent decisions. But if the groups are interdependent and must share scarce resources, they must engage in joint decision-making. Under these ubiquitous conditions the political perspective has the most relevance.

But the pluralism implied by such views can be questioned. Zald (1970) for example has suggested that interdependence may become so routinized that it ceases to be perceived as interdependence, and Gamson (1968) and Dahl

(1968) have drawn attention to the existence of unused political potential in social systems, all of which suggests that the political potential of interdependence can in some cases be inoperative. Wallimann *et al.* (1980), discussing their translation of Weber's definition of power: 'Within a social relationship, power means any chance, (no matter whereon this chance is based) to carry through one's own will (even against resistance)', point out that the word 'chance' in this definition not only allows for the inclusion of the structural dimension of power, but also for the possibility that the opportunity for power may not be used.

The strategic contingency view of power (for example Hickson *et al.*, 1971) develops the structural theme by showing that those groups in an organization which deal with its major dependencies are in a better position to exercise power than other groups. Goldner's (1970) study shows that the industrial relations specialists needed skills in dealing with the unions and with their colleagues, but these personal abilities alone did not give them power. Power came from the combination of these abilities with the fact that the unions were regarded in the organization as a major threat. The importance to the social system of the issue to which the group's activities (and therefore the individual group member's) are applied is a major consideration in the development of the power of individuals and groups into a relatively permanent power distribution. Mangham (in conversation) has suggested that the contingency view of political structure needs refining to account for the shifts in salience of particular issues, which mean that the 'chance' to carry through one's will is a matter of timing as well as structural opportunity. Pettigrew (1975) makes a similar point when he suggests that the organizational consultant should 'time his influence attempts to coincide with periods when his assessed stature is high'. Such views tend to emphasize the relatively unstable nature of power structures, those individuals and groups in the ascendancy at one time being less powerful at another. But these ideas have to be set against the views dealt with in the next section about the way in which political structures can be rendered permanent through the learning of values.

4. VALUES

The ideas about legitimacy and about social control referred to earlier raise the question of the relationship between values and power. This relationship can be seen from a number of different angles.

In the discussion on structure the way in which task differentiation results in divergence of norms (consensus of values) between groups was briefly referred to, and several writers demonstrate the links between structure, values and power. Pettigrew (1973), in considering the factors which are likely to be sources of conflict and give rise to political activity, draws attention to the way in which people learn to adopt certain values through being in differentiated groups, so that political conflict is to some extent a legacy of the organization's history and the learned values of individuals within its structure. Miliband (1969) and Freire (1973) contend that the existing political structure is perpetuated through socialization, which is the means by which individuals come to adopt values favourable to the ruling élite and by which the ascendancy of the values of the powerful is maintained. Bucher (1970) shows how, in a medical school (which she characterizes as a non-hierarchical organization) there are structures in the form of committees and role-sets which provide the means by which people gain and exercise power. Crucial to their gaining power—getting on to the committee—is their 'assessed stature'—a judgment made by their peers about their value to the school. Looked at through Miliband spectacles, this value judgment could itself be seen as a political and historical matter. What is considered 'valuable' in the school being what those with power (who had assessed stature in the past) say it is. This is not to say that committee members are entirely conformist, since Bucher observes that you do not have to be a tame supporter of status quo to be on the committee. Nevertheless those characteristics which render a person acceptable or not as a committee member are those defined by the reigning value system. This value system determines who gains access to the political structure, and this structure in turn determines whose ideas will be heard. These ideas presumably include recognition of which issues are to be considered important, and which should be ignored. Thus one can suggest that the structure and prevailing values of an organization have additional political significance in the inclusion or exclusion of issues from the agenda in decision-making, to which Bachrach and Baratz (1962) and Lukes (1974) refer.

The idea that if you have power your values will prevail is reflected in the definitions of power of several writers, for example 'to carry through one's own will' (Weber in Walliman *et al.*, 1980); the ability to impose your point of view on others (Strauss, 1962); 'ability of an individual or group to act out successfully its character or impose extrapolations or projections of its inner structure upon its environment' (Deutsch, 1963 in Harvey and Mills, 1970). Salancik and Pfeffer (1977) offer a different viewpoint on this issue when they suggest that the way to gain power is to get your perception of the priorities of the organization, that is your values, accepted. It is not enough to be able to deal with the critical contingencies of the organization, you must first be able to define what these are and have your definition prevail.

The connection between values and power is central to the notion of authority. Winch (1959) considers that the notion of 'the right and wrong way of doing things' is inherent in the concept of authority, which he sees as fundamental to the possibility of human decision-making. Day (1963), who considers that authority cannot be a coercive power, points out that the authority of governments includes the authority to coerce within certain limits, and that the assessment of whether a government has overstepped those limits and used excessive coercion depends on the values of the observers of such governments. The crux of authority is seen as the voluntary acceptance of it by those over whom it is exercised, and thus it is similar to the ideas of the 'acceptance' of the power of *A* referred to in the section of the *A–B* model. Bacharach and Lawler (1980) seem to be confusing the notion of authority when they say that the 'unique aspect of authority is that subordinates acquiesce without question and are willing to (1) suspend any intellectual or moral judgements about the appropriateness of the superior's directives, or (2) act as if they subscribed to the judgement of the superior . . .' and agree with Bierstedt (1950) that authority implies involuntary submission (pp. 28–29). This suggests not only the right to decide, but also the right to be right, and that authority is at its root coercive rather than based on a consensus of values.

Gouldner (1970), however, points out the danger of seeing power and authority as mutually exclusive terms, since those with authority have other forms of power as well. 'Power exists quietly, as it were. . . It makes its presence felt continuously, underneath and alongside of 'legitimacy' and all moral motives for obedience. . . authority is not merely some unanchored 'legitimacy', but the legitimacy of power' (p. 294).

Day (1963) by contrast suggest that if people obey a government through fear of punishment they are responding to the power of that government, not to its authority. 'When a person acknowledges another's authority, it cannot be because he is forced to. This is not what authority means.'

Talcott Parsons has been criticized for basing his analysis of social structure on a theory of consensus of values, ignoring the conflicts of interest between groups and therefore political processes, and in his later writings for trying to show that all power is legitimized, that is based on authority and is therefore part of the value consensus (see Lockwood, 1956 and Giddens, 1968, in Worsley, 1970; Gouldner, 1970). Weber has distinguished different types of values on which authority may be based—traditional, legal-rational, and charismatic—but Winch (1959) argues that these are not distinct concepts but are all based on tradition, since all conceptualizing is based on the traditional authority inherent in having a language, where rules about meanings attached to words are legitimized by usage. This suggests that the values on which authority is based are rooted in time and stability and also in a more fundamental consensus of meanings, rather than just a consensus about rights to decide particular issues.

It seems clear that these somewhat diverse notions about authority are based on the concept of 'legitimacy', but there is also a divergence of view as to what 'legitimacy' is. Schaar (1970) draws attention to the difference between older definitions of legitimacy in which any claim to power had to be justified by reference to some authority beyond and above the claimant (such as the law) and the later definitions of legitimacy. These later definitions 'dissolve legitmacy into belief or opinion. If a people holds the belief that existing institutions are "appropriate" or "morally proper", then those institutions are legitimate. That's all there is to it'. Helm and Morelli (1979) suggest that such definitions make it impossible for a group or individual in a society to say that they refuse obedience to a regime or institution on the grounds that it is illegitimate, but this seems to ignore the possibility that such a regime may be in power because of its ability to coerce the people, rather than because the people think it 'morally proper'. These arguments, in drawing attention to the distinction between legitimacy based on the consensus of values amd that based on an external power source, suggest that, since the consensus of values may exist in the form of unwritten rules, legitimacy may have an informal, as well as or instead of a formal basis, and raise the question of the circumstances under which the act of someone with authority may be said to be 'illegitimate'—could it be said to be illegitimate simply on the grounds of a consensus that it was not 'morally proper'? If legitimacy is based on formal rules, it can be assumed that such rules exist before the act of a person to whom such rules apply; but if it is based on an informal consensus, there is the possibility that the act may become illegitimate in retrospect, at least from the actor's point of view, if the act prompts the emergence of a consensus which did not previously exist, or which was not perceived by the actor. There is also the possibility that the consensus within a group may be at odds with the consensus outside the group—honour among thieves being denigrated as conspiracy by the wider society. Can a minority inside the group therefore claim that acts of group members are illegitimate, even though they accord with the group consensus, on the grounds that they are not supported by the consensus outside the group?

This brings us to the question of the relationship between values and resistance to power, which is also discussed in the literature. The resistance of B to the power of A (using the word power in its general sense) has been discussed in the literature, and it can be suggested that where the values of A and B are not congruent, resistance to the political activities of A, and to the political structure, will arise. Where these activities and structure reflect the values of both A and B, inequity in the distribution and exercise of power may remain outside the conscious observation of either party. However, it appears to be common for members of a social system to notice attempts by others to control them, socialization not being complete. Crozier (1964) considers conflict to be an inevitable outcome of organizational hierarchy (structural inequality of power), since in his view the imposing of power from the top down automatically produces resistance. Other writers too, for example French and Raven (1959), consider resistance to be inherent in the exercise of power. Weber's definition (in Walliman *et al.*, 1980) allows for the possibility of resistance but does not make it inevitable.

Another facet of the connection between values and power is the attitude adopted towards the very fact of unequal power distribution. Is this a positive benefit or does power corrupt? Presumably those who set out to gain power for themselves are in favour of its unequal distribution and do not expect that it will corrupt them. Even people who do not want power for themselves because they lack the power motive (Winter, 1973) can be shown to place a high value on differential power. From the perspective of voluntarism some forms of power, such as 'authority' or 'influence' can be defended on the grounds that authority is legitimate by definition, and influence in most models of power suggests some choice by *B* or a congruence of values between *A* and *B*. 'Expert' power where *A*'s advice turns out to be in the interests of *B*, or 'referent' power, where the power of *A* is based on *B*'s liking for *A*, are other examples of more easily defensible types of power, all of which contain the assumption that *B* plays a voluntary part in bringing about the situation in which *A* has power. But this is not to say that such types of power are seen as free of all blame. Day (1963) comments of authority. 'The authority of government, even if Hobbesian, is infinitely preferable to the Hobbesian state of nature where force is the only arbiter. Yet it is also true, as Paine says, that 'government, even in the best state, (is) a necessary evil'. There is also the problem of how *A* and *B*'s values came to be congruent in the first place, since it is possible for socialization to produce values which benefit *A* rather than *B*, but to which both subscribe.

Some writers clearly see grounds for disapproving of power, at least in some of its forms, particularly because of its consequences for the development of the human personality. Freire (1973) for example sees those with power (the oppressors) and those without it (the oppressed) as being equally damaged by the power imbalance. The adverse effects of power on creativity have also been discussed. Writing from a psycho-analytic viewpoint, Marion Milner (1950) comments: '. . . the restraint of one's will imposed by authority could at times feel like a threat to one's whole existence, an attempt to separate one from the very source of one's creative relation to the world'. Winnicott (1974) in discussing the development of creativity asserts:

> It is creative apperception more than anything else that makes the individual feel that life is worth living. Contrasted with this is a relationship with external reality which is one of compliance . . . many individuals have experienced just enough creative living to recognise that for most of their time they are living uncreatively, as if caught up in the creativity of someone else, or of a machine.

His view does not ignore the need for the individual to adapt to the environment, of which other people form a part, but does suggest that a degree of personal autonomy for *B* is necessary for creativity and psychological health. Argyris (1972) considers that autonomy is necessary for the full development of psychological maturity, and further suggests that the modern organization will tend to prevent this process by subjecting the individual to control by others, thus keeping him or her in an infantile, that is a psychologically unhealthy, state.

Organizational Development theorists and practitioners frequently adopt power-sharing approaches to organizational change through participative decision-making, thereby implying that the uneven distribution of power, especially that associated with centralized forms of management, is to be deplored. Smith and Drake (1972) point out that OD practitioners introduce their own values into the organizations they work with, and that these values are often of a humanistic-democratic kind. OD is seen as a way of adapting the organization to the needs of individuals, and a healthy organization is one which sees these needs as legitimate (Clark, 1970). Organizations should develop along the lines of giving more responsibility and therefore more power to more people if they are to have the capacity to adapt to the ever increasing rate of environmental change. This power must be based on 'collaboration and reason', rather than coercion and fear. It has been recognized that these values, based on Human Relations theories, can lead to behaviour which amounts to no more than manipulation (Miles, 1965) and that there is considerable practical difficulty in maintaining the authentic relationships based on trust which are advocated by OD theorists. Kelman (1965) shows the tension between the consultant's power and the consultant's values when he says

> . . . valuing free individual choice is a vital protection against tyranny. . . . I recognise that freedom of choice is . . . a rock-bottom value for me . . . But we must remain aware that the nature of the relationship between influencing agent and influencee is such that inevitably . . . a certain degree of control will be exercised.

Though writing from a different standpoint, Friere (1973) has a similar difficulty in reconciling the needs of individuals for personal autonomy and the needs for concerted action. How can you ensure that those who voluntarily join your revolution do not equally voluntarily go over to the other side and betray you? The answer is called 'discipline' but really amounts to being powerful enough to stop them—that is, oppression.

Emerging from this discussion is a distinction between needs for personal autonomy for oneself and the need to control other people. Although this distinction can be demonstrable in an experimental setting (Mulder, 1960), in more complex situations it is difficult to see how personal autonomy can be achieved without in some way controlling others. There is also a distinction to be made between valuing autonomy for yourself and valuing it for other people—seeing it as intrinsically desirable. Somewhere along the border between ego's autonomy and alter's, behaviour based on values of individual choice and freedom can slide into tyranny, as OD practitioners have noted. However, there have been arguments in favour of the uneven distribution of power. Salancik and Pfeffer (1977) see it as a necessary mechanism for aligning the organization with reality. Crozier (1964) considers that some individuals must be given freedom of action to make decisions, and therefore have more power than others. Mechanic (1962) asserts that organizations must control their 'lower participants', meaning of course that the higher participants must control the lower ones, that is that there must be an uneven distribution of power. Hall and Wamsley (1970) argue that an even distribution of power in an organization is a disadvantage, causing the organization to stagnate. Blau (1970) sees the sharing of power as risky for an organization, and tries unconvincingly to show that you can reduce the risk of decentralization by a simultaneously high degree of formalization. Bacharach and Aiken (1976), dealing with a similar dilemma—how the higher echelons of an organization can gain reliable information for decision-making and at the same time avoid losing control of subordinates who supply it—suggests that the answer lies in the distinction between the use of authority and of influence. Authority, they argue, which is the right to make final decisions, must be retained by the higher echelons while influence should be widely distributed within the organization. This suggests that some forms of power should be more equally distributed than others.

There seems to be a problem about reconciling the perceived need for some people to have more power than others, and the idea that there is something wrong with having power. The reasons why *A* is exercising power or wants to have power throw some light on this issue. Winter (1973) suggests that people can strive for power for either neurotic or healthy reasons. Healthy reasons are that they feel they have 'superior strength', which in organizational terms might be translated as meaning that they feel they have some special skills and knowledge to contribute to the decision-making process. A neurotic reason would be striving for power through fear of being dominated by others (see also Sanford, 1964). Adler also distinguishes between people's striving to improve things for the future through a capacity for altruism or 'social interest', and their unhealthy striving for power as a compensation for feelings of inferiority.

> With great avidity, directly or by detours, consciously or unconsciously, through appropriate thinking and action or through the arrangement of symptoms, the neurotic strives for increased possession, power and influence and for the disparagement and cheating of other persons' (Ansbacher and Ansbacher, 1958).

Looked at from the point of view of the psychology of the individual, the difference between acceptable and unacceptable political behaviour seems to rest on whether it is derived from an inward-looking need for gratification, or from the capacity for outward looking 'social interest', for although Adler does not say so, striving to improve things within the individual's social context suggests political behaviour of some kind. Mangham (1979) by contrast takes the view that all behaviour is political and arises out of self-interest, so that concepts of 'selfishness' and 'altruism' have no intrinsic validity (although they may, of course, be used as social control devices). Perhaps one reason for the distaste expressed for at least some aspects of power is to be found in the tactics people use for gaining it. Martin and Sims (1956), having interviewed a large number of top executives and studied the biographies of powerful people, produced a list of the tactics reportedly used by these people. They include the following: false compromise, that is, pretending to agree to a compromise solution while knowing that you have no intention of acting on it; delaying action—when a decision has gone against your wishes, taking so long to carry it out that it becomes impossible or irrelevant to implement; manoeuvrability—not committing yourself to any project, person or group, so that you can always back down from a project, change your job, and act against the interests of an individual 'friend'. Dalton (1959) recommends similar 'adjustments' which a departmental head should make when dealing with the competing claims of subordinates and their attempts to counteract his power. Kotter (1978) speaks with approval of a young man who initiated a social activity for political purposes. Bailey (1977) considers that the only way in which a departmental head can keep a balance between academics and bureaucrats in a university is by lying, and observes that it is necessary for principles to be upheld in public but compromised in private. Most of these activities recommended or condoned by such writers could be categorized by Adler as neurotic 'cheating of other persons'. No doubt this would be countered by saying, as Bailey (1977) does, that it is only by such cheating that reality can be dealt with, so paradoxically the argument can be facilitated that the rules of conduct of the highest order must regrettably be infringed in the name of the interest of the enterprise, thus meeting Adler's criterion of 'social interest' as an indication of healthy political behaviour. This argument is undermined by the problem of assuming the objectiveness of 'reality'. It is interesting to note that whereas Bailey is opposed to the idea of a 'real' person behind the role being played, he is willing to believe that there is an objective 'reality' beyond the subterfuges and beyond the definitions of reality proposed by the role-players.

5. RULES

There are indications in the literature that among the norms of behaviour in an organization there are always some rules which draw the line between acceptable (if disagreeable) political activity and what is unacceptable. Bucher (1970) for example, suggests that in the medical school 'not being a bastard' in political behaviour meant not keeping all the benefits of the exercise of power for yourself. Bailey (1977) notes that the roles that people choose to play, the masks they choose to wear, must not differ too greatly between one situation and another. Too much unpredictability or inconsistency of behaviour is unacceptable. The interaction between power and rules has been commented on by several writers and is particularly relevant in organizational life. Bailey (1969) distinguishes between normative rules and pragmatic rules, the latter being tactical guides about how to win in political struggles, coming into play when normative rules are not available or are insufficient to guide behaviour. But within normative rules there is also the need to distinguish between explicit organizational rules, such as 'no smoking', and the unwritten norms which draw the ambiguous line between what is and is not acceptable in political behaviour.

It has been suggested that, within an appropriate technology, behaviour can be so prescribed by the explicit rules of the organization that it would become 'power-free' since the dependencies between persons in the structure would be removed by these rules (see Crozier, 1964 and Ouchi, 1977). As long as there is some possibility of freedom of action, some gaps where the rules do not exist or cannot be enforced, political activity is facilitated. Where *A* can give or refuse permission for *B* to bend or break the rules, *A* has the possibility of exercising power in relation to *B*. Moreover, Dalton (1959) points out that rules can become outdated, and that a weak manager is one who does not recognize this and who cannot 'improvise' in a changing situation where there are no rules to guide behaviour. The strong, on the other hand, 'quickly turn ambiguous situations to their needs'—in other words, they use the rules or their absence, in the exercise of power. Astute politicians are, presumably, those who note that there is no rule prescribing their behaviour, or that it cannot be enforced, or that it has become outdated, and accurately predict what they can get away with as a result. They may face charges of deviousness, especially from those who are adversely affected by their activities, but they could equally claim with Dalton (1959) that such is the complexity of political life, no matter *what* their action *someone* would regard it as an infringement of an implicit rule of conduct. Perhaps tolerance of a degree of obliquy is also necessary to the astute politician, but since the participants in the enterprise must maintain a certain level of co-operation if it is to function at all, the politician must also retain sufficient support among colleagues. Walton (1965) has drawn attention to this dilemma, in which *A*, while on the one hand making political gains at the expense of *B*, needs at the same time to secure the positive attitude of *B*. However, some writers have demonstrated that it is possible to do both. Lukes (1974) and Hall (1972) for example show that power can be exercised by *A* without the knowledge or understanding by *B* that there is a conflict of interests between them. De Crespigny (1968) also observes that A can have 'impedimental power'—the ability of A to affect outcomes for B without B being aware of this.

What Bailey (1977) has called the myths of the organization, embodied in such slogans as 'managers must be allowed to manage' and 'business is business' may be used to rationalize the activities of A and substantiate a claim that no normative rule has been broken. Such myths may also help to accomplish the situation noted by Crozier (1964) whereby A can be said to have power in relation to B because B's behaviour is narrowly prescribed by rules but A's is not. Success in the power struggle can therefore be seen to depend on a number of factors; the ability to perceive and manipulate rules, whether explicit or implicit, to judge accurately where the line is drawn between acceptable (if regrettable) action and unacceptable action, to justify one's use of rules especially by reference to some superordinate rule (an appeal to legitimacy); and the ignorance of B.

6. THE CONSCIOUSNESS OF A AND B

Some writers (for example Winter, 1973 and Adler, 1958) consider that the exercise of power can be unconscious, but in most of the literature the assumption is made that the people involved in the political process are aware of the political nature of their interactions. They are assumed also to be aware of the issues and to adopt deliberate strategies for getting their own way (see for example Bacharach and Lawler, 1980). Among contingency theorists, with the exception of Pfeffer and Salancik, the identification of the major dependencies of an enterprise is not considered to be in dispute. Moreover the problem of cause and effect, though noted by Dahl (1968) as a problem of power theory, is not given much consideration. This problem raises the question of how you know that B's action was a response to A's action, rather than some other cause. It is only by being able to make the causal link that one can say that A is exercising power, but in complex political situations this may be in doubt. This difficulty relates to methodological problems of studying power but one can note here that one aspect of power which receives little attention in the literature is the consciousness of A and B. What do A and B think they are doing? To what extent do they see themselves as having power and exercising power, and how do these perceptions relate to their value systems and their behaviour? To what extent is there consensus among participants as to political cause and effect? Do the concepts of power, if any, held by participants match the views of theorists, and under what circumstances?

There are a few references in the literature to the ways in which people can perceive political activity. Allison (1971) for example, suggests that there are three different models (at least) by means of which people analyse the activities of governments: the 'rational actor' model, in which the government is seen as a monolith, or as though it were an individual, making a rational decision among alternatives in order to meet its objectives; the 'organizational' model, which focuses attention on the various departments involved, their routines and their objectives; and the 'governmental politics' model, which considers the competing interests, skills and political resources of individuals. Kaplowitz (1978) has put forward a number of propositions, based on a combination of power literature and attribution literature, about how power is attributed to other people and the consequences of such attributions. Kanter (1972) draws attention to differences in perception when she points out that people inside a political arena may see it as having infinite gradings of complexity, and rate the question of who wins a particular battle as being of great importance, but outsiders may see only a simple division of haves and have-nots, and the issue of who wins as trivial. Dearlove (1973) quotes Sprout and Sprout (1965) '. . . from the perspective of decisions and decision-making, what matters is how the individual or group imagines the milieu to be, not how it actually is' (p. 75).

7. CONCLUSION

It will be seen from this review of the literature that writers on power cover a wide range of views on the subject, and that it is a topic which crosses several discipline boundaries. There is no all-inclusive theoretical perspective, perhaps because writers tend to stay within their particular disciplines when considering this topic, and some power-related concepts, such as 'authority', are seen in radically different ways by different authors. While there is no shortage of literature about power, there is relatively little based on field research in organizations, and hardly any which gives consideration to the perceptions which participants in a social system have of the political processes or structures in that system.

It can be suggested that some general concepts from the social sciences such as 'structures', 'groups', 'values', and 'norms' seem of importance to the understanding of power in its various forms. The interactionist viewpoint seems also particularly relevant to theories based on the $A-B$ model, and all it implies, and to notions of political tactics, bargaining behaviour, the 'struggle for power' and the pursuit of self-interest within organizational settings. Central to theories about power is, of course, the idea that it can be differentially distributed—some individuals or groups having more of it than others, and this in turn raises questions about whether this ought to be the case, and about the legitimacy of political action. However, if the concept of power is to be useful in helping us to understand the behaviour of individuals and groups, particularly in organizational settings, what seems called for now is a great deal more field research, so that theories of power can be more soundly based in real events, the actions, thoughts, and feelings of organizational actors, than they are at present.

REFERENCES

Adler, A. (1958). *The Individual Psychology of Alfred Adler*, H. L. Ansbacher and R. R. Ansbacher (eds), London: Allen and Unwin.

Agger, R. E., Goldrich, D., and Swanson, B. E. (1964). *The Rulers and the Ruled: Political Power and Impotence in American Communities*, New York: John Wiley.

Allison, G. T. (1971). *The Essence of Decision*, Boston. Little, Brown.

Ansbacher, H. L. and Ansbacher, R. R. (eds) (1958). *The Individual Psychology of Alfred Adler*, London: Allen and Unwin.

Argyris, C. (1972). *The Applicability of Organizational Sociology*, Cambridge: Cambridge University Press.

Bacharach, S. B. and Aiken, M. (1976). Structural and process constraints on influence in organizations, *Administrative Science Quarterly*, **21** (4), 623–642.

——and Lawler, E. J. (1980). *Power and Politics in Organizations*, San Francisco: Jossey-Bass.

Bachrach, P. and Baratz, M. (1962). Two faces of power, *American Political Science Review*, **56**, November 947–952.

Bailey, F. G. (1969). *Strategems and Spoils*, Oxford: Basil Blackwell.

——(1977). *Morality and Expediency*, Oxford: Basil Blackwell.

Bates, F. L. (1970). Comments on 'Political Economy: A Framework for Comparative Analysis', by M. N. Zald, in *Power in Organizations*, M. N. Zald (ed.), Nashville: Vanderbilt University Press.

Bierstedt, R. (1950). An analysis of social power, *American Sociological Review*, **15**, 730–738.

Blau, P. (1964). *Exchange and Power in Social Life*, New York: Wiley.

——(1970). Decentralization and bureaucracies, in *Power in Organizations*, M. N. Zald (ed.), Nashville: Vanderbilt University Press.

Bradshaw, A. (1976). A critique of Steven Lukes' 'Power: A Radical View', *Sociology* **10** (1), January, 121–127.

Bucher, R. (1970). Social process and power in medical school, in: *Power in Organizations*, M. N. Zald (ed.), Nashville: Vanderbilt University Press.

Clark, J. V. (1970). A healthy organization, in *The Planning of Change*, W. G. Bennis, K. D. Benne, and R. Chin (eds), London: Holt, Rinehart and Winston.

Crespigny, A. de (1968). Power and its forms, *Political Studies*, **XVI** (2) 192–205.

Crozier, M. (1964). *The Bureaucraic Phenomenon*, London: Tavistock.

Dahl, R. A. (1957). The concept of power, *Behavioural Science*, **2**, July, 201–205

——(1968). Power, in *International Encyclopaedia of the Social Sciences*, Vol. 12, 405–415.

Dalton, G. W. Barnes, L. B. and Zaleznik, A. (1968). *The Distribution of Authority in Formal Organizations*, Cambridge, Mass: Harvard University Press.

Dalton, M. (1959). *Men Who Manage*, New York: John Wiley.

Day, J. (1963). Authority, *Political Studies*, **XI** (3), 257–271.

Dearlove, J. (1973). *The Politics of Policy in Local Government*, Cambridge: Cambridge University Press.

Deutsch, K. (1963). *The Nerves of Government*, Glencoe: The Free Press.

Emerson, R. M. (1962). Power-dependecy relations, *American Sociological Review*, **27**, February, 31–41.

Etzioni, A. (1961). *A Comparative Analysis of Complex Organizations*, Glencoe: The Free Press.

——(1964). *Modern Organizations*, New Jersey: Prentice-Hall.

Freire, P. (1973). *The Pedagogy of the Oppressed*. Harmondsworth: Penguin Books.

French, J. R. P. and Raven, B. (1959). The bases of social power, in *Group Dynamics Research and Theory*, L. Cartwright and A Zander (eds), London: Tavistock.

Gamson, W. A. (1968). *Power and Discontent*, Homewood, Illinois: The Dorsey Press.

Giddens, A. (1968). 'Power' in the recent writings of Talcott Parsons, in *Modern Sociology*, P. Worsley (ed.), Harmondsworth: Penguin Books.

Goldner, F. H. (1970). The division of labour: process and power, in *Power in Organizations*, M. N. Zald (ed.), Nashville: Vanderbilt University Press.

Goldthorp, J. H. (1966). Attributes and behaviour of car assembly workers, *British Journal of Sociology*, **17** 227–245.

Gouldner, A. (1970). *The Coming Crisis in Western Sociology*, London: Heinemann.

Hall, P. M. (1972). A symbolic interactionist analysis of politics, in *Perspectives in Political Sociology*, A. Effrat (ed.), Indianopolis: Bobbs-Merrill.

Hall, R. H. and Bates, F. L. (1970). Comments on 'Decentralization in Bureaucracies' by P. Blau, in *Power in Organizations*, M. N. Zad (ed.), Nashville: Vanderbilt University Press.

——and Wamsley, G. L. (1970). Comments on 'Social Process and Power in a Medical School' by R. Bucher, in *Power in Organizations*, M. N. Zald (ed.), Nashville: Vanderbilt University Press.

Handy, C. (1976). *Understanding Organizations*, Harmondsworth: Penguin Books

Hawley, A. H. (1963). Community power and urban renewal success, *American Journal of Sociology*, **68**, 422–531.

Helm, C. and Morelli, M. (1979). Stanley Milgram and the Obedience Experiment, *Political Theory*, **7** (3), August 321–345.

Hickson, D. J., Hinings, C. R., Lee, C. A., Schneck, R. E., and Pennings, J. M. (1971). The strategic contingencies theory of intraorganizational power, *Administrative Science Quarterly*, **16** (2), 216–229.

Horwitz, M. (1964). Managing hostility in the laboratory and refinery, in *Power and Conflict in Organizations*, R. L. Kahn and E. Boulding (eds), London: Tavistock.

Hurwitz, J. I., Zander, A. F., and Hymivitch, B. (1968). Some effects of power on the relations among group members, in *Group Dynamics Research and Theory*, D. Cartwright and A. Zander (eds), London: Tavistock.

Kanter, R. M. (1972). Symbolic interactionism and politics in systemic perspective, in *Perspectives in Political Sociology*, A. Effrat (ed.), Indianapolis: Bobbs-Merrill.

Kaplan, A. (1964). Power in perspective, in *Power and Conflict in Organizations*, R. L. Kahn and E. Boulding (eds), London: Tavistock.

Kaplowitz, S. A. (1978). Towards a systematic theoty of power attribution, *Social Psychology*, **41** (2), 131–148.

Kelman, H. C. (1965). Manipulation of human behaviour, *Journal of Social Issues*, **XXL** (2), 31–46.

Kotter, J. P. (1978). Power, success and organizational effectiveness, *Organizational Dynamics*, **6**, Winter, 26–40.

44 Power, Politics, and Organizations

Lasswell, H. D. (1930/1960). *Psychopathology and Politics*, Chicago: Chicago University Press.

Lemert, E. M. (1964). Deviance and social control, in: *Modern Sociology*, P. Worsley (ed.), Harmondsworth: Penguin Books.

Lockwood, D. (1956). Some remarks on 'The Social System', in *Modern Sociology*, P. Worsley (ed.), Harmondsworth: Penguin Books.

Lukes, S. (1974). *Power: A Radical View*, London: Macmillan.

Mangham, I. (1979). *The Politics of Organizational Change*, London: Associated Business Press.

Martin, N. H. and Sims, J. H. (1956). Power tactics, *Harvard Business Review*, November–December, 25–29.

Mechanic, D. (1962). Sources of power of lower participants in complex organizations, *Administrative Science Quarterly*, 7, December, 349–364.

Miles, R. E. (1965). Human relations or human resources? *Harvard Business Review*, 43, July–August, 148–163.

Miliband, R. (1969). *The State in Capitalist Society*, London: Weidenfeld and Nicolson.

Milner, M. (1950). *On Not Being Able to Paint*, London: Heinemann.

Mulder, M. (1960). The power variable in communication experiments, Human Relations, 13, 241–257.

Olsen, M. (1970). *Power in Societies*, London: Macmillan.

Ouchi. W. G. (1977). Relations between structure and control, *Administrative Science Quarterly*, 22, March, 95–113.

Perrow, C. (1970). Departmental power and perspectives in industrial firms, in *Power in Organizations*, M. N. Zald (ed.), Nashville: Vanderbilt University Press.

Peters, R. S. (1959). Authority, in *Social Principles and the Democratic State*, S. E. Benn and R. S. Peters (ed.), London: George Allen and Unwin.

Pettigrew, A. (1973). *The Politics of Organizational Decision-making*, London: Tavistock.

——(1975). Towards a political theory of organization intervention, *Human Relations*, 28 (3) 191–208.

——(1979). On studying organizational cultures, *Administrative Science Quarterly*, 24 (4) December, 570–581.

Roy, D. (1955). Making out: A worker's counter-system of control of work situation and relationships, in *Industrial Man*, T. Burns (ed.), Harmondsworth: Penguin Books.

Salancik, G. R. and Pfeffer, J. (1977). Who gets power—and how they hold on to it: A strategic contingency model of power, *Organizational dynamics*, 5 Winter, 3–21.

Sanford, R. Nevitt (1964). Individual conflict and organizational interaction, in *Power and Conflict in Organizations*, R. L. Kahn and E. Boulding (eds), London: Tavistock.

Schaar, J. H. (1970). Reflections on Authority, *New American Review*, 8, 44–80.

Smith P. and Drake R. (1972). Behavioural Sciences in Industry, New York: McGraw Hill.

Sprout, H. and Sprout, M. (1965). *The Ecological Perspective on Human Affairs with Special Reference To International Politics*, Princeton: Princeton University Press.

Strauss, G. (1962). Tactics of lateral relationships, *Administrative Science Quarterly*, 7, September, 161–186.

Tannenbaum, A. S. (1973). *Social Psychology of the Work Organization*, London, Tavistock.

Tushman, M. L. (1977). A political approach to organizations, *Academy of Management Review,* **2** (2), 206–216.

Walliman, I., Rosenbaun H., Tatsis, N., and Zito, G. (1980). Misreading Weber: the concept of 'Macht', *Sociology*, **14** (2), May, 261–275.

Walton, R. E. (1965). Two strategies of social change and their dilemmas, in *The Management of Change and Conflict*, J. M. Thomas and W. G. Bennis (eds), Harmondsworth: Penguin Books.

Weber, M. (1948). *From Max Weber* (translated and edited by H. H. Gerth and C. Wright Mills), London: Routledge and Kegan Paul.

Winch, P. (1959). Authority, in *Social Principles and the Democratic State*, S. I. Benn and R. S. Peters (eds), London: George Allen and Unwin.

Winnicott, D. W. (1974). *Playing and Reality*, Harmondsworth: Penguin Books.

Winter, D. G. (1973). *The Power Motive,* New York: The Free Press.

Worsley, P. (ed.) (1970). *Modern Sociology*, Harmondsworth: Penguin Books.

Wrong. D. (1979). *Power: Its Forms, Bases and Uses*, Oxford: Basil Blackwell.

Zald, M. N. (1970). Political economy: a framework for comparative analysis in *Power in Organizations*, M. N. Zald (ed), Nashville: Vanderbilt University Press.

Zaleznik, A. (1970). Power and Politics in Organizational Life. *Harvard Business Review*. 3. May–June, 47–60.

Power, Politics, and Organizations: A Behavioural Science View
Edited by Andrew Kakabadse and Christopher Parker
© 1984 John Wiley & Sons Ltd

Chapter 3

The Legitimacy Cycle: Long-term Dynamics in the Use of Power*

WILLIAM E. HALAL

THE IMPENDING SHIFT IN POWER

The use of power has always been a central concern in organizations, of course, but the turbulent events of the past decade or two have raised the serious possibility that a subtle but important shift may be imminent in the power structure of modern organizations.

One prominent indication of such a shift can be seen in changing attitudes towards institutional authority. Most developed nations, such as the USA, the European states, and Japan, experienced a rather unusual wave of 'liberation' movements during the past two decades among minorities, students, women, and other relatively powerless groups, which now show signs of spreading to employees as well (Harris, 1974). Rising affluence, guaranteed job security, incomes from two-career families, the heightened sophistication fostered by electronic media, and other developments have produced a new breed of workers who are often less respectful of their superiors (Fritz, 1979; Kerr and Rosow, 1979; Jenkins, 1974; Berkeley, 1971). This has been further aided by the 'me-decade' of the 1970s that encouraged self-fulfillment values, especially among the younger cohort of the post-world-war baby boom that is now maturing (Yankelovich, 1974). As one executive in a major corporation candidly told the author, 'Young business people comprise a quiet revolution from within the firm.

A second cause for change in the use of organizational power emanates from the revolution in office technology that is spreading like wildfire (Drucker, 1980; Hiltz and Turoff, 1978). The use of computerized information networks tends to 'short-circuit' the traditional hierarchy, and many

*For a fuller treatment of this theme and related topics, see the author's book *The New Capitalism: Democratic Free Enterprise in Post-Industrial Society*, John Wiley & Sons Inc., New York, 1984.

authorities claim that an electronic equivalent of the old cottage industries should soon become common in which employees may work from their homes rather than under the thumbs of their supervisors (Toffler, 1980b). The implications for altering the traditional superior-subordinate relationship are awesome. One manager expressed a typical reaction: 'We're trained to supervise people who are sitting there and who look like they're working hard' (*Business Week*, 1981).

Finally, a third major force for change lies in the urgency of developing more productive institutional relationships. Almost the entire developed world has been experiencing an economic crisis during the past few years, and an important focus of this crisis seems to involve structural changes that are intended to bring relevant parties into business policy-making (*Business Week*, 1980). Such changes would involve employees in what have heretofore been exclusively managerial decisions and responsibilities, and some authorities also suggest that corporate governance should represent a political coalition or 'social contract' among management, investors, labour, customers, the public, suppliers and distributors, and possibly other constituencies of large 'quasi-public' firms (Nader *et al.*, 1976; Stone, 1975; Halal, 1978). Institutional changes of this type represent social upheavals that only occur during periods of profound social transition, but there are many signs that they may be required to cope with the erupting complexity of a 'post-industrial' world. Noted business professor George Steiner believes that 'we are redefining capitalism' (Steiner and Miner, 1977).

In view of such widespread prospects for important change in power structures, there is considerable confusion and uneasiness about how organizational power should be used by managers and executives, politicians and government officials, workers and labour leaders, representatives of public interest groups, and others who are involved. What do trends on the changing use of power actually suggest? Which areas of managerial prerogatives should be opened to the influence of other parties? How will managers maintain effective control over organizational performance in the face of these numerous and conflicting power centres?

This chapter presents a conceptual framework and empirical data that provide some answers to these questions. An analysis of research data from previous studies conducted by my associates and I supports the view that there exists a long-range tendency towards increasing freedom of subordinates from supervisory control. This conclusion is further clarified using the concept of a 'legitimacy cycle' which provides a model for understanding the dynamics of organizational power over the long term. Implications of this work are then explored to forecast future changes in the way power is likely to be used in organizations, and to suggest how managers may develop strategies for controlling such changes effectively.

CONCEPTUAL FRAMEWORK

For the purpose of this study, *power* is defined as the potential or ability to exercise influence over the decisions of others, to determine their behaviour to some degree, to establish the direction of future action. *Leadership* is the use of power for these purposes. That is, leaders employ various forms of influence to mobilize followers effectively. *Control* is the end result or objective of influence. The central concept that is fundamentally involved in these related concepts of power, leadership, and control, then, is *influence*. Influence is regarded in this framework as the underlying process through which leaders obtain their power to control events. Leaders may derive their power from a variety of different types of influence, such as the use of physical coercion or force, money and economic resources, formal and legal authority, social pressure or status, special skills and knowledge, personal vision and charisma, and possibly other such sources (Cartwright, 1965).

An aspect of influence which is particularly important is the issue of *legitimacy*. Influence becomes legitimate when followers accept a leader's power because they believe it to be sufficiently just and rightful to comply willingly, rather than to submit grudgingly or to oppose the leader. Furthermore, legitimacy is essential to the successful conduct of leadership. As Chester Barnard pointed out some time ago, the power of managers may appear to flow from higher authorities in the organization, but true power ultimately is obtained by gaining the support of subordinates (Barnard, 1938). In other words, influence may be exercised from the top-down, but its legitimacy is drawn from the bottom-up. When legitimacy is lost, the influence of the leader will usually wane as well, as dramatically illustrated by some notorious political instances recently, such as the revolutions in Iran, Nicaragua, and even the Watergate crisis in the United States. Former US Secretary of State Cyrus Vance stated this fundamental axiom in the use of power effectively: '[Once] a government has lost its legitimacy if the eyes of its people, no amount of outside intervention can secure its long-term survival' (Vance, 1979).

A recent but growing literature exists in the field of organization studies concerning the legitimacy of management influence. Schein and Ott (1962) conducted a seminal study that analysed attitudes concerning the legitimacy of supervisors influencing various types of subordinate behaviour. Other studies have subsequently utilized this same conceptual framework to investigate different aspects of the topic. Schein and Lippitt (1966) correlated supervisor attitudes towards the legitimacy of influence with key organizational variables; Davis (1968) studied attitudes towards managerial efforts to influence employees; Heizer and Litton (1972) surveyed the legitimacy of influence among minorities; Kemp (1973) investigated the relationship between legitimacy and leadership; and Bedian (1975) provided a cross-cultural comparison between the attitudes of managers in the USA and Germany. As a result of this accumulation of research evidence, the concept of legitimacy of influence has become well-established and there now exists a reasonably accurate understanding of how norms of legitimacy are distributed.

The conceptual framework developed by Schein and Ott (1962) essentially describes the extent of agreement within an organizational culture as to whether it is legitimate or not for supervisors to influence various types of subordinate behaviour. This is measured along a 'legitimacy scale' that varies between two bipolar concepts. At one ends, there is complete consensus that it is legitimate to influence some particular form of behaviour; this is the 'maximum legitimacy' end of the scale, or what would be described as total supervisory *control* over subordinates. At the opposite end, complete consensus exists that it is *not* legitimate to influence some form of behaviour; this is the 'minimum legitimacy' or 'maximum illegitimacy' end of the scale, or what could be called total subordinate *freedom*. The legitimacy of various particular forms of behaviour will usually lie at different points along this scale. As Schein and Ott (1962) pointed out, forms of behaviour lying near either end represent high agreement, while the middle of the scale represents disagreement or conflict.

Although this framework seems well-designed to study influence in static terms, such norms are actually dynamic because they are likely to move along this scale with time. There is a need, therefore, to extend this framework to the measurement of *changes* in norms of legitimacy. This study is unique because it uses time-series data to investigate these long-term dynamics in the legitimacy of influence.

EMPIRICAL DATA BASE

The study is based on earlier research conducted by Halal and Nakshbendi (1980) that replicated the original survey of Schein and Ott (1962). Both surveys measured attitudes among a large sample of organizational members in the Northeastern United States concerning the legitimacy of supervisors influencing various forms of subordinate behaviour. These two studies, therefore, comprise a simple time-series data base covering approximately a 13-year interval that brackets the past period of critical social change.

Both surveys were based on the instrument development by Schein and Ott (1962) which contains 55 items measuring attitudes towards various types of subordinate behaviour. Respondents were asked to answer 'Yes' or 'No' to the statement—'It is legitimate for a superior to attempt to influence his subordinate in terms of:'—which was followed by individual statements describing the 55 different types of behaviour. Aggregate responses were reduced into a single index for each item that represents the degree of legitimacy along a scale from +100 to −100; '+100' indicates maximum legitimacy, while '−100' indicates minimum legitimacy or maximum illegitimacy. The validity and reliability of the instrument were confirmed before its use.

Table 1 Legitimacy of Influence Indices
(+100 = Maximum legitimacy, −100 = Minimum legitimacy

Item[a]	1962 Study	1975 Study Original sample	1975 Study Adjusted sample[b]	Change in legitimacy (1975 adjusted indices − 1962 indices)
7 Alcohol during work	+84	+76	+73	−11
27 Working hours	+84	+81	+83	− 1
34 Temperament on job	+82	+81	+86	+ 4
1 Getting along with people	+79	+68	+75	− 4
44 Tidiness of office	+79	+53	+56	−23
36 Criticism of compamy	+76	+56	+58	−18
10 Family calls	+74	+74	+75	+ 1
25 Job-related education	+74	+59	+65	− 9
6 Use of profane language	+72	+72	+65	− 7
45 Use of working time	+65	+62	+68	+ 3
19 Job-related reading	+64	+45	+52	−12
26 New job relocation	+59	+32	+27	−32
52 Alcohol during lunch	+58	+33	+43	−15
37 Supervision of secretary	+54	+51	+66	+12
16 Type of clothing	+47	+20	+16	−31
38 Form of addressing colleagues	+46	+41	+50	+ 4
13 Help in recruiting	+28	−23	−18	−46
39 Formality of clothing	+26	− 4	− 2	−28
5 Attitude towards unions	+24	−62	−54	−78
14 Competition with peers	+12	+ 8	+32	+20
42 Taking work home	+ 6	− 7	+ 5	− 1
40 Use of company products	− 1	−46	−36	−35
53 Public activities	−11	−72	−65	−54
48 Company social functions	−13	−77	−76	−63
35 Sexual morality	−19	−76	−71	−52
11 Organizational politics	−19	−40	−23	− 4
55 Organizational athletics	−21	−70	−66	−45
32 Attitude towards money	−37	−77	−58	−21
4 Wearing beard or moustache	−39	−83	−81	−42
24 Leisure time with subordinates	−49	−77	−72	−23
46 Faithful to spouse	−54	−90	−81	−27
43 Attitude towards savings	−57	−89	−81	−24
47 Drinks at home	−59	−83	−76	−17
30 Affiliation with clubs	−59	−79	−75	−16
3 Leisure time with superiors	−63	−80	−73	−10
20 Use of credit	−65	−86	−74	− 9
2 Donation to charity	−68	−95	−94	−26

Table 1 Legitimacy of Influence Indices *continued*
(+100 = Maximum legitimacy, −100 = Minimum legitimacy)

Item[a]	1962 Study	1975 Study		Change in legitimacy (1975 adjusted indices − 1962 indices)
		Original sample	Adjusted sample[b]	
28 Leisure time with peers	−68	−87	−81	−13
18 Personal friends	−70	−87	−74	− 4
51 Friendship in rival company	−70	−84	−75	− 5
41 Life insurance	−72	−91	−86	−14
12 Location of residence	−74	−90	−86	−12
33 Attitude towards smoking	−77	−83	−76	+ 1
8 Ownership of home	−81	−95	−90	− 9
49 Amount of entertaining	−83	−96	−93	−10
23 Type of home	−84	−97	−93	− 9
54 Employment of spouse	−87	−95	−92	− 5
17 Choice of spouse	−88	−95	−91	− 3
9 Type of car	−89	−95	−94	− 5
15 Political party	−92	−98	−96	− 4
21 Number of children	−92	−93	−89	+ 3
31 Children's school	−94	−95	−87	+ 7
50 Choice of charge accounts	−94	−98	−95	− 1
22 Vacation plans	−95	−98	−96	− 1
29 Church attendance	−96	−97	−95	+ 1
Mean	−17.2	−36.7	−32.3	−15.0[c]
S.D.	64.4	63.0	59.7	19.9

[a] Item descriptions are abbreviations of the complete items originated by Schein and Ott (1962).
[b] Adjusted sample is the original sample corrected to match the 1962 sample.
[c] Significant at the 0.05 level.

The principle results are presented in Table 1 which contains legitimacy of influence indices arranged in decreasing order. The original data (collected in 1975) have been adjusted to match the sample characteristics of the 1962 survey in order to make the two sets of results comparable.

Both sets of data agree closely regarding what constitutes legitimate versus illegitimate forms of influence. Behaviour which is considered to be legitimately influenced tends to be more directly related to job performance—'alcohol during work', 'working hours', 'temperament on job', and so forth. At the other end of the legitimacy scale, behaviour that is considered illegitimate tends to be of a more personal nature—'church attended', 'vacation plans', and so forth. This close agreement is confirmed by the high correlation between rank orders of the two studies (Spearman's rho = 0.98).

As further shown in Table 1, algebraic differences were also obtained between the legitimacy indices of the two studies to determine the change in legitimacy which occurred during the intervening 13-year period. Legitimacy decreased for 45 of the items, with some having decreased considerably. The greatest decreases occurred over 'attitudes towards unions', 'company social functions', 'public activities', and 'sexual morality', which have all decreased by more than 50 index points, or a quarter of the entire scale. The greatest increase was over 'competition with peers' which has gained 20 points. The changes were generally much greater for instances of decreasing legitimacy than for the few cases of increasing legitimacy. The mean decrease for all 55 items was 15.0 index points, or 7.5 per cent of the legitimacy scale, which is significant at the 0.05 level.

If changes in legitimacy are studied as they vary along the legitimacy scale (that is, from the top to the bottom of Table 1), some interesting observations are suggested about the dynamic process by which norms of legitimacy change. Most items are concentrated at the two extreme ends of the scale, and these items change so little that there seems to be a rather clear and stable concensus as to what constitutes legitimate verses illegitimate forms of influence. However, the greatest and most varied changes appear to take place in the neutral, middle range of the scale where opinion is more evenly divided over controversial types of subordinate behaviour. This curvilinear tendency towards greater changes in the middle range of the legitimacy scale was confirmed by analysis of variance (ANOVA) which shows the relationship to be significant at the 0.001 level. This would suggest that the consensus of opinion shifts in a rather well-defined, turbulent, and controversial period that marks the passage of organizational norms of influence as they make a transition from the status of legitimacy to illegitimacy.

A TENDENCY TOWARDS DECREASING LEGITIMACY

One of the more important conclusions of this study is that there exists a long-range tendency towards decreases in the legitimacy of organizational power. Over the 13-year period between studies, the vast majority of behavioural areas showed a decrease in legitimacy and only a few items increased. Also, the magnitude of change was much greater for instances of decreasing legitimacy than for the few cases of legitimacy increases. As a result, the mean change for all items represented a statistically significant decrease. On the basis of this evidence, we conclude that significant decreases in legitimacy appear to have occurred during the period from 1962 to 1975 for large organizations in Northeastern areas of the United States.

Naturally, these findings should be accepted with some caution. Although the 1975 data are believed to represent a reasonably faithful replication of the 1962 survey, it is always possible that the observed changes may be attributable to spurious results from unknown causes, such as unrecognized differences in the sample, or possibly other factors. However, multiple regression studies (Halal and Nakshbendi, 1980), and adjustments that were made in the 1975 sample to match the 1962 sample indicate that these data are not particularly sensitive to sample differences. It should be noted that other comparable studies also indicate that significant decreases in legitimacy have taken place recently (Papp, 1976).

It seems more likely, therefore, that these data actually do reflect changes in attitudes which have occurred during this period. This conclusion would support the common observation that a relaxation of organizational control appears to have taken place during the past few years, in contrast to the more conforming period of the 'organization man' that prevailed prior to the cultural changes of the past decade or two (Whyte, 1956).

Furthermore, although this study seems to have covered a somewhat unusual period of social turbulence, there is good justification for believing that these findings are generally representative of long-term trends. If one examines the history of industrial relations (Bendix, 1956; Wren 1972), it seems clear that almost *all* forms of subordinate behaviour were legitimately influenced by employers at the beginning of industrialization, including the most highly personal areas such as church attendance and marital practices. A quaint old sign that was once displayed in a New England factory reads: 'The Company will not employ any one [sic] who is habitually absent from public worship on the Sabbath, or whose habits are not regular and correct'.

Thus, almost all of the behavioural items of this study were at one time located at the legitimate end of the scale and they have progressively spread towards the illegitimate end over a very long time. It is undoubtedly true that such attitudes may oscillate somewhat, but over the long term there appears to exist an historical tendency towards decreasing legitimacy of influence which seems to be reflected in these data. One of the main conclusions of this study, therefore, is to confirm the theory that institutional power continuously evolves towards increased subordinate freedom and participative forms of organizational governance. In the words of Warren Bennis: 'Democracy is Inevitable' (Bennis, 1966).

THE LEGITIMACY CYCLE

Perhaps the most intriguing and central outcome of this study concerns the dynamic process by which norms of legitimacy change. Our findings suggest that attitudes regarding legitimacy pass through a fairly orderly and predictable sequence of stages that could be best described as a 'legitimacy cycle'. Figure 1 illustrates a proposed 'flow model' of this cycle, which is superimposed over the principal study results; legitimacy indices of Table 1 comprise a scatter plot of the data, and the ANOVA results provide a trend line for these data points.

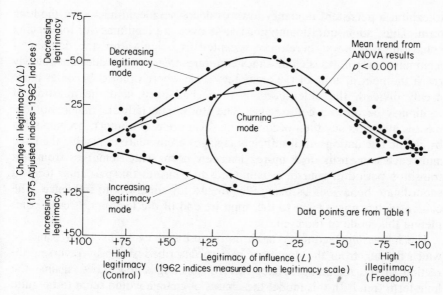

Figure 1 The legitimacy cycle

The legitimacy cycle constitutes a 'flow model' in the sense that the two variables of Figure 1 are logically related in a recursive fashion such that all data points move with time in a clockwise direction along various trajectories. As indicated, data points representing decreases in legitimacy will form a trajectory as they move to the right with time, those representing increases in legitimacy will flow to the left, and those near the origin will tend to move in a clockwise circle. Using this concept of the legitimacy cycle, the data in this study can be usefully interpreted as representing three corresponding components, or modes of change, that comprise basic variations in the long-term dynamics of legitimacy: the 'decreasing legitimacy' mode, the 'increasing legitimacy' mode, and the 'churning' mode.

The most common of these is the *decreasing* legitimacy mode, which roughly approximates the average trend of the data because of the general tendency towards decreasing legitimacy that was demonstrated above. Interpretation of these data shows the following sequential stages seem to take place in this mode as organizational norms proceed through a transition from legitimacy to illegitimacy over the long term.

As indicated, most types of behaviour appear to cluster at either end of the legitimacy scale. That is, there apparently exist stable norms within an organizational system which are widely agreed upon as to which types of subordinate behaviour are either legitimate or illegitimate for superiors to influence. However, the findings indicate that the majority of items appear to exhibit a persistent tendency towards decreasing legitimacy over the long term. Thus, some questioning must arise over the legitimacy of influencing behaviour which was heretofore accepted as being within the domain of legitimate control. As such deviancy continues to grow, attitudes must slowly reach the neutral zone of the legitimacy scale where opinion becomes more evenly divided, the older norm is then challenged, and the question of legitimacy becomes a controversy. The study data indicate that major decreases in legitimacy then occur during this period of conflict, accompanied by erratic fluctuations until sufficient changes accumulate to resolve the issue and reach consensus once more. The new norm which emerges from this transition period of course, usually tends to consider this particular form of subordinate behaviour as being illegitimate for superiors to influence. The consensus has now swung to the opposite end of the legitimacy scale, completing this mode of the cycle.

The *increasing* legitimacy mode is represented by items 14, 37, and 38 which deviate from the dominant pattern described above by reversing direction in the legitimacy cycle, thereby forming a 'backflow' against the long-term trend. In this mode, the phases of change would seem to be quite similar to those of the decreasing mode, although they occur in reverse order. Various forms of behaviour that have become controversial are likely to undergo erratic changes as before, but ultimately this conflict would be resolved to reach consensus that such behaviour is again legitimate for supervisors to influence. This component of the legitimacy cycle may thereby produce a complete cycle by causing behaviour that had been considered controversial, or possibly even illegitimate, to retain legitimacy once again.

The third possible component of the legitimacy cycle, the *churning* mode, is a combination of the previous two. In this case, illustrated by items 11 and 42, a temporary decrease in legitimacy is followed by a temporary increase, which may be followed by another decrease, and so on. This would constitute long periods of controversy in which the margin of opinion swings in one direction and then another, forming a clockwise churning action about the origin of the legitimacy scale.

An interesting question remains unanswered by this concept of the legitimacy cycle. How is it possible to know which of these three trajectories, any particular issue will take? That is, if various types of future behaviour are possible, what determines which one will be chosen?

This question can be understood by recognizing that the relationships in Figure 1 describe a recursive function. That is, indices measured along the legitimacy scale for the independent variable, *legitimacy of influence* (L), will at later points in time ($t+1$) be equal to the indices at some earlier time (t) plus the associated value of the dependent variable *change in legitimacy* ($\triangle L$). This relationship can be expressed as:

$$L_{t+1}=L_t+\triangle L$$

Where:

$$\triangle L = F(L_t)$$

And combining produces the recursive function:

$$L_{t+1}=L_t+F(L_t)$$

Thus, future legitimacy is determined by the previous level of legitimacy plus some change that is also a function of the earlier level. In effect, this means that norms of legitimacy are self-determined, which is a characteristic feature of living systems. Organizational systems, like all other living systems, are largely free to choose their future. So it is impossible to *predict* future behaviour of this type in some strictly deterministic sense, and the best we can hope for is to track past trends in order to project these into the future and thereby estimate the most likely outcome.

To summarize, we propose a cyclical theory of change in which attitudinal norms concerning the legitimacy of influence trace curvilinear trajectories that flow clockwise through two-dimensional legitimacy space, as illustrated in Figure 1. The individual paths of different behavioural items may follow either of the three modes of change outlined above, or they may follow various combinations of these modes which are possible. Of course, the range of time involved in passage through these paths of the legitimacy cycle must be quite long, of the order of several decades. It is important to emphasize that this is a general model that can accommodate patterns of change in either direction, although there seems to be a strong tendency to move in the direction of decreasing legitimacy over the long term.

From a holistic viewpoint, the legitimacy cycle describes the universal process by which individuals tend to gain increasing freedom to act as more responsible human beings. At early stages of development the behaviour of subordinates is almost fully constrained by their superiors, much like the relationship between a child and its parents. However, humans have a persistent and tenacious attraction to freedom in order to realize their own power, and this tendency continually results in a cyclic process by which the least critical areas of behaviour are challenged for legitimacy and ultimately released to the control of subordinates. This process of 'liberation' occurs for individuals as they mature, and collectively for organizations and societies as well on a larger macro scale.

MANAGING THE IMMINENT POWER SHIFT

The previous analyses have concluded that the power of American managers to control the non-performance-related behaviour of their subordinates has decreased significantly during roughly the past two decades and this decline in managerial influence can be effectively understood as part of a long-range process in which organizational norms tend to pass through a transitional cycle from legitimacy to illegitimacy. We now turn our attention to the implications of these findings for managing such power shifts in the future. By drawing on the data reported here concerning changes in legitimacy, the concept of the legitimacy cycle, and other related trends, a forecast is offered describing how organizational power seems likely to change over the long-term period of the next 20 years or so, roughly to the year 2000. This forecast is then used as a basis for defining what appears to be the most effective strategy for organizational governance in the future.

If the trends reported here hold true, the following scenario suggests what organizations may expect over the next two decades. Although quite specific predictions could be made by extrapolating the future location of each item on the legitimacy scale, only general tendencies are indicated because these data are not sufficiently accurate or complete to warrant detailed projections.

Those behavioural areas that are now illegitimate to influence are unlikely to experience large further changes because they have now become stable organizational norms. Only modest moves consolidating the existing consensus may be expected. This type of forecast seems likely for items that have moved well into the illegitimate end of the scale (about −50 to −100): 'political party', 'leisure time with subordinates,' 'sexual morality', and so on. There seems to be wide general agreement that employees should be free to control these private, non-work related areas of behaviour themselves, and this seems unlikely to change.

Employee behaviour that is now in the central, controversial region (about +50 to −50) where there are sharp differences of opinion should experience the greatest changes as these prominent issues are resolved. This would include such items as 'new job relocation', 'types of clothing', 'help in recruiting', 'alcohol during lunch', and so on. Because of the long-term tendency towards decreasing legitimacy, most of these items are likely to pass into the control of employees themselves, although some may regain the legitimacy for managerial control, and others may simply churn as the controversy over them continues. This central zone is characterized by great turbulence over such controversial issues, so it is difficult to make accurate forecasts over individual forms of behaviour.

Attitudes towards forms of behaviour which are now fairly legitimate for supervistors to influence (about +100 to +50) are likely to move towards this central region and become controversial issues in turn. Some areas that may be expected to become increasingly questioned include: 'criticism of company', 'job-related reading', 'tidiness of office', and so forth. If this process of decreasing influence continues over a sufficiently long time, one wonders if even behaviour that is quite directly related to work performance will become illegitimate to influence, such as 'working hours', 'temperament on job', 'getting along with people', 'use of working time', and so on. Of course, such possibilities seem outlandish at first thought, so it may be that the trends observed in this study will not hold true for the future. However, it would be wise to remember that many employee policies of today would have been considered equally preposterous just a decade or two ago.

Serious signs of this sort of liberation can be seen even now in some prominent trends: the increasing acceptance of flexi-time schedules, the emphasis on maintaining privacy of personnel files, greater tolerances for individual idiosyncrasies like homosexuality, increasing interest in employee rights, and other such prerogatives that are being gained by organizational members. For example, IBM, a firm with a past reputation for having a 'button-down' culture of organization men, has moved strongly away from prescribing the behaviour of its employees (*Newsweek*, 1975).

Of course, these forecasts should be treated with some caution because of unavoidable limitations in this study, and wide variations will undoubtedly occur among regional areas, organizational cultures, individual persons, and different points in time. It is also important to recognize that this does not mean 'looser' forms of control will permit anarchy, for the loss of organizational control over critical aspects of organizational performance cannot exist for long without destroying the system. A more reasonable scenario would be that organizational members are likely to be accountable for the work-related *outcomes* of their behaviour—that is, their job performance proper—rather than their behaviour itself. Attempts to control employee behaviour can be quite arbitrary because individuals with idiosyncratic qualities may nonetheless perform as well as others, although in their own unique way, and a variety of approaches always exist to accomplishing most tasks.

Thus organizations are likely to face increasing demands for freedom of employee *behaviour*, but this should also be accompanied by greater accountability for employee *performance*. The economic crisis that grips the developed world can be best understood as the evolution of modern societies into a new era (Toffler, 1980a). Now that the rapid physical growth and material affluence of the industrial era appear to have reached their limits, a keen scrutiny will undoubtedly continue to grow in order to ensure that resources are allocated more effectively to encourage economic productivity, and more equitably in order to foster social well-being. Demands for accountability have been especially severe during the past few years among workers, professionals, managers, private organizations, and governments, which have been increasingly subjected to rigorous new standards of performance. As Peter Drucker (1981) expressed it, '. . . the battle cry for the Eighties and Nineties will be the demand for performance and accountability'.

Furthermore, this transition to a new era has produced new political forces focusing on these two central issues of freedom and control, which are now restructuring the role of government around the developed world. Voters in

Europe, England, the United States, and even workers in Poland have rejected the continued growth of the centralized welfare state, and have firmly indicated that it is time to restore individual freedoms along with individual responsibility for initiative and self-reliance.

The unique significance of the present transition from the industrial era of the past into a new and dimly understood 'post-industrial' era of the future seems to be rather well characterized by this conflict between two very powerful and apparently contradictory trends that are likely to change the use of organizational power. On the one hand, Western culture is becoming far more sophisticated of late, so that it is increasingly unacceptable to hold organizational members to standards of behaviour that involve personal choices that are arbitrary or that are only indirectly related to performance. The genie of employee freedom has been released from the bottle, and it seems highly unlikely that it can be imprisoned again. On the other hand, this same historical transition is placing tough new demands on individuals and institutions to become truly productive in order to restore economic health.

The key to progress in the years ahead seems to require a creative resolution of the tension between these two poles of freedom and control, which may then produce a synergistic release of energy to drive organizations into a new era that lies ahead. Organizations may adapt to these changes by developing more effective systems for ensuring accountability of performance, by creating more organic forms of organization, and by encouraging more sophisticated forms of leadership.

The first of these recommendations requires distinguishing clearly between those uses of power that are legitimate and those that are not. Our findings show that organizations continue to have a legitimate claim on the performance of their members. Unfortunately, this claim is often not enforced effectively because of a poor definition of responsibilities, the absence of sound performance measures, the lack of will to insist on accountability, and other such failings. But organizations have also failed to safeguard adequately the freedoms of their members. Managers often provoke unnecessary obstacles and resistance when they attempt to extend their control to those personal prerogatives that are weakly related to performance and which individuals increasingly cherish.

As a consequence of this failure to clarify both employee accountability and freedom adequately, most organizations suffer from a hazy and muddled fog of uncertainty as to what is expected of their members. A recent study of 190 organizations revealed that more than two-thirds of their managers '. . . have no idea what their standing is in the organization' (*Washington Post*, 1981).

There are a number of ways in which this crucial distinction between legitimacy and illegitimacy may be identified and enforced. One obvious suggestion is to employ the type of methodology that has been developed by studies of this type. It seems entirely feasible in principle to conduct periodic surveys in order to define the boundary of behaviour which can be legitimately influenced, and to monitor changes in this boundary over time in order to provide a rational system for organizational governance. This could then suggest various legitimate forms of accountability, such as the types of behaviour to be evaluated in performance reviews, the feasibility of incentive systems, acceptable measures of performance, equitable productivity standards, realistic job descriptions, and other such definitions of what constitute the essential responsibilities for which organizational members must be held accountable—as well as those areas over which they should retain individual discretion.

If this fundamental imperative for ensuring control over critical aspects of organizational performance can be assured, it would then be far easier for managers and employees to consider structural changes in various systems for accomplishing these results with greater flexibility. Organizations around the world are now experimenting with a very wide variety of innovative methods to provide 'alternative work patterns' to suit the needs of modern organizations. These include quality of work-life programmes, various forms of participative management, industrial democracy, employee rights, management by objectives, automomous work teams, organizational development, matrix organizational structures, the introduction of computerized information networks, and other possibilities that offer a more organic and flexible working environment that is better suited to the complex tasks organizations now face in a turbulent new environment, and that enhance the freedom which sophisticated personnel value (Mills, 1978; Kerr and Rosow, 1979).

Changes of the above two types both seem necessary if modern organizations hope to resolve the increasing tension between control and freedom. Bringing this about, however, will also require far more powerful forms of leadership. Many of the problems facing modern economies stem from the fact that these two fundamental issues have not been addressed very squarely. Studies show, and the author's experience confirms, that most executives continue to rely on a rather authoritarian approach to leadership, albeit concealed thinly behind a rather manipulative facade of 'human relations' skills (Halal and Brown, 1981). The truth of the matter is that most organizations today continue to be managed as benign dictatorships.

The consequence of this outmoded leadership is that the two critical issues of freedom and control have not been addressed very effectively, and this is reflected in the evasive quality of the dilemma facing industrialized economics. The root causes of these problems do not involve macroeconomic policies primarily, but rather a deeply engrained set of cultural traits concerning the way power is used within institutions. The Japanese and German economies are generally healthier than other industrialized nations principally because Japan and Germany have distinctive cultures that embody more effective forms of leadership—not because they have discovered some superior combination of macroeconomic variables. To paraphrase Shakespeare a bit, Prime Minister Thatcher is discovering in England, and President Reagan is learning in the US that 'The fault, dear Brutus, is not in our (government,) but in ourselves. . .'

So the key to resolving the current economic malaise, from this view, involves creating new forms of leadership that may reconcile this perennial conflict between control and freedom that societies have always wrestled with. Because of the wide diversity that increasingly characterizes developed regions of the world, there is no single approach to these issues that can be recommended. Methods of accountability, organizational structures, and leadership styles are likely to grow increasingly complex and varied, which is precisely why there had occurred recently a growing interest in contingency approaches to management.

It is clear, however, that effective leadership will require some form of participation between those exercising power and those subjected to it in order to establish legitimate forms of governance that are acceptable to each unique working group, organization and society. The essential challenge is for organizational leaders to confront their followers with the two most prominent issues that dwell on most peoples minds today, but which we avoid almost daily; the inadequacy of performance, and the inadequacy of freedom. To do so, however, will require heroic leaders who are able to bring that rare but extremely powerful quality of personal charisma into their leadership. Charisma is one of those often discussed but poorly understood terms in leadership. It can be simply thought of as instilling a vision of the future into an organization, a sense of mission and purpose which is so highly valued that it can inspire others. And in an age of such transition that most of us have lost our moorings, it is precisely this renewed dedication to substantive values and goals that is badly needed to guide the way ahead (Gallup and Poling, 1980).

If people can be found to provide this leadership, it is likely that they would be accorded the power to strike an historical bargain between these two demands of control and freedom. Now, as always leaders must negotiate a renewed 'social contract' with their followers that may help to strengthen those fragile psychological ties that hold institutions together. And the heart of this contract today requires that organizational members assume greater responsibility for their performance—in return for obtaining greater freedom from supervisory influence.

REFERENCES

Barnard, C. (1938). *Functions of the Executive*, Cambridge, Mass: Harvard Press.

Bedian, A. G. (1975). A comparison and analysis of German and United States managerial attitudes toward the legitimacy of organizational influence, *Academy of Management Journal*, December, **18**, No. 4, 897–904.

Bendix, R. (1956). *Work and Authority in Industry*, New York: Harper & Row.

Bennis, W. (1966). *Beyond Bureaucracy*, New York: McGraw-Hill.

Berkeley, G. (1971). *The Administrative Revolution*, Englewood Cliffs, NJ: Prentice-Hall.

Business Week (1970). The re-industrialization of America, 2 June.

——(1981). The potential for telecommuting, 26 January, p. 94.

Cartwright, D. (1965). Influence, leadership and control, in March (ed.), *Handbook of Organizations* New York: Rand McNally.

Davis, K. (1968). Attitudes toward the legitimacy of management efforts to influence employees, *Academy of Management Journal*, **2**, 153–162.

Drucker, P. (1981). The coming changes in our school system, *The Wall Street Journal*, 3 March.

——(1980). Managing the information explosion, *The Wall Street Journal*, 10 April.

Fritz, S. (1979). New breed of workers, *U.S. News and World Report*, 3 September.

Gallup, G. and Poling, D. (1980). *The Search for America's Faith*, Nashville Tenn: Abingdon.

Halal, W. E. (1978). Beyond the profit motive, *Technological forecasting & Social Change*, June **12**, No. 1.

——and Brown, B. S. (1981). Participative management: myth and reality, *California Management Review*, Summer.

——and Nakshbendi, G. F. (1980). Changing legitimacy of influence, *Business Journal*, Autumn, **6**, No. 1, 3–9.

Harris, L. (1974). *The Anguish of Change*, New York: W. W. Norton.

Heizer, J. H. and Litton, D. H. (1972). Some negro and white views of organizational legitimacy, *Southern Journal of Business*, August, **7**, 1–7.

Hiltz, S. R. and Turoff, M. (1978). *The Network Nation*, Addison-Wesley.

Jenkins, D. (1974). *Job Power: Blue and White Collar Democracy*, Baltimore, Maryland: Penguin Press.

Kemp, W. B. (1973). Organizational influence and its relation to perceived leader behaviour, in Green and Ray (eds), *Management in an Age of Rapid Technological and Social Change*, Mississippi State: Southern Management Association, pp. 52–59.

Kerr, C. and Rosow, J. (1979). *Work in America: The Decade Ahead*, New York: Van Nostrand Reinhold.

Lasch, C. (1979). *The Culture of Narcissism*, New York: Morton.

Mills, T. (1978). Europe's industrial democracy: an American response, *Harvard Business Review*, November–December, **56**, No. 6.

Nader, R. *et al.* (1976). *Taming the Giant Corporation*, New York: W. W. Norton.

Newsweek (1975). Corporate life: butting out, 10 November.

Papp, J. E. (1976). The legitimacy of organizational influence: a comparison of the attitudes of two generations of management students. Working Paper WP. Massachusetts Institute of Technology, pp. 836–876.

Schein, E. H. and Ott, J. S. (1962). The legitimacy of organizational influence, *American Journal of Sociology*, May, **67**, 692–699.

——and Lippitt, G. L. (1966). Supervisory attitudes toward the legitimacy of influencing subordinates, *The Journal of Applied Behavioural Science*, **2**, No. 2, 199–209.

Steiner, G. and Miner, J. (1977). *Management Policy and Strategy*, New York: Macmillan, p. 46.

Stone, C. (1975). *Where the Law Ends*, New York: Harper & Row.

Toffler, A. (1980a). *The Third Wave*, New York: William Morrow.

——(1980b). The electronic cottage, *Creative Computing* reprinted from *The Third Wave*, December.

Vance, C. (1969). Speech delivered by the US Secretary of State on 23 July as reported in *The Washington Post*, 2 August.

The Washington Post (1981). Report of the Work in America Institute as reported in Careers: the ratings game . . . at work, 25 March.

Whyte, W. H. (1956). *The Organization Man*, New York: Simon and Schuster.

Wren, D. (1972). *The Evolution of Management Thought*, New York: Ronald Press.

Yankelovich, D. (1974). *The New Morality*, New York: McGraw-Hill.

Power, Politics, and Organizations: A Behavioural Science View
Edited by Andrew Kakabadse and Christopher Parker
© 1984 John Wiley & Sons Ltd

Chapter 4

Organizational Development: A Missing Political Dimension?

RONALD G. HARRISON and DOUGLAS C. PITT

INTRODUCTION

As it moves into the 1980s Organization Development (OD) seems to be experiencing something of a hiatus. By contrast with the exuberance and optimism which accompanied its launch in the early 1960s, OD now stands in a more melancholy mood of self-doubt, a posture of defence replacing that of evangelism. The movement which appeared poised to free Western Industrial Man from the chains of unresponsive, inhuman, inefficient, and bureaucratic organizational structures seems itself ironically impotent. OD languishes in a period of criticism and decline.

Some observers would trace these developments to the collapse of the assumption of growth—both personal and economic—upon which the early optimism and success of OD were based. But OD's current defensiveness also stems from a growing body of critical writings which have attacked the crude theoretical bases of OD practice. Our aim in this chapter is to examine this literature which has thrown OD on to the defensive. In our view certain criticisms which it has had to face are well-founded and should be used constructively to point out directions for change in both the theoretical base and the practical applications of OD work. This we attempt to do in the concluding sections of the paper where we argue for a rededication of OD. This, we believe, should be based upon a more explicitly *political* appreciation of organizational life. Other criticisms we find to be unsubstantiated.

Our reasons for being interested in the rehabilitation of OD are related to our belief that the problems to which OD was originally a response have been neither resolved nor substantially diminished. As a diverse literature reveals, the problems of industrial society remain as acute as ever. See, for example, Illich (1973), Higgins (1978), Henderson (1978), Skolimowski (1981), Jenkins and Sherman (1979), and Robertson (1978).

Arguably, the problem of organizations is more pervasive and intractable in modern society than ever before. There is, for example, as Blau and Schoenherr (1973) pointed out, a continuing concern about the accountability of multinational corporations. In the field of public administration, confidence in bureaucratic agencies has been eroded, to be replaced by a disconcerting cynicism. This sees government institutions merely as machines for the mutilation and frustration of public policy. In all organizations, both public and private, one may observe what is best described as the tyranny of job dissatisfaction. The dehumanizing thrust of many current approaches to job design finds its expression in the sheer waste and inefficiency which characterizes the performance of many contemporary organizations, and which reduces all notions of commitment to a strictly calculative one. Added to this are the growing problems of unemployment and the 'new technology' (Showler and Sinfield, 1980).

This raises a puzzle and a paradox. Arguably, the merit of OD lay in the concern of its adherents to address precisely these problems of human satisfaction and organizational performance and, in so doing, to generate the kind of social science theory which, in Argyris' (1972) terms is 'applicable' and yet, precisely at the moment when the problems to which OD was directed have increased in their salience, OD itself seems unable to respond to the challenge of change.

Undeniably, OD has been the target of some extremely negative criticism. It has been subjected to serious and protracted censure from a variety of sources. See, for example, Stephenson (1975), Strauss (1968), Nord (1974), Goodge (1975), Burke (1976), Buchanan (1971), Bennis (1969a), Walton (1965), Pettigrew (1975), and Nichols (1975). Crudely, such criticism has collectively thrown doubt on to OD's applicability. In reviewing this barrage of critical literature we propose to consider several questions: Who are the critics? What precisely are they saying about OD? Do they have reasonable grounds for their criticisms? What might be said by way of counter-criticism? Answers to these questions are essential if we are to evaluate effectively the future biography and relevance of OD. Moreover, exploration of the issues raised by such writers may be one way to distinguish the destructive and, at times, polemical charges to which OD has been, in our view, subjected, from useful areas of feedback which can form the basis for a considered revision of OD theory and practice.

WHO ARE THE CRITICS?

It seems reasonable to ask what sort of motives, background experience, and theoretical preconceptions have influenced the writings of those critical of the OD approach. One of the interesting points which emerges from even a superficial examination of these issues is the observation that many of the critics write from a base within OD itself.

Surprisingly, perhaps, many of the more helpful and critical insights into the OD enterprise have come from figures who have been, or continue to be, mainstream contributors to OD theory and practice. See, for example, Bennis (1969a), Walton (1965), Pettigrew (1975), Mangham (1978), and Friedlander (1976). This would seem to imply that OD has at least some capacity for what Gouldner (1971) termed 'reflexive self-criticism'. The commonly held view that OD has been forced on to the defensive as a result of devastating external criticisms clearly needs modification. Careful scrutiny of the backgrounds of OD critics reveals another interesting finding. The great majority of such criticism is derived from what might be termed academic sources. This may be partly a reflection on the fact that academics operating under a 'publish or perish' reward system do more reporting of their OD work than do freelance consultants or internal change agents. However, it is perhaps significant that managers and workers in organizations which have made use of OD techniques in the implementation of change have not been the loudest voices in the chorus of criticism. Nor is there, as some might have expected, a conspicuous trade union lobby against OD. In fact, Partin (1973) provides evidence in the opposite direction that the experience of both participants and managers with OD programmes is typically enthusiastic.

Another, perhaps rather cheap, point may be made about several of the critical essays which have appeared on OD. A casual reading of this literature might leave the reader with a strange feeling of *déja vu*, for many of these writings are nothing more than poorly rewritten attacks in classic Human Relations thinking: see Strauss (1963).

Now it must be said that Human Relations-bashing is a very popular and bracing sport amongst social science academics. It even forms a basic part of the curriculum in many first- or second-year degree courses for our students. Small wonder then that some academics should be on the lookout for further opportunities for their entertainment. But simply to designate OD as the 'New Human Relations' does scant justice to OD. The serious critic must ground his analysis upon the 'charity principle'; he must characterize the position he wishes to attack at its strongest. Many of OD's critics seem to neglect this fundamental rule of criticism, preferring instead to demolish a 'straw man' concept of OD based upon an often simplistic appreciation of contemporary theory and practice. But, whatever their motives, there may be something in what OD's critics have to say and it is now time to turn our attention to the substance of the criticisms which have been levelled against the field.

CURRENT CRITICISMS OF OD

An examination of the literature critical of OD not surprisingly reveals a number of common areas of concern. Collating the dominant themes across a range of sources we find the critics in broad agreement that OD appears vulnerable to a triple assault. It stands accused of failure to confront three basic issues. First, criticism has been levelled against the 'model of man' at the centre of OD formulations. Secondly, and no less problematically, its practitioners are accused of failing to take proper account of the complexity of organizational functioning. This amounts to the accusation that the 'model of organization' at the centre of OD accounts is naive and simplistic. Thirdly, to complete the assault, we find a criticism of the putative failure of OD practitioners to develop a sophisticated 'model of organizational intervention'. This last may, of course, be seen as a corollary of the earlier criticisms since the emergent consequence of incorrect diagnostic models is incorrect prescription. Taken together, these criticisms imply that OD is faced by *three central crises*: reductionism at the level of the individual; reductionism at the level of the organization; and reductionism at the level of the intervention process. We shall deal with each in turn.

An Amputated Model of Man?

An interesting paper by Blackler and Brown (1978) suggested that 'self-actualization' models of the individual have acquired paradigm status in organizational psychology as they represent 'models of reality which provide the basis for coherent bodies of scientific inquiry'. Most commentators on OD confirm that this self-actualization view of human proclivities and predispositions does indeed provide the key core assumptions about human behaviour within OD writing. Greiner (1980) for example, acknowledges that OD approaches have been dominated by a 'love/trust' view of individuals which values personal growth, autonomy, authenticity, openness, and emotional expression. Similar themes characterize Tannenbaum and Davis' (1969) discussion of their own OD practice. French and Bell (1973), two figures of key importance in the OD literature, articulate essentially the same assumptions in their summary of the work of leading organizational psychologists. Illustrating the dependency on Maslovian and Rogerian-type thinking contained in OD writings, they note that . . .

> Most people have drives towards personal growth and development . . . wish to become more of what they are capable of becoming . . . desire to make and are capable of making a higher level of contribution to the attainment of organizational goals than most organizational environments permit.

In short, in the field of OD, the influence of 'self-actualization' models is strongly felt and, without doubt, the concept of self-actualization has a compelling appeal. As Wilson (1972) notes, such theories have centred upon the necessary and sufficient conditions of psychological 'health', thereby refocusing Freudian theory. In contrast to the negative and deterministic position of the Freudians, self-actualization theory revealed a basically optimistic model of the individual based on a 'free-will' perspective: man can become what he chooses to become. His achievement is a matter of choice and courage, not of circumstances. A morbid view of the personality was thus replaced by one optimistically charting human potential for improvement. See Heather (1970) and Shotter (1976). The implication seems to be that removing barriers to individual achievement will release a tidal flow of human energy, such that the age-old anarchist dream of a mutually cooperative society may be achieved in which one man's freedom of action is limited only by the legitimate aspirations of others.

Arguably, one of the most significant contributions rendered by the 'self-actualization' school to a developing understanding of organizations has been its concentration on the individual, thus providing a necessary antidote to earlier analyses of organizations which demonstrated a theoretical amnesia by forgetting the individual in the analysis. With the publication of the Hawthorne studies and the ensuing 'Neo-Human Relations' writing, the individual was rehabilitated: men were 'brought back in'. In recent years, however, the resultant model of the 'self-actualizing' individual has been subjected to a rising chorus of criticism. Though, in spite of the development of such thinking, it has remained surprisingly resilient. And yet, for all its seductive qualities, there is an important sense in which the model is troublesomely deficient. Simon (1973) has waspishly pointed to the 'herculean' assumptions enshrined in self-actualization writing leading to an 'inexhaustibly creative picture of man'. Ironically, it is this essentially optimistic thrust in the theory which has provided its critics with ammunition. The essential problem would appear to lie in Maslow's synergistic proposition that the goals of individuals and organizations are compatible. This presents what might best be called a 'fallacy of misplaced optimism', for if one thing is clear in the contemporary organization literature it is that the 'happy family' view of organizations must be renounced in favour of a more pluralistic model of their working. Conflict is as endemic in organizations as co-operation. Maslow's insistence that such conflict can be legislated out by enlightened adoption of a 'self-actualization' strategy begs the question. The hostility and suspicion of trade unions, for example, to 'Human Relations' solutions to the present distribution of the 'corporate cake' signal a warning that the move into a 'self-actualization' future may be fraught with difficulty. On this point at least we find sympathy with Nichols' (1975) perspective.

Such difficulties with the self-actualization formulation suggest real problems with the model. As Pitt and Webb (1978) have argued, the Achilles heel of such thinking resides in its basic failure to acknowledge that organizations are, partially, political systems. The merit of a political model of the organizations is that it deals with questions of human motivation and ensuing behaviour as operating within an environment of power and negotiation; neither is central to a self-actualization account.

If the 'self-actualization model' of individual human behaviour has been demonstrated to manifest important weaknesses why, it must be asked, is it still adhered to in much current writing? Such a paradox suggests that the answer might lie in Kuhn's (1970) celebrated analysis of 'scientific revolutions'. Reluctance to abandon 'paradigms' may arise from the perception of painful conceptual readjustment to new ones: the result is inevitable intellectual inertia, one of the major complaints about contemporary OD. The self-actualization model appears, in fact, as an unhappy amalgam of description and prescription. As such, it manifests an important philosophical weakness. 'Is' and 'ought' statements are combined within it in a confused fashion. Self-actualization writers are engaged in an act of analysis and advocacy without clarifying when they are involved in the first or second activity. Resident, too, within this stance is an important problem of value-relativism. Theorists frequently impute their own values to the subjects of their analysis, thereby accelerating the possibility of differences in individual interpretations of 'development'. Such hardly seems an accidental omission. The feelings of the individual are characterized by reference to the dominant value system of the OD specialist, rather than *a posteriori* after empirical analysis.

Such a criticism reveals a curious irony—a theory based on trust and democracy seems destined to deny both! From a professedly humanistic position, self-actualization theorists thus end up in an *authoritarian denouement*. Despite liberalizing intent, OD writers often conclude by defining the organizational (and individual) purpose from a top management perspective; leading in the name of individual growth and development to some very skilful manipulation of people. Blackler and Brown argue that self-actualization doctrines may thus encourage a crude exploitative view of the individual in relation to other individuals and his surrounding society. Self-actualization emerges as a new hedonistic calculus in all but name.

An Amputated Model of the Organization?

A second important criticism of the OD school concerns its characterization of the structural aspects of organizations. Max Weber, the foremost biographer of the bureaucratic phenomenon, showed characteristic percipience in his insistence that, while it displays all-too-familiar disadvantages, certain positive benefits accrue from its technical rationality.

Perhaps misled by the tendency of post-Weberian scholarship to concentrate on the debilitating features of large-scale organization, OD theorists have uncritically allowed themselves to be infatuated by the 'seamy side' of bureaucratic life. This over-concentration on bureaupathology, 'vicious circles', 'dysfunctions' and the like, obscures for them Weber's insightful point that bureaucracy has positive virtues. Such an observation as this may be 'fleshed out' by examination of the organizational writings of one of OD's most prolific authors—Warren Bennis. Bennis has been credited with putting forward . . . 'probably the most widely-publicised view of the organizational future' (Waldo, 1973). He can justifiably be seen as the exemplar of much contemporary writing critical of existing organizations which Wilcox (1969) has suggested has accompanied a period of undoubted social and cultural change. For Bennis, bureaucracy is flawed on two counts. First, as a moral organization, it is acutely disappointing. It truncates the lives of the individuals within it and is ill-suited to their individual needs. It dehumanizes the individual and prevents him achieving self-actualization. Secondly, the organization is out of phase with its environment. Not only is it 'internally' unsatisfactory from the point of view of those 'condemned' to work within it, it is subject too to a 'second and more major shock . . . caused by the scientific and technological revolution' (Bennis, 1969b).

Bennis has constantly reiterated this theme that bureaucracy has outlived its usefulness and must be replaced by more satisfactory organizational forms. The primary alternative for Bennis is the democratic organization. Rejecting criticism of democracy that it is 'nice but inefficient', he insists that it is a functional necessity wherever a social system has to compete for survival under conditions of chronic change. Democratic values are peculiarly well adapted to changing conditions, based as they are on principles of free communication, consensus, and influence based on technical competence as opposed to positional (hierarchical) authority. The climate of the democratic organization supports emotional expression, giving the organization a 'human bias', ensuring simultaneous achievement of efficiency and moral approbation. Bennis (1966) concluded that, 'if bureaucracy was a monumental discovery for harnessing the muscle power of the Industrial Revolution', it had become a 'lifeless crutch that is no longer useful'.

It was Bennis' discontent with the technical and moral performance of bureaucracy that triggered his involvement in the OD movement. For him, OD is a response to the pressures of the 'spastic' times within which we live. The organization is seen as facing a set of exigencies as a result of changes in its environment. The key problem for organizations is learning to deal with the pressures of change. Contemporary organizations cannot cope and they fail to take account of the complex needs of the human organism. They thus work on simplistic models of man and the environment. Bennis therefore formulates the task of OD as a planned, deliberate effort to change and revitalize bureaucratic organizations by reconstituting them. The preferred organizational alternative is the 'organic' form. Within this, collegiate relationships replace those based on hierarchy, greater collaboration is encouraged, and the utilization of 'love/trust' approaches to the inhabitants of the organization replaces more 'authoritarian procedures typical of bureaucracy'. In OD then, we have a programme for the activist intervention of change agents in the reconstitution of organizational society. An activist orientation, moreover, founded upon a philosophy of change enshrining strong negative evaluations of 'bureaucracy'.

The key question, which arises in any attempt to evaluate the 'organizational' writing of Bennis—and, by extension, the other members of the OD movement, is that of asking whether the models of organization provided, both negative and preferred, are useful in evaluating the nature and impact of organizational change, or whether, like the 'model of man' on offer, they are unsatisfactory and amputated. In the view of OD's critics, it is certainly the case that it is seen to be operating with truncated models of organization.

Some of the most trenchant criticisms of Bennis' formulations have been levelled by Perrow (1979). In essence, he suggested that Bennis' writing on organizations is too sweeping and too simplistic. Stigmatizing him as a leading member of the 'science fiction' wing of organizational analysis (elsewhere he refers to Bennis as the Buck Rogers of organizational analysis), Perrow argues that the abandonment of bureaucratic hierarchy may be a misconceived enterprise. In the successful achievement of organizational goals, he insists that a degree of order will be necessary, and bureaucratic rule systems are a key means of providing this. Even OD's so-called 'temporary' organization will require rules once its initial purposes have been met. It too will be subject to omnipresent pressures for bureaucratic routinization.

In terms of his characterization of the 'environmental' problems of bureaucracy, Stephenson (1975) also finds Bennis unperceptive, accusing him of taking an over-deterministic approach to this issue. He confronts Bennis' position that bureaucracy has become a victim of the environment with which it cannot cope, with the question . . . 'Whence arose the technological and scientific changes deemed by Bennis to mark the beginning of the end of bureaucracy?' He concludes that the very changes held to contribute to the demise of bureaucracy are often themselves the product of those same bureaucracies which 'are claimed to suppress and distort growth and innovation'. This point has also been addressed by Vickers (1972), who has taken the view that bureaucratic rule-systems are a necessary condition for successful adaptation to the pressures of a changing environment. On this argument, we must 'design for change by designing for stability'.

Not only can Bennis be criticized for his simplistic account of organization-environmental relations, his characterization of the internal workings of bureaucracy is similarly vulnerable. Stephenson and others attack Bennis' rather deterministic view which treats the individual in a bureaucracy, as a 'victim', presenting a plastic model of organizational behaviour as the product of extraneous impersonal forces. No mention is made of the way in which the individual can 'make out' in the organization. One of the most powerful critiques of deterministic views of bureaucracy has been offered by Gouldner (1955). Referring to the pessimism of these perspectives he insists that they downgrade the role of the individual. Gouldner's corrective indicates that the individual is not merely the passive recipient of rule-systems but is highly creative in negotiating his organizational role. The 'metaphysical pathos' of thinking such as that of Bennis resides in his too-willing assumption that individuals have little part in the construction and reconstruction of the bureaucratic reality which surrounds them. Edmonstone (1979) addresses a similar point when he argues 'that man is capable of forgetting his own authorship of the human (and organisational) world'. On this view the key fault with Bennis' formulation of the organization as transcendent over the individual is that of reificationism. On Edmonstone's argument the organization is best seen as structured through a continual process of negotiation and politicking. See, for example, Mechanic (1962), Child (1972), Strauss (1963), and Elger (1975). Their work stresses that in this 'process of negotiation and bargaining the lower-order' participants have a key activist role to play.

Bennis' conceptual failure on these counts is intimately linked to the model of man fallacy which we dealt with in the last section. The assumption that individuals wish to achieve infinite increments of 'self-actualization' quickly dissolves into an argument that the key factor preventing this heroic achievement is organizational structure. To a truncated model of individual personality is now added an unsatisfactory account of organizational structure. The ultimate development of this analysis may be seen in the writing of radical critics such as Illich (1973) and Pym (1978). The essential yet unresolved problem of their positions is that they employ *a priori* assumptions that the abandonment of organizations and the renunciation of contemporary social forms will release abundant—and hitherto untapped—reserves of self-actualization energy. A realistic corrective to such thinking takes the form of an argument that individuals can (if not invariably) achieve a higher measure of freedom and satisfaction in organizations (including bureaucracies) rather than outside them.

An Amputated Model of Intervention?

A corollary of these reductionist models of the individual and the organization, is a weakness in the model of diagnosis and intervention at the heart of the OD enterprise. OD employs an individualistic/interpersonal approach to organizational renewal. The central diagnostic thrust is psychological rather than socio/political. Such an orientation offers at most limited leverage for designing strategies for organizational change. Such psychologistic intervention strategies are typically underwritten by a concept of the 'organization as a person'. The implications of this *personological metaphor* are that methods and techniques used in the counselling of individual patients are seen as applicable to the organization as a whole. It is our contention that there has been a steady and marked monopolization of the theory and practice of Organization Development by individuals committed to this narrow psychological intellectual tradition. Evidence for this contention emanates from three major sources:

1 Key contemporary writers in OD—as we suggested above—are, as a matter of fact, psychologists.
2 As Sofer (1972) has made clear we can trace the intellectual ancestry of these writers back to the seminal contributions of Freud, Lewin, Rogers, and Maslow.
3 The key competences and skills employed in OD interventions are psychologically-derived. The briefest examination of the OD literature reveals a typical model of intervention not dissimilar to the phases encountered in psychological counselling.

OD interventions typically follow the approach of counselling the 'head' of the organization, rather than examining its 'body'. This anthropomorphic view carries attendant dangers. As Argyris' (1970) work hints there are risks in simply merging the perspective of the interventionist with that of top management. What is worrying here is the development of a peculiarly unitary view of the organization which neglects the 'political' processes within a wider organizational constituency. This may lead to the premature abandonment of a perspective taking as axiomatic the ubiquity of conflict and dissensus as common currencies of organizational exchange. Thus blinkered, OD theorists may be justly alleged to have abdicated concern with organizational politics in favour of a roseate consensual view of organizational life. If substantiated, such criticism amounts to a particularly telling attack on OD and raises an exquisitely excruciating irony. For the moment of abandonment of such a perspective in OD is precisely the moment at which theorists within a 'sociology of organizations' literature have 're-discovered' the political. See Pettigrew (1973), Child (1972), Salaman (1979), Benson (1977), and Pfeffer (1981).

In ignoring the variable of the political dimensions of organizational life, the change agent displays a curious reluctance to discuss questions of organizational power, presumably on the grounds that such a notion does not easily accord with his dominant effective (truth/love) organizational view. The secondary consequences of such abandonment are, presumably, that the OD practitioner condemns himself to irrelevance at the level of his intervention. By ignoring the political dimension in organizational life, he condemns himself to a position of impotence, for he cannot use power to bring about his desired changes,

Now disquiet about the naive political sensivity of OD seems to be gaining ground amongst practitioners. But in so far as there is discussion of the politics of intervention strategy it remains based on theoretically unsatisfactory social psychological notions of power. This 'psychobabble' stresses the need for OD practitioners to find ways of 'empowering' key individuals in their client-systems. Such a process of empowerment is to be accomplished, one gathers, by the judicious use of the myriad technologies of personal growth, sensitivity training, counselling, and so on. From such encounters the individual hopefully emerges, empowered by being more truly centred upon his needs and therefore able to deal more influentially with others. But as Emerson (1962) and others have pointed out there are formidable intellectual difficulties locked into any view of power as the attribute of particular social actors. Power is more helpfully construed as a *property of social relationships* rather than an individual psychological resource which one either possesses or lacks. Political sensitization of OD must then move beyond its current rather narrow preoccupation with social-psychological formulations of interpersonal influence to confront the structural realities of organization power conflicts. Other writers have been no less critical. Burke (1977) suggests that in its treatment of organizational politics, OD would not receive more than a passing grade in any examination, while Herman (1977) and Srivastva (1977) argue that such behaviours as anger, coercion, hate, and aggression are just as normal and human as love, compassion, and peacefulness. OD experts, on this analysis, have shown a total lack of skill in dealing with the so-called 'darker aspects of human behaviour'. OD's commitment to a politics of intervention based on therapeutic ideals leaves it singularly ill-equipped to influence the *realpolitik* of organizational decision-making. The remaining sections of this chapter are dedicated to an exploration of the likely implications of a reconstructed 'politicized' OD.

THE REHABILITATION OF OD?

In summing up the case against OD we find ourselves sympathetic to many of the criticisms which have been raised. But in accepting the validity of these charges against OD we do not necessarily agree with those observers who have gone on to call for its wholesale dismantling. The problem as we see it, is to develop a remedial programme for OD capable of successfully rehabilitating it as a coherent and credible area of theory and practice. In pointing out specific areas for revision we shall make further use of the framework around which our review of the criticisms of OD was organized. The construction of a more politically aware OD enterprise must obviously begin with a reassessment of the meta-theoretical models of man, organization, and intervention currently deployed. Let us begin, therefore, with the model of human nature upon which OD bases its interventionist stance. In calling attention to the question of personal growth and the conditions required to sustain and nurture it, OD has certainly performed a useful function. So far as their members are concerned, many organizations remain—to use Rattray Taylor's (1972) phrase 'psychological slums' where the personal environment at work is more conducive to apathy, alienation, and frustration than fulfilment and growth. But it is clear that in its efforts to confront these issues OD has retained a far too limited conception of personality development. Despite Schein's (1970) advocacy of the need to recognize a model of 'Complex Man', OD clings sentimentally to a simplistic, self-actualizing account of man's essential nature. Scant attention has been paid to the many European research studies which have shown patterns of work motivation and commitment somewhat at variance with the Maslovian formulation (Gallie, 1978).

As Goldthorpe *et al.'s* (1968) discussion of the *Affluent Worker* has emphasized, there may be considerable variation in individual orientations to work. OD has to come to terms with the notion that many organizational members (managers as well as workers) may see their commitment to the organization in strictly limited terms, preferring (perhaps realistically) to look for their peak experience outside the employment situation. One implication of this is the theoretical need to accommodate to the growth of work-instrumentalism with its associated account of the motivational phenomenon as a calculative and strategic process. OD can no longer afford to operate with models of individual behaviour which ignore the differential, and possibly conflicting, orientations, commitments, and involvements of actors occupying different positions in the social structure of the organization. As Silverman (1970, p. 176) notes, 'many studies of organisations have tended to assume . . . that the character of the attachment of members is determined either by the nature of the organisation or the psychological propensities which they bring to it'. In leaving out of account whose definitions of 'development' will prevail in the political arena which is organizational life, OD is seriously unfaithful to its espoused view of man as agent of his organizational fate.

A further charge we have found to be broadly substantiated against OD is the claim that its exponents have operated with overly simplistic models of the organization. In particular, we accept Stephenson's claim that OD treatments of the bureaucratic form of organization have been cavalier to the point of irresponsibility. Bennis' extravagant predictions made in the 1960s about the 'death of bureaucracy' for example, now have a quaintly lunatic flavour. Bureaucracies remain central features on the organizational landscape. What is at issue here, as we have suggested, is OD's inadequate conception of the peculiar strengths of the bureaucratic model coupled with too vicious an attack on its dysfunctions. But this problem of the conception of organization at the heart of OD theory is more deeply rooted. OD emerged out of an American social psychological tradition itself inextricably identified with the social systems perspective. As Weeks (1973), Dawe (1970), and Silverman (1970) have tried to demonstrate, this 'way of seeing' organizational life yields only part of the picture needed for full understanding. Moreover, social systems formulations tend to stress the pre-eminence of overall system goals, promoting a unitarist conception of organizational politics which in turn emphasizes the stability of patterns of structure. There is a macabre irony in this observation that the professional practice of organizational change agency has been founded on an epistemological approach which celebrates the stability of structural arrangements seeing the individual not as an agent of change but as a passive recipient of role demands. This attachment of OD to the social systems perspective may also offer a partial explanation of its failure to do justice to the political dimensions of change already noted and its tendency to see problems from a top management (= total systems?) perspective.

A related point is the need to give greater recognition to the interaction between organizations and their environments. A great deal of current OD work focuses exclusively upon the internal processes of the organization, such as communication networks, small group decision-making, and the leadership styles of its managers. It is, of course, not surprising that OD has concentrated upon such factors since they are seen as potentially manipulable. But it should be emphasized that a theory of organizational behaviour which limits its attention to those factors operating 'inside' the factory gates must have severely impaired predictive power. What is required is a new form of organizational ecology which will trace the multiple connections between the organization and its significant environments: social, political, and economic. Theories of change and intervention which neglect the forces that environmental pressures exert upon the internal system of relationships will always give partial and incomplete insights and thus provide a poor basis for action. OD must thus recognize the significance of 'politics' at two levels. There is the level of internal politics among strategic coalitions (Child, 1972) and competing interests. There is, too, the level of macropolitics concerned with the question of societal allocation of values. Organizational development can escape neither macro nor micro politics without committing the error of seeking technicist solutions to what are essentially political issues.

In suggesting that OD should reconceptualize the organizational/environmental nexus, we are also insisting that it should give greater attention to the mechanisms by which organizational goals are established. The OD exponent, in coming to terms with the organization as a micro-political system, will be forced to take into account the struggles for competitive advantage and the bargaining about rewards, stakes, and prestige which are constant in all organizational life. One of the persistent naiveties of OD work is the notion that the consultant intervenes to help the whole system to become more healthy. Implied in this kind of formulation is the clear non-sense that the organization is a single, unified entity. In this, OD seriously underestimates the problematics of change and injures (perhaps fatally) its own intellectual credibility by propagating the 'happy family' model of organizations.

Proposals for the rehabilitation of OD must, therefore, address themselves directly to some of these underlying theoretical weaknesses. In previous paragraphs we have argued for more sophisticated theories of organizational behaviour, a more considered treatment of the bureaucratic phenomenon and the creation of new studies of organizational ecology and micro politics. Another way of restating these themes is to suggest that OD must show greater willingness to move towards an action sociology of organizations as evidenced in recent European literature (see Salaman, 1980; Watson, 1980; and Elger 1975).

Thus far our discussion of the future prospects for OD has centred upon the need to revise the models of man and theories of organization currently in use. But what of the models of intervention presently favoured? Several changes must be insisted upon here if the practice of OD is to remain viable. First, OD practitioners must give greater attention to what Friedlander and Brown (1974) have called the 'techno-structural' levers for change. It remains sadly a fact that much current OD work concentrates upon the human-processual strategies for change. This infatuation with behavioural techniques also carries implications for the development of OD practitioners which is often dominated by training in interpersonal skills and small-group dynamics. As we have earlier suggested, the theory of consulting which presently un-derscores OD strategy is based upon the simple transfer of concepts, tech-niques, and approaches developed for helping and counselling individuals about personal problems to the more difficult task of organizational renewal where economic and political considerations often place severe constraints upon action. The classic contributions to OD's theory of consultancy (such as Argyris' discussion of the primary tasks of the interventionist (1970); Blake and Mouton's (1976) consulcube model; and Watson *et al.*'s (1958) phase model for consultancy episodes), all systematically blur this distinction between persons and organizations-as-clients. There is an assumption of continuity in consulting theory and practice across client systems that to the present authors at least seems unwarranted and possibly misleading.

Thus, our call for more politically informed models of organization must be supplemented with a greater sensitivity to the politics of the intervention process itself. OD practitioners must learn to cope more effectively with, and where necessary confront, existing patterns of influence and domination in work organizations. One aspect of this is the delicate professional politics of the multi-consultant situation. As more organizations are penetrated by OD practitioners, theory must give greater attention to these issues of inter-consultant politics and their impact upon the effectiveness of intervention. The practice of OD itself may be testing the limits here of those collaborative and collegial ideals which it itself has suggested its client systems should adopt in place of conventional, hierarchic social controls, see Klein (1976). Another neglected aspect of OD intervention theory is the role of internal change agents. The dilemmas of the internal OD practitioner who risks his career development in what most find (at the very least) an exposed and vulnerable role have received scant attention. Theory remains infatuated with the near-mythical figure of the 'invited-in' consultant. Internal change agents find existing theories of intervention politically barren, a weakness all the more apparent to the internal practitioner since he confronts daily the exigencies of the micro-political system as a matter of routine survival.

The connecting theme within these criticisms of OD's models of man, organization, and intervention may be summarized as a demand for a more politically eloquent OD. We recognize, however, that it is simpler to call for such theoretical revision than to provide it. In the following sections, there-fore, we outline some contours of a political model proceeding via a critical review of what is arguably the most considered statement of present theories of intervention extant in the OD literature, notably Argyris' discussion of the primary 'tasks of intervention'. Our intention is to demonstrate how a determination to confront the political realities of organizational affairs might strengthen Argyris' analysis.

The Argyris model identifies three core tasks as central to the change agent's role. His is a universalist formulation in the sense that these tasks are considered the key elements whatever the size or type of client system (individual, group, total organization, or larger social institutions). Basically the goals of the change agent may be summarized in Argyris' own vocabulary as the requirements to:

(1) 'Generate valid information' defined as 'that which describes the factors, plus their inter-relationships which create the problem for the client system'.
(2) 'Encourage free and informed choice' which 'places the locus of decision-taking in the client system' making it 'possible for the clients to remain responsible for their destiny' thus 'the clients can maintain the autonomy for their system.'
(3) 'Ensure internal commitment' so that clients experience a 'high degree of ownership and have a feeling of responsibility about the choice and its implications'. This means that individuals reach 'the point where they act on the choice because it fulfils their own needs and sense of responsibility, as well as those of the system'.

A critical political theorist reviewing this account might legitimately entertain several misgivings about its central axioms. In the first instance the concept of 'valid information' begs a number of questions. While Argyris concedes that the interventionist's diagnosis 'must strive to represent the total client system and not the point of view of any such group or individual' he appears over-confident that consensus about what is problematical will emerge. In our view he pays insufficient attention to the ability of certain organizational groups to promote their definitions of the situation through the use of strategic power resources. There is also considerable ambiguity about exactly which groups in the organization form the diagnostic constituency. Nor is any treatment given to the ability of key participants to structure the pattern of diagnostic inquiry by preventing certain issues coming on to the agenda for change. Such activities now enjoy a central position in the research manifesto of contemporary political science, see Crenson (1971).

There are also difficulties with Argyris' resolve to anchor his approach to notions of 'free, informed choice' for the client system. This formulation appears insensitive to the problems which attend conceptions of 'freedom'. Closer familiarity with the literature of political science might obviate such shortcomings by emphasizing the bounded character of freedom. In a world where 'ends collide' one man's definition of freedom may require constraints to be placed on the legitimate aspirations of others. Whose 'free, informed choice' prevails is clearly related to the system of power distribution within the organization.

Argyris' analysis reflects at this juncture a simple but fatal category mistake. He, like many other OD consultants, seems guilty of personalizing the organization and treating it in by now familiar 'unitary' terms. It is simply unsatisfactory to suggest that the responsibility for change decision-making should be placed squarely back into the client system without contemplating where in the political constituency choice eventually lies. This leaves the interventionist committed to Argyris' guidelines in grave danger of capture by sectional interests—most usually top management.

The force of this kind of criticism is to cast doubt on Argyris' third proposition about intervention activity, that concerning internal commitment. Argyris' anxiety to secure such commitment derives from his conviction that problems of implementation recede as a direct function of the level of ownership of the changes. As writings in the field of policy implementation demonstrate, however, sheer psychic energy is an insufficient, albeit necessary, precondition for successful reform. Power to mobilize support and resources is arguably as critical a variable as commitment. The change agent operating according to political maxims would place greater emphasis on the role of ideological legitimations in sustaining the momentum for change. In short, Argyris' formulation appears to manifest a political insensibility which severely impairs its potential as a satisfactory basis for effective intervention.

REVISIONIST TRENDS WITHIN OD?

So far, this chapter has remained within a dominant, if somewhat ecumenical, tradition of dissent in the literature on OD. We have outlined many of the contemporary criticisms which abound, and probably given the impression that we agree with much of what they have to say on the OD phenomenon. It seems only right to point to one or two hesitations which should appropriately attend such criticisms. These arise out of our earlier mentioned conviction that some of the most thoughtful criticisms of the role and nature of OD have emanated from practitioners playing a central role in applying OD methods to organizations. Typical of such 'internal' criticisms are those of Warren Bennis, earlier identified in this paper as one of the central contributors to the literature and practice of OD. Bennis' own thinking has not remained static but has been subjected, autodidactically, to a thorough-going revisionism. One of the fascinating features of such a change of heart on the part of Bennis is how early it took place in his thinking and how his change of heart has failed to impress his followers. As early as 1969, for instance, in a paper evocatively entitled 'Unsolved Problems Facing Organisation Development', Bennis appears well aware of the central crisis of OD namely, that in establishing its rationale in the area of change and development, OD has remained curiously insensitive to the problematics of change episodes. This early paper is a thoroughgoing critique of the state of then-existing theory. Suggesting that OD would be unable to reach its true strength unless it confronted a series of practical, tough problems, Bennis castigated OD for basing its practice on the unsatisfactory philosophy that only two sources of influence—'truth' and 'love'—were available to it. In adopting such a view, practitioners were effectively condemning themselves to irrelevance, straitjacketing OD by arguing that it was most appropriate under conditions where truth, love, and collaborative strategies were applicable. This diverted it away from those (increasingly evident) situations in which the truth/love approach seemed peculiarly redundant and in which the dominant medium of exchange between organizational participants was distrust, violence, or conflict. In producing such a critique, Bennis makes explicit his view that OD has 'systematically avoided the problem of power or the politics of change'.

Interestingly this important renunciation of existing theoretical statements in the Organization Development literature has been openly acknowledged by Pettigrew (1975), one of the few OD contributions to grapple directly with the political aspects of intervention theory. His work is testimony to the value of an expressly 'political' orientation in the organizational analysis, an orientation which he insists has added weight to the literature. His main point is that there is a significant lacuna in the writing of Organization Development specialists, namely that they avoid dealing with political questions at precisely that moment in the life of organizations when a 'proper' concern of the theorist must lie in articulating sophisticated political theories. As Pettigrew insists, political activity in organizations tends to be particularly associated with change, since internal (and external consultants) are the initiators of organizational change their activities and plans are inextricably bound up with the politics of change. Innovations in organizational design are likely to threaten existing parts of the working community of an organization. In brief, major structural changes have political consequences. There are additionally, encouraging indications from other quarters of movement in such a direction. Mention should be made of the willingness to grapple with the realities of organizational politics evident in the work of Mangham (1978), Kakabadse (1982), Klein (1976), Blackler and Brown (1980), Borum (1980), and Golembiewski (1980) amongst others. These are useful contributions upon which a theoretical reconstruction of OD might be founded. Rehabilitation of OD requires a strenuous effort to be launched from within to return practice closer to the intellectual leading edge of organization theory, a position it once occupied in its early history but which it appears to have vacated in recent years. In essence what we are arguing is that OD practice must somehow regain that rapport with theory it once enjoyed and which remains one of its important bases for credibility.

Whilst OD remains a technology for changing organizations available only to certain interests and working only towards certain kinds of 'adjustment' change, its moral bankruptcy will increase and intensify. Organizational change strategies must be developed and made available to a wider range of participants to enable them to recover control over organizational arrangements in ways which allow the reinstatement of human dignity as a condition of modern industrial employment.

Yet whilst an attempt to rededicate OD seems a necessary precondition of its continuing viability, the move to strengthen its 'political' appreciation carries possible dangers. The ultimate cost of embracing a political version of change dynamics may be that the OD practitioner must sacrifice the convenient professional fiction which legitimates his role as that of neutral facilitator. In a politicized OD partisanship thus emerges as the most urgent item on the agenda for debate.

REFERENCES

Argyris, C. (1970). *Intervention Theory and Method*, Reading Mass.: Addison Wesley.
——(1972). *The Applicability of Organisational Sociology*, Cambridge University Press.
Bennis, W. G. (1966). Changing organisations, *Journal of Applied Behavioural Science*, **2**.

——(1969a). Unsolved problems facing organisational development, *The Business Quarterly*, **34**, (4) 80–84.

——(1969b). Beyond bureaucracy, reprinted in Etzioni, A. (ed.), *Readings on Modern Organizations*, Englewood Cliffs: Prentice-Hall.

Benson, J. K. (1977). Organisations: a Dialectical View, *Administrative Science Quarterly*, **22**, 1–21.

Blackler, F. and Brown, C.A. (1978). Organisational psychology: good intentions and false promises, *Human Relations*, **31** (4), 333–351.

——and Brown, C. A. (1980). *Whatever Happened to Shell's New Philosophy of Management*? London: Gower Press.

Blake, R. R. and Mouton, J. S. (1976). *Consultation*, Reading Mass.: Addison Wesley.

Blau, P. and Schoenherr, R. A. (1973). New forms of power', in Salaman, G. and Thompson, K. (eds), *People and Organisations*, London: Longmans.

Borum, F. (1980). A power alternative strategy to O.D., *Organisation Studies*, **2**, 123–146.

Buchanan, P. C. (1971). Crucial issues in organisation development, in Hornsten, H. A. *et al.* (eds), *Social Intervention*, New York: Free Press.

Burke, W. W. (1976). O.D. in transition, *Journal of Applied Behavioural Science*, **12** (1), 22–43.

——(1977). Some neglected issues in O.D., in Burke W. W. (ed.), *Current Issues and Strategies in O.D.*, New York: Human Sciences Press.

Child. J. (1972). Organisational structure environment and performance: the role of strategic choice, *Sociology*, **6** (1), 1–22.

Crenson, M. (1971). *The Unpolitics of Air Pollution*, Baltimore: Johns Hoplins Press.

Dawe, A. (1970). The two sociologies, *British Journal of Sociology*, **21** 207–218.

Edmonstone, J. (1979). *O.D. Regulation or Revelation*, paper presented at the OD Network Annual Conference, November.

Elger, A. (1975). Industrial organisations: a processional view, in Mackinlay J. B. (ed.), *Processing People*, London: Holt Rinehart.

Emerson, R. (1962). Power dependence relations, *American Sociological Revuew*, **27** 31–41.

French, W. L. and Bell, C. H. (1973). *Organisation Development*, Englewood Cliffs, NJ: Prentice-Hall.

Friedlander, F. (1976). O.D. reaches adolescence: an exploration of its underlying values, *Journal of Applied Behavioural Science*, **12** (1), 7–21.

——Brown, L. D. (1974). Organisation development, *Annual Review of Psychology*, **25**, 313–341.

Gallie, D. (1978). *In Search of the New Working Class*, Cambridge University Press.

Goldthorpe, J. H., *et al.* (1968). *The Affluent Worker: Industrial Attitudes and Behaviour*, Cambridge University Press.

Golembiewski, R. T. (1980). O.D. in industry: perspectives on progress and structures, in Smith, P. B. (ed.), *Small Groups and Personal Change*, London: Methuen.

Goodge, P. (1975). The 'love/trust' model and progress in organisation development, *Journal of European Training*, **4** (3), 170–184.

Gouldner, A. (1955). Metaphysical pathos and the theory of bureaucracy, *American Political Science Review*, **49**.

——(1971). *The Coming Crisis of Western Sociology*, London: Heinemann.

Greiner, L. E. (1980). O.D. values and the 'Bottom Line', in Burke, W. W. and Goodstein, L. D. (eds), *Trends and Issues in O.D.: Current Theory and Practice*, San Diego: University Associates.

Heather, N. (1970). *Radical Perspectives in Psychology*, London: Methuen.
Henderson, H. (1978). *Creating Alternative Futures*, New York: Berkley Publishing.
Herman, S. M. (1977). 'The shadow of organisation development, in Burke, W. W. (ed.), *Current Issues and Strategies in O.D.*, New York: Human Sciences Press.
Higgins, R. (1978). *The Seventh Enemy*, London: Hodder and Stoughton.
Hill, S. (1981). *Competition and Control of Work*, London: Heinemann.
Illich, I. (1973). *Tools for Conviviality*, London: Caldar Boyars.
Jenkins, C. and Sherman, B. (1969). *The Collapse of Work*, London: Eyre Methuen.
Kakabadse, A. (1982). Politics in organizations, re-examining O.D., *Leadership and Organization Development Journal*, **3** (3).
Klein, L. (1976). *A Social Scientist in Industry*, London: Gower Press.
Kuhn, T. S. (1970). *The Structure of Scientific Revolutions*, London: University of Chicago Press.
Mangham, I. (1978). *The Politics of Organisational Change*, London: Associated Business Press.
Mechanic, D. (1962). Sources of power of lower order participants in complex organisations, *Administrative Science Quarterly*, **7**, 349–364.
Nichols, T. (1975). Some comments on the 'New Socialism' of management, *Sociological Review*, **23** (2), 245–265.
——and Armstrong, D. (1976). *Workers Divided*, London: Fontana.
Nord, W. R. (1974). The failure of current applied behavioural science: a marxian perspective, *Journal of Applied Behavioural Science*, **10** (4), 357–378.
Partin. J. J. (ed.) (1973). *Current Perspectives in Organisation Development*, Reading Mass.: Addison Wesley.
Perrow, C. (1979), *Complex Organisations: A Critical Essay*, Glennview: Scott Foresman.
Pettigrew, A. (1973). *The Politics of Organisational Decision-Making*, London: Tavistock.
——(1975). Towards a political theory of organisational intervention, *Human Relations*, **28** (3), 191–208.
Pfeffer, J. (1981). *Power in Organisations*, London: Pitman.
Pitt, D. C. and Webb, K. (1978). Management theory: observations on a contemporary orthodoxy, *Journal of the Conflict Research Society*, **1** (3), 75–91.
Pym, D. (1978). In quest of post industrial man, in Armistead, N. (ed.), *Reconstructuring Social Psychology*, Harmondsworth: Penguin Books.
Rattray Taylor, G. (1972). *Rethink: Radical Proposals to Save a Disintegrating World*: Harmondsworth, Penguin Books.
Robertson, J. (1978). *The Sane Alternative*, London: Villiers.
Salaman, G. (1979), *Work Organisations Resistance and Control*, London: Longmans.
——(1980). *Class and Corporation*, London: Fontana.
Schein, E. H. (1970). *Organisational Psychology*, 2nd edn, Englewood Cliffs, Prentice-Hall.
Shotter, J. (1976). *Images of Man in Psychological Research*, London: Methuen.
Showler, B. and Sinfield, A (1980). *The Workless State*, London: Martin Robertson.
Silverman, D. (1970). *The Theory of Organisations*, London: Heinemann.
Simon, H. A. (1973). Organisational Man: rational or self-actualising?, *Public Administration Review*, **33**, 346–353.
Skolimowski, H. (1981). *Eco-philosophy: Designing New Tactics for Living*, London: Caldar Boyars.
Sofer, C. (1972). *Organisation in Theory and Practice*, London: Heinemann.
Srivastva, S. (1977). Some neglected issues in O.D., in Burke, W. W. (ed.), *Current*

Issues and Strategies in Organisation Development, New York: Human Sciences Press.

Stephenson, T. E. (1975). Organisation development—a critique, *Journal of Management Studies*, **12**, 249–265.

Strauss, A. (1963a). The hospital and its negotiated order, in Freidson, E. (ed.), *The Hospital in Modern Society*, London, MacMillan.

Strauss, G. (1963b). Some notes on power equalisation, in Leavitt, H. J. (ed.), *The Social Science of Organisations*, Englewood Cliffs, Prentice-Hall.

Tannenbaum, R. and Davis, S.A. (1969). Values Man and Organisation, *Industrial Management Review*, **10** (2), 69–80.

Vickers, G. (1972). *Freedom in a Rocking Boat*, Harmondsworth: Penguin Books.

Waldo, D. (ed.) (1973). Organisations of the future symposium, *Public Administration Review*, **33** (4), 249–335.

Walton, R. E. (1965). Two strategies of social change and their dilemmas, *Journal of Applied Behavioural Science*, **2** (2), 167–169.

Watson, J. *et al.* (1958). *The Dynamics of Planned Change*, New York: Harcourt Brace.

Watson, T. J. (1980). *Sociology, Work and Industry*, London, RKP.

Weeks, D. (1973). Organisation theory: some themes and distinctions, in Salaman, G. and Thompson, K. (eds), *People and Organisations*, London: Longman.

Wilcox, H. G. (1969). Hierarchy, human nature and the participative panacea, *Public Administration Review*, **29**. 53–63.

Wilson, C. (1972). *New Pathways in Psychology*, New York: Mentor Books.

Power, Politics, and Organizations: A Behavioural Science View
Edited by Andrew Kakabadse and Christopher Parker
© 1984 John Wiley & Sons Ltd

Chapter 5

Towards a Theory of Political Behaviour in Organizations

ANDREW KAKABADSE and CHRISTOPHER PARKER

Analysing organizations in terms of political behaviour is nothing new in the Organization Psychology field. Over 20 years ago, well-known theorists such as French (1956), Burns (1961), and March (1962), indicated that the political aspects of life in organizations required substantial exploration. Only in the last decade has the challenge been accepted as greater attention has been given to the field of politics in organizations. However, in the literature, different interpretations of politics have developed.

Writers such as Schein (1977) and Porter, Allen, and Angle (1981) have treated power and politics as additional subjects tacked on to Organization Behaviour (OB). In contrast, other writers such as Nord (1974) and Warner Burke (1976) have developed an interest in power and politics largely because of a dissatisfaction with the underlying values and practical application of behavioural science knowledge and technique—Organization Development (OD).

Others analyse politics at the organization level as opposed to the individual level. Hinings *et al.* (1974) attempt to measure political activity at the subunit (group) level in organizations, whilst Mintzberg, Raisinghani, and Theoret (1976) relate corporate decision-making processes to political behaviour in organizations.

There is most certainly a mix of meanings on the subject in the available literature. Therefore, we first explore the different meanings attributed to politics in organizations and analyse why writers have opted for certain interpretations of political behaviour by relating politics to the longer-term preferred behaviour strategies that individuals adopt which in turn determine their pattern of behaviour. We relate preferred behaviour strategies to the personal values people develop and the norms of behaviour with which they identify. Thereby, all behaviour in organizations is considered potentially political, as the strategy that one individual has adopted may not be compatible with the strategy of another person. We explore a cognitive model of individual behaviour and pay attention to the range of behaviours people seem to exhibit consistently in normal work relations.

By concentrating at the individual level, we do not assume that analysis at the group or total organization level is unimportant. On the contrary, examining group and organization processes are important areas of activity. However, a fundamental proposition that we offer is that politics involves influencing key persons (actors). The process of political influence is best examined at the individual level, exploring the relationships amongst the key actors involved. Thereby it is necessary to focus on the recurring and non-recurring patterns of behaviour of individuals and their attempts to influence others through interpersonal interaction. But first let us examine the mix of meanings surrounding the terms 'politics' and 'power'.

MIX OF MEANINGS

A literature search of eight journals and numerous books has produced over 350 relevant journals articles and 38 books on the subject of power and politics in organizations. From this plethora of material, three key categories have been identified.

(1) Studies examining the *intents* and the *means* of individuals and organizational subunits. Intents relate to the salient intentions or objectives that individualss wish to attain and the means identify how those objectives are to be achieved. Within the category are included studies of political behaviour at the individual level, the group level, and an examination of the processes of collective bargaining, especially the behaviour of individuals who occupy organizational boundary roles. In addition, the budgeting process is recognized as a political method of allocating financial resources.

(2) Organizations are examined in terms of the dominant shared values, myths, rituals, and symbols, under the general heading of studies of organization culture.

(3) Diagnostic case-studies of decision-making practices in organizations are presented, from which are deduced the political and power-oriented behaviour of key individuals.

1. Intents and Means Approach

Political behaviour at the individual level

The intentions of actors and the means by which those intentions are operationalized has received the greatest attention in the literature. For a large number of writers, identifying the likely operational steps (means) towards more effective individual political behaviour has produced numerous check-lists of appropriate political behaviours to suit certain situations (Schein, 1977; Cobb, 1980; Pettigrew, 1972; 1973; 1975; 1977).

Pettigrew (1977) has probably been one of the more influential writers identifying five potential power resources available to internal consultants (expert control over information; political access and sensitivity; assessed stature and group support). Schein (1977) adds to Pettigrew's (1977) work by identifying six power strategies that change agents require in order to accomplish effective change (aligning with a powerful other; trade-off; re-search; using a neutral cover; limiting communication; withdrawing). Hersey, Blanchard and Nortemeyer (1979) add connection power to French and Raven's (1959) classic work on the five bases of social power. Numerous other writers adopt similar sorts of approach whereby if the x number of appropriate behaviours are applied, the chances of the actor obtaining what he wants are vastly improved.

Political behaviour at the group level

Other writers have attempted to measure political behaviour at the organizational subunit level. Hickson *et al.* (1971) hypothesizes that organizations are systems of interdependent subunits who compete for a finite distribution of power within the organizational system. Power for Hickson is the ability of the organizational subunit to determine its own strategies and activities. As subunits are likely to have to co-ordinate with other subunits, the power of subunit A can only be measured by its ability to ensure that subunit B falls in line with the demands of A. Hence the power of a subunit is increased or diminished by its ability to cope with uncertainty, changes in the organization, and the activities of other units. Essentially, Hickson *et al.* (1971) offer a strategic contingencies approach to political behaviour which Hinings *et al.* (1974) and others (Benson, 1961) have found suitable for further exploration. Surprisingly, both Hickson and Hinings side-step the problem of identifying the intents and the means necessary for the acquisition of greater power. Further, they offer no indication as to how key individuals within subunits perceive or even influence organizational trends and then attempt to influence their unit members as to the immediate and strategic contingencies that have to be considered. By concentrating at the subunit level, the above writers provide organizational maps of subunit behaviour, and attempt to explain that behaviour within a strategic contingencies framework.

Dilemmas for organisation development (OD)

Out of 15–20 years of behavioural science application known as OD there has emerged an espoused philosophy of care, trust, and affection for the individual. Although these key values have dominated the field of organization development, certain writers have questioned the practicability of such norms. Bennis (1969) recognized this development, stating that OD practitioners 'rely exclusively on two sources of influence, truth and love', (p. 81). Such an approach is justified under conditions of collaboration. What of the other side of humanity?—behaviours which Herman (1974) identifies as anger, coercion, hate, and aggression which are as usual as love, peacefulness and compassion. There certainly has been a reluctance to develop conceptually what Warner Burke (1976) calls the 'darker side of humanity', lest it should taint and corrupt and give licence to practise the 'blacker arts of human behaviour'.

Until now, writers on OD have equated politics with behaviours which are considered unpleasant, but nevertheless practical, pragmatic and necessary. Unpleasant as politics may seem to be, the need to find a new philosophical and conceptual base for OD and a disappointment with the operational results of OD interventions have stimulated a number of writers (Nord, 1974; Beer, 1976; Bowen, 1977) to explore the field of political behaviour.

Studies of political behaviour in OD, circles have concentrated on examining both the intended outcomes of interventions and the necessary means of achieving those intents. Beer (1976) for example, emphasizes an intents/means approach to interventions. Conceptually, however, the arguments have not progressed, as OD writers find themselves unable to develop beyond the good/evil view of political behaviour in dealings with human beings. Notions of power and politics have been identified as *A* intending to influence *B*, but in a way that *B* might not approve if he became sufficiently aware of *A*'s intentions.

Boundary roles

A recent development is the recognition that persons occupying positions at the boundary between groups who hold different values, or who are pursuing different objectives or are at the boundaries between organizations, are involved in political behaviour. In themselves, boundary roles and organizational boundary management are not a new area of study (Thompson, 1967; Cyert and March, 1964). However, the recognition that boundary management is essentially a process of influencing the decisions and behaviours of individuals, well encompassed within an organizational boundary, has stimulated a new interest in boundary management processes as political processes. In order to be an effective boundary-role influencing agent, it is necessary to recognize that political tactics and strategies of 'bureaucratic gamesmanship' (Strauss, 1962) have to be utilized by the actor to enhance his position of influence. How can this be done? Some of the recent studies on boundary-role management have utilized previous work on power/politics as the basis of their study. Spekeman (1979) simply adopts French and Raven's (1959) five power bases in order to discover, through empirical study, which of the five power bases boundary-role agents and negotiators tend to favour most.

Perry and Angle (1979) adopt a more complex approach. By observing trade union and management negotiators, they noticed that certain 'key influences' such as the need to display loyalty, goal ambiguity, and past experience, affect the relationship between the negotiator and his constituents. The greater the psychological distance of the negotiator from his constituents, the less the likelihood of success in negotiations. Hence, in order to achieve certain objectives the means must include reducing the anxiety, goal ambiguity, and role contradiction of the negotiator in order to shorten the psychological distance between him and his constituent members.

Policy preferences

Wildavsky (1968) suggests that the budgeting process is a political method of allocating financial resources; a notion consistent with Cyert and March's (1964) proposal that the budget represents the outcome of bargaining and leads towards organizational coalitions. For Wildavsky (1968), politics is seen as the conflict over whose preferences are to prevail in the determination of policy. Hofstede (1978) endorses the view, by indicating that many management control systems, such as PPBS and MBO are ineffective as they are based on a cybernatic philosophy which is homeostatic in approach as opposed to organizational environments which are heterostatic-oriented.

To limit political behaviour simply to conflict over policy decisions is too narrow an approach. The identification and development of policy involves political action in its own right. A number of writers have recognized that the determination of policy preferences in addition to policy implementation is a form of political activity. Warmsley and Zald (1973), in their work on public service organizations, define politics as the structure and process of the uses of authority and power to define goals, directions, amd the major parameters of the economy of an organization. In addition, Dirsmith and Jablonsky (1979) explicitly identify zero-based budgeting (ZBB) as both a management technique and a political strategy to apply to poorly understand key problem areas. the technique takes into account discrete decisions of which key actors in the situation may be only partially aware.

Again, discussions on policy preferences centre around attempting to identify the particular means that could be adopted by actors (whether they fully or partially understand key problem areas) at the senior levels of the organization, in attempting to ensure that their policies are adopted.

2. Study of Organization Cultures

Studies exploring the culture of organizations have developed quite independently of any work on power and politics. For example, culture has been defined in terms of Social Dramas (Turner, 1957), Organizational Sagas (Clark, 1972), Symbolism (Cohen, 1974), Language (Berger and Luckman, 1966), and Myths and Rituals (Bocock, 1974). It is only recently that a few writers have identified the interaction between the individual and others of similar or different cultures in terms of political behaviour (Pettigrew, 1979; Mangham, 1978). Hence this area of study has only recently been recognized as worthy of debate in the area of power/politics.

In contrast to the intents and means approach, the writers on culture attempt to show why things are happening as they are, rather than attempting too precise an elaboration of the current structures and mechanisms that maintain, initiate, or do away with systems of power. This more existentialist approach to organizational study is practised by adopting a longitudinal-processual approach to the study of organizations, relating the history and future of the organization to the present. As Pettigrew (1979) indicates, analysis of cultures could produce useful results in a number of areas such as exploration of the political process of legitimation and delegitimation in organizations, or the leadership components of entrepreneurship.

Mangham (1978) follows similar lines to Pettigrew (1979) and specifically adopts a 'social dramas' approach to the analysis of interventions in organizations. He concludes that the power of an interventionist is dependent on his ability to diagnose the kinds of 'scripts' he sees his clients adopting (individual social dramas) and the scripts he encourages his clients to accept. The professional interventionist is in as powerful a position to determine the direction of the play, as are the performances of the actors on stage.

3. Case-studies into Decision-making

Certain researchers have studied decision-making patterns, at the individual and organizational levels, in particular organizations, and have presented their data as case-studies. However, their conclusions emphasize behaviour in terms of political processes in organizations rather than as explicit decision-making behaviour.

Hammer and Stern (1980) examine the role perceptions of workers and management in a furniture factory and conclude that worker directors in general considered full-time management as the true owners of the firm. They did not view themselves as partners and indicated that they preferred an internal distribution of power that favoured management as opposed to power equalization.

Hall (1976) develops a system pathology approach in his study of the fall of the newspaper the *Saturday Evening Post*. His analysis concentrates at the organizational subunit level in an attempt to understand how the management system of the newspaper reacted both in the short and long run, to changes of management control variables such as subscriptions and advertising rates. Hall postulates that a series of group sub-cultures had developed in the magazine industry and that by providing a model of management's collective decision-making behaviour, reliable estimations of any publishing organization's future growth or demise can be made.

Teulings, Jansen, and Verhoeven's (1973) study of hospitals and Salancik and Pfeffer's (1977) study of a university specifically examine the trends of organizational decision-making by exploring the power of key organizational subunits. In both studies, the authors discovered that those units who could obtain and control the resources most sought after by the institution held power to determine the direction and operationalization of other resources. In the university case, departmental power correlated highly with the departments' ability to obtain grants and contracts. Power once obtained was utilized in other areas such as the allocation of graduate university fellowships.

ISSUES EMERGING

As indicated by Lord (1977), Pandorus (1973), Allen *et al.*, (1979), and Mowday (1975), there seems to be little common agreement as to the meaning of two key words—politics and power. To what do politics and power relate—intents, means, strategies, personal values, group norms of behaviour acts, or events in the life of individuals and organizations? Further, what is the appropriate unit for analysis—individual, group, division within an organization or the total organization? Each unit of analysis would presumably require a different methodological approach to suit the original hypotheses.

However, certain trends can be identified and the writer who links seemingly incompatible streams of thought is Lukes (1974), in his analysis of power.

Historically, the use of the term power by community development theorists, such as Dahl (1957) and Wolfinger (1971) was based on the Weberian approach: 'A having power over B to the extent that he can get B to do something that B would not otherwise do' (Lukes, 1974, pp. 11–12). Thus for Dahl (1957) power is only meaningful after a careful examination of a number of observable decisions. Lukes (1974) terms this process the 'One Dimensional View' of power, in that emphasis is given to observable overt conflict and hence decision choices are relatively clear cut. Schein (1977),

Porter, Allen and Angle (1981), Lee (1977), Zaleznik (1979), Hall (1976), and Salancik and Pfeffer (1977) pursue this line of thought by examining the appropriate behaviours required at the individual or group level in order to achieve particular objectives. The writers exploring power/politics at the group or subunit level conclude that subunit power is increased by attracting and controlling key resources.

Yet Bachrach and Baratz (1962; 1963) strongly disagree with Dahl's (1957) view. They state that by concentrating on observable decisions and actions, the potent power of a silent majority is not appreciated. In addition to participating in decision-making, power can further be exercised by individuals devoting their energies to reinforcing the predominant norms and values. Hence, the range of issues under public consideration are limited. Schattschneider (1960; p. 71) stated, 'some issues are oganized into politics, while others are oganized out'. Lukes (1974) considers Bachrach and Baratz's examination of decision-making and non-decision-making processes, observable overt and convert conflict, and terms their combinations of active/passive behaviour as the 'Two Dimensional View' of power. Pettigrew's (1977) analysis of discrete and actual decisions probably falls into this category. Similarly, Provan (1980) draws a similar distinction between potential and enacted power, stating that both must be taken into account in macro level organizational research.

Luke's (1974) criticizes Bachrach and Baratz's view on two counts. First, whether covert or overt, Lukes states they eventually concentrate on overt actual behaviour. Decisions and choices are consciously and intentionally made by individuals between alternatives, even if the intention is towards the exclusion of key issues. Second, power is associated with conflict in that power is utilized either to satisfy personal needs or in a preventive way to minimize the degree of threat to oneself. Luke states that power is more than that.

As an alternative, the 'Three Dimensional View' of power is offered, indicating that key actors and institutional practices are instrumental in developing social agendas, commonly known as norms. Most people are aware to some extent of the norms that influence their own and others' behaviour in the work place. However, a number of people in work organizations are not aware of the future potential issues likely to arise and hence have no way of assessing whether their interests are threatened or not. It is the ability to generate and understand potential issues in situations through an understanding of organizational norms that distinguishes the three-dimensional view from the other two.

The views of few writers in the literature on politics in organizations, other than the writers on culture, resemble the three-dimensional view. Probably the closest are Mitroff and Emshoff (1979) who indicate that political behaviours occur when key organizational actors are asked to deal with ill-structured organizational problems. The greater the ambiguity that surrounds particular problems, the more political the behaviour required by the actor. They suggest that political behaviour is an ability by organizational actors to accept and work with persons who hold different values to their own. Hence, an ability to understand and generate acceptable potential issues is important for actors operating on a three-dimensional model of power.

The one area that is not explained in the literature is the ability or inability of actors to discern appropriate from inappropriate behaviours to suit their particular objectives in a situation. This begs the question as to how each actor sees a situation and how their interpretation is influenced by their behaviour in the past, their needs for the present, and their requirements for the future. We have seen that the literature on power/politics is strongly influenced by the intents/means philosophy, whether applied to individuals, organizational subunits or total units. It is a pointless exercise to recommend that five, or whatever number of political behaviours, if adopted, will lead to success, as it is first necessary to establish whether the actors involved are able to recognize appropriate 'means' behaviours as worthwhile. Second, it is also necessary to determine whether they are capable of implementing such behaviours. Lukes (1974) and Mitroff and Emshoff (1979) indicate that the process of *recognitions* and *enactment* will vary with each individual, without exploring why individual differences occur.

Our concern is to bridge the gap between individual motivation and organizational situations by concentrating at the individual level. We do this by relating the concept of politics to the longer-term preferred behaviour strategies individuals adopt. In so doing, we distinguish between politics and power. Politics are the resultant interactions that arise from the consistent (or inconsistent) behaviours that an individual adopts in reaction to actual or latent issues in the situation. Power is the ability to develop, to the actor's satisfaction, particular changes in context by adopting one or more of the strategies of behaviour.

In this chapter, we concentrate on an analysis of politics in organizations. In effect, our approach to organization politics examines how consistent or inconsistent individuals are at responding to external potential or actual stimuli compared to how successful they are at putting their intentions into practice.

COGNITIVE MAPS AND POLITICAL ACTIVITY

A wealth of evidence exists in the psychological literature supporting the argument that individual behaviour is driven by cognitive maps. Bartlett (1932) and Neisser (1977) suggest that humans operate on cognitive schema, that is, the way each individuals receives, organizes, plans, regulates and transmits information to other humans or things. In other words, people are capable of choice and self-regulation. Initially, Kelly (1955) and later Slater (1976) developed the Repertory Grid technique as a means of identifying cognitive schema. Piaget (1978) and Bruner (1972: 1981) offer similar arguments in the field of developmental psychology. Bandura (1977) and Mischel (1977) suggest that people use symbolic processes to represent events and to communicate with others. Goffman (1974) suggests that 'Frames' of individual reference are created through subjective interpretations of social interaction.

Tolman (1924) suggested that we structure our experience to form 'purposive maps' which drive behaviour. Broadbent (1978) has suggested that subjective maps may be structured on a hierarchical basis forming global and local schema through association networks, with local schema nested in the global schema. In addition, Salancik and Pfeffer (1978) offer a 'social information processing' model to describe how salient 'purposive maps' can be developed and drive behaviour. The principle is that behaviour can be explained in terms of a reciprocal interaction between personal and environmental determinants. People are influenced by environmental forces, but they also make choices as to how they should behave. People are responsive to situations and also influence situations. Through personal values, thoughts and symbols, people anticipate future experiences and attempt to prepare the present for the future.

Through the process of reciprocal determinism (i.e. the process of valuing certain environmental events, discriminating among situations in terms of their potential, judging one's ability to cope, deciding which situation to enter and how to behave) and through using feedback to ascertain the results of decisions, the individual is developing a repertoire of *cognitive competencies*. This repertoire of cognitive competencies, we call the perception/ enactment model.

1. The Perception/Enactment Model

From our experiences as Organization Development interventionists, we assert that successful or unsuccessful interaction between people in organizations is dependent on each individuals's repertoire of cognitive competencies. Each person's repertoire of cognitive competencies involves different perceptions of organization values and roles; task and power dependencies in the total organization, subsystems, and small groups.

From our observation of people's behaviour in organizations (in the role of third-party agents) we offer a model which identifies two fundamental drives which lead to the formation of purposive maps in individualss:

(1) the stimuli which lead to the determination of peoples' perceptions, views, and beliefs;

(2) the way people attempt to put their beliefs into practice.

In Figure 1, the *horizontal axis* represents the determinants of peoples' perceptions. The two extreme ends of the continuum are inner directedness and outer directedness. People who are inner-directed develop their perceptions and views of the world with little reference to external conditions. People who are outer-directed feel a need to comply with the perceived norms and values of the situation.

Complying with the perceived norms of the situation is termed 'shared meaning'. People who need to operate under conditions of shared meaning identify with the organization's values and roles, the power dependencies in the system, and the monetary and status rewards the organization offers.

People who generate their own values of life and norms of behaviour are self-dependent. They live with unshared meaning. In addition, they appreciate and tolerate that a number of the people with whom they will interact, think and feel differently to themselves.

The *vertical axis* represents peoples' abilities to put into practice their views, norms, and values; their repertoire of enactment strategies. Again, a bi-polar continuum is identified with two alternate types of action strategies— simple and complex. Those who practise strategies classed as simple, aim for consistency. Irrespective of whether the people in the situation work on shared or unshared meaning, the behaviours they feel they should adopt are predictable, commonly recognized, and probably previously practised. In this way, individuals and groups are seen to be consistent and previous experience of those behaviours reduces the degree of felt threat.

Complex enactment strategies involve people behaving in ways that they consider suitable to meet their needs in the situation. To the outsider, the individual may exhibit no consistent pattern of behaviour. Only by possessing

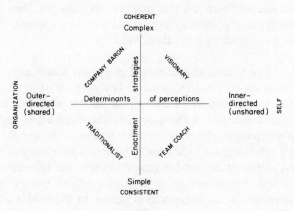

Figure 1

knowledge of the individuals's objectives or by observing his behaviour for some time, will any sort of picture emerge. The pattern of behaviour may be inconsistent but the reasons why people act in certain ways makes sense (is coherent) if one knows the individual and his desired objectives.

The combination of the inner/outer-directed axis and the simple/complex enactment strategies axis, forms the individuals's purposive map. It is inevitable that people will interact with others who hold a different map to their own, even if the difference is slight. It is equally inevitable that people will experience elation or threat by interacting with other people. It all depends on the state of your map and the other party's map on meeting each other.

By adopting a cognitive approach to the analysis of behaviour in organizations, it is assumed that all behaviour in organizations could be interpreted as political.

The politicians

To clarify further the concept of politics, four stereotypic characters are identified, based on the Perception/Enactment model; Traditionalist, Team Coach, Company Baron, and Visionary. Below are behavioural sketches (maps) of the four characters.

Traditionalist. The values of the traditionalist match those of the organization and/or the unit in which he interacts. The individuals accepts and maintains the power dependencies and resource allocation processes within the organization. The traditionalist emphasizes control of group membership and in this way ensures that the 'right' sort of person enters the group. Once in the group, group values are maintained by paying particular attention to the interpersonal interactions of each member of the group.

Traditionalists are concerned with maintaining the status quo. By ensuring that the resources and power structures remain constant, they reduce uncertainty and minimize the anxiety associated with any change. Traditionalists tend towards conservatism and inflexibility.

Team coach. The values and beliefs of the team coach are self-generated. However, the team coach does need to belong to a group and may spend time searching for an appropriate group of people with which he wishes to associate. Once a member of the group, he/she emphasizes control of group membership and pays attention to the interactions in the group, so that group values are not fundamentally changed. The espoused values of the group and the perceived values of the total organization may be different. In fact, team coaches may see themselves as missionaries whose calling is to shift the predominant values of the organization nearer to the values of the group.

The two drives of consistency and of self-generated attitudes and ideas are likely to induce both humanistic- and task-accomplishment-oriented values in Team Coaches for two reasons. First, a sincere desire to help group members understand each other more fully (need for consistency). Second, a need to achieve high task expertise and offer a unique and creative contribution (inner directedness). Adopting consistent and non-threatening enactment strategies, such as being open, caring, trusting, and simply understanding that others in the group are different but can make a valuable contribution, achieves the people objective. Control is applied only over individual behaviour and not over individuals opinions. Pressure is brought to bear on individuals who threaten other members of the group by their actions. As a final resort, the erring individual may be expelled.

Team coaches are flexible to the extent that they are stimulated by interacting with people who think and feel differently to them. However, their need for consistency of behaviour prevents any real change of group opinion or real innovation in tasks. Task accomplishment comes to be doing what you were good at before.

Both the traditionalist and the team coach will have high concerns about 'system pathology'—that is to say, that things are getting worse in this organization. Perception of system pathology will be easily tapped when they are confronted by others holding different perceptions and enactment strategies to their own.

Company baron. The company baron is able to recognize how the power dependencies the systems of resource allocation and values in the organization, operate. What he/she finds difficult is to disengage or become separate from the majority in the organization. As a result, the company baron rarely attempts to introduce major changes which will involve shifts of organizational values and changes of structure, but rather tends instead to question the performance of particular divisions, departments, units, or work systems. He/she will have developed a fairly clear idea of how subsystems interact within the organization and will also have recognized that the situation will not improve unless other parties are involved who may think and feel differently.

The company baron holds a strong role orientation to his/her work. Whilst questioning performance and resource allocation, he will do so in such a way that his current role is maintained or more usually amplified at the expense of others. He will use role amplification incentives to gain support from others such as status, promotion, or monetary rewards, The company baron will collaborate with others and 'check the waters before making his play'. He needs others on his side before taking action.

Attempts at influence are not necessarily made to be to the advantage of all. Decisions will be arrived at on the basis of what is tolerable to the parties concerned and not necessarily consensual. The acceptance of total organization values could be utilized as justification for redistribution of power and resources.

If major changes are deemed necessary, the person appointed to master-mind the changes will have been part of the system for some time. He/she would need to be seen as representing stability. The approach to change would be to introduce phased change to the dominant values and structure of the organization. Propensity to risk dramatic change would be low and the principle of 'rolling re-organization' (phased change) is adopted. The company baron does not require other people to agree with what he does, just to accept it without too much opposition.

Visionary.   Visionary-orientated people question the power dependencies, the resource allocation, *and* the value system of the total organization. They are characterized not only by a questioning of current dominant values but also by exhibiting an ability to disengage or become separate from the previous values held by the majority in the organization. Visionary people aim towards developing new organizational values and forms. People opera-ting with visionary values believe in their visions about long-term trends in the external and internal environment. They have developed what Vickers (1973) describes as 'systematic wisdom'.

The visionaries operate in relative isolation from other organizational personnel in order to develop new beliefs. Their work philosophies and strategies are dependent on a well-identified but personal philosophy con-cerning the future.

The visionary does not value the process of 'step by step' change because he is not committed to the previous value systems. Typically, a new broom, he is able to revolutionize the work environment. Visionaries tend to manage their own change attempts, share little, organize other people to undertake certain tasks, but not get involved in the details of implementing change. In this way, they minimize their commitment to the past by not unduly inter-acting with others.

Attempts at change can concentrate at the total system or subsystem level. At the subsystem level, the visionary will be concerned with product or service improvement. He would attempt to change his own role and that of others, alter the pattern of allocation of resources and reorganize units or departments to fit in with measures to improve performance. He would 'test the waters' before making his play but would not be dependent on the support of others before stating his case. Rather he would use his influencing skills to gain support after stating his case.

At the total systems level, the visionary is able to revolutionize because he manages his own change attempts. Despite their non-commitment to the past, visionaries will have a good appreciation of how the current system has evolved and in what direction they want it to change. Typically, the visionary may be considered the 'saviour' or 'hit-man' brought into an ailing organization.

WHAT IS POLITICS IN ORGANISATIONS?

Certain writers (Pettigrew, 1975; Schein, 1977) suggest that managers, consultants, and organizational interventionists may have to adopt behaviours towards others which initially could be distasteful to them, but may in the long term prove to be an effective approach to achieving their goals. Hence, politics in organizations has largely been viewed as individuals or groups adopting certain deemed necessary behaviours in order to change or cope with strenuous circumstances. In this way, only certain behaviours are political and others are not.

As stated, adopting the Perception/Enactment model approach to the analysis of individuals behaviour in organizations assumes that all behaviour in organizations is political. Hence, what is politics? Politics is an influence process which can be perceived as positive or negative depending on whether one's own 'purposive maps' are being threatened or supported. Behaviour that is acceptable is behaviour that fits with the purposive map(s) of the incumbent. Pathological situations develop when an individual or a group rejects, misunderstands, or responds with inappropriate behaviours to the actions of another individual or group. In other words, the person concerned is unable to recognize mentally the demands and behaviours of the individuals or group with whom he is interacting. It is these negative consequences of personal and group interaction that have largely, to this day, been interpreted as individual or group political behaviour.

Simply to identify certain 'political' behaviours which, if practised, lead to greater personal effectiveness and greater personal gain, as do the majority of the writers in politics in organizations, is wasted advice. It is necessary to understand the map(s) of strategic actions that individualss have developed before being able to identify the behaviour that an individual can competently practise, bearing in mind what is appropriate to the situation. The skill is to try and prevent individual and organizational pathological circumstances from arising by recognizing the appropriate and inappropriate behaviours that individuals and groups will and will not be able to accept.

Case Example

Peter has been a personnel consultant for over 19 years in the same company; 11 years of which he has spent working with the same team. A new team leader, John, initially suggested to Peter that experience with another team or even attending a short course would be beneficial, in order that Peter could take time off to develop and reflect on his consultant style and work practice. Peter viewed John's suggestion as inconsistent with his pattern of standards and expectations and felt threatened by the suggestion. In the circumstances, being unable to avoid any interaction with John, Peter slowly developed a negative attitude towards John. He tried to avoid John whenever he could; presented John with incomplete information which enhanced his own position, and tried to ensure that John had no access to his work.

John identified Peter as out of date in terms of knowledge and work practice; as a person who attempted to prevent positive change within the work team; ineffective in client/consultant relationships and generally a symbol of passive resistance to John's authority. Over time Peter responded by indicating his past success with clients, how his long presence in the work group acted as a stabilizing force through successive changes of leadership, and generally how detrimental it would be to the group and group leader if changes in work practice were introduced too quickly.

However, the more the two interacted, the less they seemed able to appreciate each other's rationale. Gradually Peter attempted to avoid John totally as he recognized that only painful experiences followed encounters with John. Avoidance was impossible and therefore Peter entered into defensive hostile behaviours such as not presenting work for supervision, not regularly attending group meetings, questioning John's actions, sending derogatory memos concerning John's behaviour to all members of the group. John responded by adopting punishment/rejection behaviours towards Peter such as not giving Peter interesting work and criticizing him publicly.

Over time, Peter developed a pathological, dysfunctional self-evaluation such as being unable to maintain existing self-established work standards, increasing his dependency on other group members, and being disappointed if they seemed to let him down. In addition, he presented excessive defensive behaviour to any suggestion of change or new experience.

In this case, John did finally rid himself of Peter by posting him abroad and manoeuvring him to a position where Peter opted for early retirement. Ironically, Peter's assessment that the organization could not cope with too much change too quickly, was accurate. Shortly after Peter was retired, John was eased out by his own superiors.

Each of the two parties involved in these series of interactions found it impossible to assimilate the rationale of the other person. Peter seemed to have adopted traditionalist values towards his work practice, his relationships with others and the way he viewed the future. John adopted visionary values and was, in fact, brought into the organization to introduce changes and improve professional practice. The end result was that one of the faithful 'old hands' of the organization, Peter, was seemingly poorly treated, becoming more depressed with his work situation and operating below his own established standards. From this and other experiences, John was viewed as a maverick who made no attempt to understand the organization, was seen as introducing too many silly changes, and generally causing distress to those with whom he interacted. John eventually developed hostile/defensive behaviours as a response to the consistent pressure he was experiencing from his own superiors. One of John's bosses stated openly to him, 'see how you like your own medicine'.

TOWARDS MULTI-RATIONALITY

In the case example above, John found himself in a paradoxical situation. He was hired to introduce change and yet was fired, in his own eyes, for honouring his psychological contract of employment. John's problem was that he had never considered the difficulties that his colleagues, superiors, and subordinates would have in accepting and internalizing any new patterns of behaviour. An understandable error, for it is difficult to identify realistically the changes required and then further to develop a strategy of new work behaviours that are acceptable to most members of the organization. Peter, his colleagues, and superiors were persons who had adopted traditionalist values. In contrast, John operated with visionary values. He did not realize that to disturb the norms of behaviour of key actors and groups in the organization would generate substantial opposition to his policies and activities. Further, no company baron or other visionary actor was present to supervise, guide, or direct the interactions between John and the other members of the organization. The end was inevitable. Key personnel in the organization hired John to stimulate change but in reality wanted no change. There was no alternative but for John to leave.

From the above case, it can be seen that each actor develops his own beliefs, values, and norms which in turn stimulate his interactions with others. Hence, each actor behaves in a rational manner that is consistent with his norms, beliefs, and values. It is when actors, who by force or circumstance have to interact with others, are consistently unable to appreciate the rationale of others, that fundamental problems begin to arise. A way of reducing the problems that actors in organizations experience in interactions with each other is to help each interested party understand the different points of view of others. This process we term multi-rationality. In striving towards multi-rationality, the aim is to help actors understand the bounds of their belief systems; help them assert their individuality and yet appreciate the rationale of others. The key is to understand the opinions and postures of others but not to comply (except through self-choice) with their requests and demands.

Change agents, whether they be line managers, trainers, or consultants, are left with an interesting dilemma. On the one hand, they may sincerely wish to adopt a neutral stance by trying to help their client, clarify his view of his problems, possibly not interfere with the decisions the client makes within his work environment. On the other hand, the change agent may feel he clearly sees what actions are required by the client, which may or may not be in line with the client's pattern of behaviour or decision-making. Certainly, the change agent will be strongly influenced by his own purposive map. Whether the change agent works on his own issues and attempts to influence his client to accept them, or on the client's issues, one feature of client/consultant interaction emerges. In order to accomplish an intervention successfully, we postulate that the two parties have at least to share some agreement on dominant value systems. Further, by assisting the client to identify weaknesses in his existing cognitive repertoire, and by examining ways of applying particular actions to specific problematic circumstances, the change agent is promoting the position of the client within the client's work environment. The promotion of the client could be to the positive gain or detriment of others within that work environment.

In striving for multi-rationality and utilizing an individual motivational model of human behaviour, we question the degree to which an open, honest, value-free stance can be adopted by the actors involved. The issue at hand is the degree to which actors can attempt to influence each other without unduly disturbing the other party's value, beliefs or perceptions. Hence, what use is the Perception/Enactment model?

First, the model is valuable in enabling individuals to understand the previously amorphous area of politics in organizations, through classifying particular values and behaviours. Second, it moves people away from thinking of 'politics' as outcomes of unsuccessful influence attempts to the realization that maybe they too are already highly skilled as organizational politicians. Once individuals see politics as a process, they begin to realize that maybe they can have greater influence on outcomes by using their process skills more effectively.

SUMMARY

The intents/means approach to analysing politics in organizations is considered inappropriate, for it gives no indication as to whether actors are able to utilize the means and further deduce whether the identified intents and means are appropriate to the situation. As an alternative, we suggest that all individuals develop a pattern of behaviours, based on each individual's personal values, beliefs, and norms. The pattern of behaviour we term purposive maps. Two key dimensions are identified to form a purposive map—determinants of peoples' beliefs/perceptions; determimants of people's actions. It is considered that all behaviour in organizations is political, as actors, in order to interact, have to utilize behaviours from their purposive map. Behaviour that is acceptable is behaviour that fits in with the values and range of behaviours of the actor in question. Problems arise when an individual or group rejects, misunderstands, or responds with inappropriate behaviours to the actions of other individuals or groups. In the literature, it is these negative interactions that have, to date, been labelled 'political'.

We suggest that one way of reducing negative interactions is to strive for multi-rationality. Multi-rationality is a process whereby actors begin to understand their own values, beliefs, and norms; are able to assert their individuality but are equally able to accept that others hold a different rationale.

REFERENCES

Allen, R. W., Madison, D. L., Porter, L. W., Renwick, P. A., and Mayers, B. T. (1979). Organizational politics: tactics and characteristics of its actors, *California Management Review*, **XXII**, No. 1, 77–82.

Bachrach, P. and Baratz, M. S. (1962). The two faces of power, *American Political Science Review*, **56**, 947–952.

—— —— (1963). Decisions and non-decisions: an analytical framework, *American Political Science Review*, **57**, 641–651.

Bandura, A. (1977). *Social Learning Theory*, Englewood Cliffs, NJ: Prentice-Hall.

Bartlett, Sir F. (1932). *Remembering: A Study in Experiential and Social Psychology*, Cambridge University Press.

Beer, M. (1976). On gaining influence and power for O.D., *Journal of Applied Behavioural Science*, **6**, 44–51.

Bennis, W. G. (1969). Unresolved problems facing organization development, *Business Quarterly*, Winter, 80–84.

Benson, J. K. (1961). The interorganisational network as a political economy, *Administrative Science Quarterly*, **6**, 229–249.

Berger, P. L. and Luckman, T. (1966). *The Social Construction of Reality*, Harmondsworth: Penguin Books.

Bocock, R. (1974). *Ritual in Industrial Society*, London: Allen and Unwin.

Bowen, D. D. (1977). Value dilemmas in organization development, *Jounal of Applied Behavioural Science*, **13**, No. 4, 543–555.

Broadbent, D. E. (1977). Hidden pre-attentive processes, *American Psychologist*, **32** 109.

Bruner, J. S. (1972). *Process of Education*, Harvard University Press.

——(1981). *Beyond the Information Given*, London: Allen and Unwin.

Burke, Warner,W. (1976). Organization development in transition, *Journal of Applied Behavioural Science*, **12**, No. 1, 22–43.

Burns, T. (1961). Micropolitics: mechanisms of institutional change, *Administrative Science Quarterly*, **6**, 257–281.

Clark, B. R. (1972). The organizational saga in higher education, *Administrative Science Quarterly*, **17**, 178–184.

Cobb, A. T. (1980). Informal influence in the formal organization: perceived sources of power among work unit peers, *Academy of Management Journal*, **23**, No. 1, 155–161.

Cohen, A. (1974). *Two Dimensional Man: Essay on the Anthropology of Power and Symbolism in Complex Society*, London: Routledge and Kegan Paul.

Crozier, M. (1973). The problem of power, *Social Research*, **40**, No. 2, 211–228.

Cyert, R. and March, J. (1964). *A Behavioural Theory of the Firm*, Englewood Cliffs, NJ: Prentice-Hall.

Dahl, R. A. (1957). The concept of power, *Behavioural Science*, **2**, 207–225.

Dirsmith, M. W. and Jablonsky, S. F. (1979). Zero-based budgetting as a management technique and political strategy, *Academy of Management Review*, **4**, No. 4, 555–565.

French, J. R. P. Jr. (1956). A formal theory of social power, *Psychological Review*, **63**, 181–194.

——and Raven, B. (1959). The bases of social power, in Darwin Cartwright (ed.), *Studies of Social Power*, Ann Arbor MI: Institute of Social Research, The University of Michigan.

Goffman, E. (1974). *Frame Analysis: An Essay on the Organization of Experience* Penguin Books.

Hall, R. I. (1976). A system pathology of an organization. The rise and fall of the old *Saturday Evening Post*. *Adminitsrative Science Quarterly*, **21** No. 2, 185–211.

Hammer, T. H. and Stern, R. N. (1980). Employee ownership: implications for the organization distribution of power, *Academy of Management Journal*, **23** No. 1, 78–100.

Herman, S. M. (1974), *The Shadow of Organization Development*. Paper presented to the NTL Institute Conference on New Technology in OD, New Orleans, February.

Hersey, P., Blanchard, K. H., and Nortemeyer, W. E. (1979). Situational leadership, perception and the impact of power, *Centre for Leadership Studies*, Learning Resources Corporation, pp. 1–5.

Hickson, D. J., Hinings, C. R., Lee, C. A., Schneck, R. E., and Pennings, J. M. (1971). A strategic contingencies theory of intraorganizational power, *Administrative Science Quarterly*, **16**, No. 2, 216–229.

Hinings, C. R., Hickson, D. J., Pennings, J. M., and Schneck, R. E. (1974). Structural conditions of intraorganizational power, *Administrative Science Quarterly*, **19**, 22–44.

Hofstede, G. (1978). The poverty of management control philosophy, *Academy of Management Review*, July, 450–460.

Kelly, G. A. (1955). *The Psychology of Personal Construct Theory*, Vols 1 and 2, New York: Norton.

Lee, J. A. (1977). Leader power for managing change, *Academy of Management Review*, **2**, No. 1. 73–80.

Lord, R. G. (1977). Functional leadership behaviour: measurement and relation to social power and leadership perceptions, *Administrative Science Quarterly*, **22**, 114–133.

Lukes, S. (1974). *Power: A Radical View,* London: Macmillan.

Mangham, I. L. (1978). *Interactions and Interventions in Organizations*, Chichester: John Wiley.

March, J. G. (1962). The business firm as a political coalition, *Journal of Politics*, **24**, 262–278.

Mintzberg, H., Raisinghani, D., and Theoret, A. (1976). The structure of unstructured decision processes, *Administrative Science Quarterly*, **21**, 246–274.

Mischel, W. (1977). Self-control and the self, in. T. Mischel (ed.) *The Self: Psychological and Philosophical Issues*, NJ: Rowman & Littlefield.

Mitroff, I. I. and Emshoff, J. R. (1979). On strategic assumption making: a dialectical approach to policy and planning, *Academy of Management Review*, **4**, No. 1, 1–12.

Mowday, R. T. (1975). *An Explanatory Study of the Exercise of Influence in Organziations*. Unpublished Ph.D. Dissertation, University of California, Irvine.

Neisser, U. (1977). *Cognition and Reality,* New York: John Wiley.

Nord, W. R. (1974). The failure of current applied behavioural science—a Marxian perspective, *Journal of Applied Behavioural Science*, **10**, No. 4, 557–578.

Pandarus, (1973). One's own premier of academic politics, *American Scholar*, **42**, No. 4, 569–592.

Perry J. L. and Angle, H. L. (1979). The politics of organizational boundary roles in collective bargaining, *Academy of Management Review*, **4**, No. 4, 487–496.

Pettigrew, A. M. (1972). Information control as a power resource, *Sociology*, **6**, No. 2, 187–204.

——(1973). *The Politics of Organizational Decision Making*, London: Tavistock.

——(1975). Towards a political theory of organizational intervention, *Human Relations*, **28**, No. 3, 191–208.

——(1977). Strategy formulation as a political process, *International Studies of Management and Organization*, **7**, 78–87.

——(1979). On studying organizational cultures, *Administrative Science Quarterly*, **24**, 570–587.

Piaget, J. (1978). *Essential Piaget*. Gruber and Voneche, J. (eds), London: Routledge and Kegan Paul.

Porter, L. W., Allen, R. W., and Angle, H. L. (1981). The politics of upward influence, in *Research in Organizational Behaviour*, Vol 3, Staw, B. and Cummings, L. (eds), Greenwich: JAI Press.

Provan, K. G. (1980). Recognising, measuring and interpreting the potential/enacted power distinction in organizational research, *Academy of Management Review*, Vol 5, No. 4, 549–559.

Salancik, G. R. and Pfeffer, J. (1977). The bases and use of power in organizational decision making: the case of a university, *Administrative Science Quarterly*, **22** No. 3, 453–473.

—— —— (1978). A social information processing approach to job attitudes and task design, *Administrative Science Quarterly*, **23**, No. 2, 224–253.

Schattschneider, E. E. (1960). *The Semi-Sovereign People: A Realist's View of Democracy in America*, New York: Holt, Rinehart and Winston.

Schein, V. E. (1977). Individual power and political behaviour in organizations: an inadequately explored reality, *Academy of Management Review*, January, 64–72.

Slater, P. (1976). *Exploration of Intrapersonal Space*, Vol. 1, Chichester: John Wiley.

Spekeman, R. E. (1979). Influence and information: an explanatory investigation of the boundary role person's basis of power, *Academy of Management Journal*, **22**, No. 1, 104–117.

Strauss, G. (1962). Tactics of lateral relationships. The purchasing agent, *Administrative Science Quarterly*. **7**, 161–186.

Teulings, Ad W. M., Jansen, L. CW. O., and Verhoeven, W. G. (1973). Growth, power structure and leadership functions in the hospital organization, *British Journal of Sociology*, **24**, 490–505.

Thompson, J. (1967). *Organizations in Action*, New York: McGraw Hill

Tolman, E. C. (1924). *Behaviour and Psychological Man*, University of California Press.

Turner, V. W. (1957). *Schism and Continuity in an African Society*, Manchester University Press.

Vickers, Sir. G. (1968). *Value Systems and Social Processes*, London: Tavistock.

Wamsley, G. L., and Zald, M. N. (1973). *The Political Economy of Public Organizations*, Lexington. Mass.: Heath.

Wildavsky, A. (1968). Budgetting as a political process, in David L. Sills (ed.), *The*

Interventionist's Encyclopedia of the Social Services, London: Cromwell, Collier and Macmillan, pp. 192–199.

Wolfinger, R. E. (1971). Non-decisions and the study of local politics, *American Political Science Review*, **65**, 1063–1080.

Zaleznik, A. (1970). Power and politics in organizational life, *Harvard Business Review*, May–June, 47–60.

Power, Politics, and Organizations: A Behavioural Science View
Edited by Andrew Kakabadse and Christopher Parker
© 1984 John Wiley & Sons Ltd

Chapter 6

The Politics of Educational Institutions

HARRY L. GRAY

A SUBJECTIVE THEORY OF EDUCATIONAL ORGANIZATION

Schools and colleges are in essence personal experiences. The basic 'technology' of education is a personal relationship between pupil and teacher, student and lecturer. Our memories of school and student days are personal recollections about people and their uniqueness, idiosyncrasies, originality. The tales we tell about school are about exceptional events that remain in our memory; staffroom talk among teachers is about eccentricity, deviance and the unusual that brightens up the day. By and large when we think about school, we think about people, though we may recall aspects of buildings, as personally remembered smells, sights, and physical experiences. But when officials or academics write about schools they deal with intangible concepts like subjects, curriculum, and administration as if they were the embodiment of the essence of schools instead of the people who function in them.

In my view we can only properly understand schools, colleges, polytechnics, universities and so on if we concentrate on the people. To view 'educational institutions' as if they were tangible administrative creations is not only to miss the essence but it is to create artefacts that encourage us to avoid facing the real issues which concern people. Every educational institution I have ever been in has had a character that derives entirely from the people who compose it. In every case, the personality of the top person—head, principal or whatever—has been pivotal. All the manoeuvrings of staff and students to bring about changes, reforms, and improvements have had to concern themselves with the top person and adjust themselves to finding ways of dealing with him, because of the kind of person he or she was. And each other member has functioned in terms of his own personality and characteristics when dealing with his colleagues and the 'system'.

In this chapter, I wish to explore the importance of understanding educational organizations from a personal standpoint. Schools or any other educational organization are experienced by their members personally but they are also created as a consequence of personal perceptions. The organizations we belong to are in large measure the organizations we create for ourselves and if researchers and outsiders are to understand them they must look for the ways individual members perceive them. Perception is a product of experience and experience continues over time as a 'career' in an organization. As we interpret and explain our experiences to ourselves we develop a 'theory' of organization and specifically of the organization of which we are a member. Our experiences are largely in terms of people and we react to them and interact with them according to the kind of person each of us is, according to our personality. No member of an organization reacts as an inert object and it is one of the cruellest myths of organizations that 'objectivity' increases with organizational status; vice-chancellors of universities are no more 'objective' about their university than anyone else. Reality is a function not of status but of understanding.

Educational organizations well repay study from the viewpoint of 'subjective theory' because they do not depend on a technological process to determine their structure. Educational organization is largely—if not entirely—a function of quite personal choices uninfluenced by technical necessity. There is more freedom of choice over what to do and how to do it—potentially—in education than in any other form of organization. No wonder politics plays such a large part in the ongoing activity of educational institutions.

The subjective experience and perception of educational institutions may be much more significant than that of commercial and industrial organizations where reality testing is an immediate, frequent and concrete matter. Members of educational institutions can give much fuller rein to their imaginations than members of any other kind of organization (churches and religious movements perhaps excepted). Educational institutions are very much what their members make them and they do not need to check out too often that their fantasies are compatible; lecturers and students, teachers and children, can all live in their own little worlds without experiencing very much discomfort. The politics of the institution arise from individual fantasies, while the exercise of power is directed towards protecting and extending a personal fantasy. It would not be impossible, for example, for a university vice-chancellor to believe himself to be in complete control of his colleagues and their resources while in fact having no direct influence whatsoever—especially when the UGC has control of the funding.

SUBJECTIVE THEORY AND PERSONALITY

In what follows I want to attempt to outline a basis for viewing the politics of educational institutions as centring on the personality of individuals rather than on the functioning of an abstract or technical system. To do so I shall try to explain how I see people fitting into institutions where there is an unresolved conflict between the essential and personal function of education and the impersonal function of system maintenance. I use a comparatively simple model of organizations explained in terms of membership and the roles members create for themselves in order to deal with their perceived needs. I understand organizations as functioning in terms of personal value systems rather than agreed organizational goals and I believe that organizational evaluation is performed subjectively according to personal gratification rather than objective, impersonal criteria. I have expressed my own basic 'Subjective Theory' more fully elsewhere (Gray, 1980) and this chapter is an expression of the application of that theory rather than a full exposition.

In what follows, politics is an emphasis in a more general theory of organization. Politics is an expression of organizational behaviour arising from the conflicts inevitable among people who are all competing for organizational space. My personal view is that all organizations could give more space and more rewards than they do and the most dysfunctional aspect of managerial behaviour is that it is almost invariably directed at restricting or limiting opportunities under the guise of control and the need for good order. All organization raises questions of trust and the greater the trust among members the less disruptive political activity ensues. But trust depends on the perception of the one who trusts, not the one trusted, and it is the failure of managers to trust as a consequence of their own anxieties and apprehensions that leads to escalation of overtly political activity in organizations. Politics may more usually be about the lack of trust in organizations among members. In any case, the existence of trust is a matter of perception since the proof of trust can appear only after the event, not before.

THE EXPERIENCE OF POLITICS

No-one who has experienced membership of an institution of higher education in the last decade will have any illusions about the political nature of colleges, polytechnics, and universities. Schoolteachers may be less aware of institutional politics but as schools contract, political consciousness increases. A recent conference of the British Education Management and Administration Society was devoted to a discussion of 'micropolitics' (Pratt, 1982), an indication that educational administrators have at last become aware that what goes on within an organization is as political as what goes on round about it.

It would, however, be a pity if some term like 'micropolitics' were to obscure the fact that organization studies have always been concerned with internal politics. Discussing the politics of organizations is merely one emphasis among several and by no means the most significant. Organization theory has language enough to describe the exercise of power and it would be unfortunate if the language of political philosophy were to oust the language of the other perspectives that contribute to our understanding of organizations—sociology, psychology, economics, philosophy, cynbernetics, and so on.

Nevertheless, since there is likely to be an increasing interest in the politics or micropolitics of educational institutions, I would like to air the topic from the point of view of an organizational psychologist who has spent several years trying to make sense—not always very successfully—of educational organizations.

Some Definitions

While educational institutions do not appear to differ in any basically significant way from other forms of organization, there are a number of factors which need to be borne in mind when describing and generalizing about education. For one thing, there are both public and private educational organizations, which means that there are quite different market orientations, between the types, which extend beyond pure financial considerations. For another thing schools do not have a product, at least none of any coherence.*

Again, rewards and resources relate less to what schools do than to what governments and local authorities decide they shall have. (Pay schools provide scope for dreams and can never deliver a purely quantifiable return for the investment of parents' money). But above all, in a quite remarkable way, schools, organized as they are as institutions, have less to do with the needs of students than almost anyone else involved in them. The needs of students as consumers have the least regard so far as the management and administration of the institutions are concerned and this means that in any discussion of educational politics, students are little more than pawns. That is to say, from an organizational standpoint, students have little influence over determining what happens in schools.

I cannot, in the whole of over 25 years experience of education, recall an instance when the students have been able to exercise decisive and significant influence over educational decisions. The reason is, quite simply, that students have the least power of any group in the system: whatever influence they have—as for example in the student rebellions of the 1960s—has been short-lived and effectively countered by other interests in the system.

Perhaps it is because educational institutions exist within such a large and determinative system (the national/local education service) that internal politics have been overlooked in favour of the politics of the macro system. But each school, college or whatever does have a distinctive existence as an

---

*Students are not a product of schools in the manufacturing sense and it is unhelpful so to describe them because they are as much a part of the process of education as their teachers. Students are not inert material which teachers convert into some form of artefact.

organization and the nature of its organization is constrained in some way by its legal standing as defined by its instrument and articles of government or whatever legal statutes apply to it as a trust, charity, or manifestation of local government provision. My personal preference is to speak of 'educational institutions' and to subsume such within the concept of organization.

Politics is concerned with the deliberate and purposeful attempt to change the balance of power in an organization, usually in favour of the protaganist. Politics is defined in Collins *English Dictionary* (1979) as 'the complex or aggregate of relationships in society, especially those relationships involving authority or power'. But power is an exceedingly difficult concept to define; it appears to be a portmanteau word for a variety of ideas such as influence, coercion, authority, and even leadership. In the political sense, power means a form of compulsion in which the subject of power/influence is in some measure unwilling to have power exercised over him. (In which case, students must be a fairly downtrodden class of people!) Most of the time, when we describe power and politics in educational institutions, we refer to the teaching members and occasionally to wage-earning members such as laboratory assistants, secretaries, caretakers, and cleaners. In the normal way of things student politics is merely an adjacent matter of interest or irritation.

Politics and Membership

Presumably, people join an organization because they consider it to be in their interests to do so and in those instances where their membership is not, or is only partly, voluntary their satisfaction with their membership is related to how they value the rewards or returns of membership. Some kind of 'exchange' theory (e.g. Homans, 1961) would appear to provide a reasonably fundamental explanation for why people join, remain in, and leave organizations. Exchange and return, for instance, seems to account for the financial viability of a company as well as indicating why people do jobs they do not like for sums of money that they do like. I attempted an application of exchange theory to schools in a paper entitled 'Exchange and Conflict in the School' (Gray, 1976) in which I discussed ways in which schools have no satisfactory mechanisms for resolving conflict. This implies that they are also politically immature.

Students join educational institutions with a different kind of psychological contract from other members. Students do not require any material rewards nor other material resources and as a consequence have virtually no bargaining power. It is paradoxical that those who want more from the institution (salaries) have potentially the greatest power over the institution—not just in terms of withdrawal of labour but in the whole network of 'professional' activities which they come to control. The examination system in most educational organizations is the most powerful controlling mechanisms. Power in the examination system (whether internal or external examination systems, no matter) is the most critical source of power in educational institutions while the most powerful mechanism is the administrative system. Students have virtually no influence with either.

Power and Careers

The concept of staff and line sometimes proves useful in distinguishing roles in industry; for one thing it helps us to explain why 'power' appears to be somewhere else other than with a given individual. In education, it is useful to distinguish between professional and administrative careers. In order to 'succeed' in education (that is, command the highest salaries) an individual must engage in an increasing amount of administration. Yet the over-riding evaluation of anyone in education is that he should be essentially a 'good teacher' whatever else he may be. Indeed, lip-service is paid to 'being a good teacher' as the essential qualification for promotion to most levels. Even (*sic*) a Director of a Polytechnic is expected to be a 'good teacher' whatever else he may be—though no-one would expect the manager of an opera house to be a good musician. This is undoubtedly the greatest basic tension in educational organizations—the distinction between teaching (line) and administration (staff).

The financial and status rewards in education do not relate to competence purely as a teacher (or researcher in the case of higher education) but to progression up an administrative ladder. Furthermore, the rewards are determined by the administrative structure in that individuals cannot be rewarded individually and uniquely but only in so far as they fulfil positions hierarchically arranged. By and large the hierarchy of position is determined by the size of the institution, as is the salary paid to each position. A 'successful' career in education is determined by progression up the administrative ladder since all 'promotions' carry increased administrative responsibilities. By and large there is little experience of collegiality in educational institutions. For instance, polytechnics often exhibit the worst qualities of administrative politics—a strong sense of hierarchy and administrative systems that are ostensibly used to depersonalize decision-making while in fact they are used in an entirely personal way.

One manifestation of this situation is the kind of stress to which many teachers find themselves subjected. Because teaching has become a career-orientated profession, many teachers seek fulfilment in promotion. Aspiring to a headship is an almost universal hope for teachers at some period in their career. To achieve career success, they identify with 'the school' in such a way that they take lack of promotion in a strongly personal way. By seeing themselves as 'committed to the school' they somehow depersonalize what was in reality no other than personal ambition. In the contracting educational system, more and more teachers are unable to find promotion as a reward but they have lost all interest in intrinsic satisfactions and have become embittered and disillusioned. I would make a guess that over the last 30 years the most important feature of educational politics has been the amount of opportunity for promotion which has been characterized by institutional (as opposed to personal) involvement or commitment. Now that promotion is comparatively rare, many teachers are withdrawing from involvement and the location of power in the system has changed quite remarkably. Teachers who were once supportive of their organizational superiors are now no longer prepared to follow where others try to lead.

Describing Educational Politics

It is not enough to analyse institutional politics in purely descriptive terms. Political analysis in education is often little more than a description of what is believed to have happened or an account of the overt behaviour of actors in the political drama. Organization theory attempts to provide a conceptual framework for explaining behaviour and to that extent is more than merely descriptive. An organizational perspective is concerned to explain how people are motivated and what are the causes of behaviour as well as explaining why behaviour takes the forms it does.

Because educational institutions are so large and complex, it is tempting to explain behaviour by taking events at their face value. The problem is that it is very difficult to 'know' what is going on and none of the vast quantity of documentation is much help. For example, there have been a number of *causes célèbres* in higher education in recent years that have been recorded over a period of months and even years in the daily papers and educational journals. No-one believes that what is made public is anywhere near the whole story and those of us who have been internally involved know that what the public knows is nothing to, what we on the inside, know.

One of the difficulties of analysis is a blending of two concepts of 'politics'—the local government side which is expressed as a game with highly stylized rituals, and the power struggles between individuals. It is tempting to assume that these great political battles are 'impersonal'—one aspect of the game; people as counters not real people, cyphers not personalities. But everyone knows that politics is essentially a matter of personalities in conflict not because of the circumstances they find themselves in but because of the people they are (though some political theorists take a more 'objective' view of the determinants of behaviour.) It is my view that the greatest insights into institutional politics come from an understanding of personality rather than from an analysis, for example, of role and role behaviour.

The Problem of Role

My experience of counselling managers in education is that they often become confused over the nature of their role. The problem is not simply role
conflict but a confusion over whether behaviour is determined by their role
or their self-perception. Headteachers, principals, etc., tend to assume that
what they do is objectively determined by their role rather than by their
personal inclinations and dispositions. I am not denying that there is a role
syndrome for each position in an organization for there clearly are problems
of role expectation for everyone involved with an organizational position.
But most people find it very difficult to understand that they do not fill a
position objectively but only in terms of their perception of the role and that
this perception is subjectively determined. Most of the political behaviour in
organizations is a consequence of failure to discriminate between objectivity
and subjectivity in positional behaviour. In educational institutions most
problems (if not all) are simply a consequence of varied interpretations of
situations rather than wrong interpretations. A 'good' interpretation is one
that is capable of accommodation with the other interpretations of those also
involved in the situation.

In education nothing is quantifiable against a 'correct' measure. Because
education is a process and ultimately an individual experience, no decision
or action is capable of an 'objective' evaluation; that is because there is no
tangible product. Everything that is decided in education is a matter of
opinion or is capable of an alternative opinion. This puts administrators in
a very difficult position because they can never be proved right (nor wrong
either). And even when they are 'right', a teacher may quite legitimately and
professionally deny the validation of the claim. Thus there are very few
educational issues that have a single 'correct' answer.

Because educational administrators have no special status with regard to
educational issues, they resort to administrative issues to assert their power,
though they know that such issues are spurious because they are remote
from the basic activity of the institution. Administration should serve the
purposes of the institution (i.e. teaching) but administrators try to make the
institution (i.e. teachers) serve the needs of administration. This is the classic
educational dilemma because pedagogic expertise lies with the teaching
rather than the administrative role, yet the institutions are so organized that
power is exercised by the administrators. As the administrators become
increasingly frustrated by the unwelcoming responses of the teachers, they
devise more and more complex ways of increasing their power and the best
teachers can do is retreat within their own classrooms.

Power and Personality

Relationships among people are an expression of the kinds of people they are, perhaps a function of their liking for one another. The more people actively like one another, the better they get along together. Organizational position often affects the relationship because of the additional factor of role expectations. But roles are merely opportunities for further self-expression so if an individual allows role to come between him and a colleague (say on being promoted) that difference is a consequence of a changed self-concept. It is an important question to ask why a change of position leads to a change in behaviour for a given individual. The answer reveals the way in which he regards the positional change to be significant to him. For example, does he see promotion as a confirmation of his view that he really is a better leader than his colleagues? Or that being promoted to Head of Department (an administrative job) proves he is a better teacher?

It must be obvious that the same organizational position occupied by two different people will be to all intents and purposes a different position simply because they act differently. We have all experienced changes in position— a new head, principal, registrar, etc., and noted how important the changes are because of a different personality. In my view the particular politics of any organization stems from this fact of different personalities because it is the personality of an individual we each have to contend with. Furthermore, it is not just because the principal is a certain sort of person but because he functions in terms of a unique personal value system that organizational conflicts arise.

The Politics of Organizational Values

The concept of organizations as values systems (Hodgkinson, 1978) is an important aspect of organization theory. Organizations function as value systems because values are the basis of consistency in decision-making. Though no two individuals will have exactly the same value system congruence of values will lead to consistency while conflict may lead to friction. Powerful individuals often do not negotiate their values and so the conflicts go unresolved. Organizational power relates to the perception colleagues have of the ability to promote growth or reward—hence the 'ultimate' power of the principal. Where the head of an organization so identifies with the organization as to view his personal interests and the organization's interests as identical, he behaves as if no other values were valid. In so doing, he incapacitates those who do not share those values because they cannot make decisions in value terms they do not hold. The complication is that values and personality correlate so that by merely being himself the principal expresses his values in all his actions.

We can explain how political situations arise in organizations if we analyse personal behaviour and gain an understanding of the organizational ways in which personal idiosyncrasy becomes a pervading value system or ideology.

Some examples will help to explain this approach though they are somewhat brief in form. Only a complete analysis of a particular personality can fully explain the origins and character of political behaviour around an individual but the examples will go some way to illustrating how educational institutions depend on the personality of key individuals whereas one might expect them to be more vaguely collective or collegial.

The Person as Source of Political Behaviour

'If the Principal told me to throw myself off the top of the building, I'd do it.' These are the words of an assistant principal of a polytechnic spoken not in fun but with seriousness. In a nutshell they sum up his behaviour in political terms because they explain many of his public actions. Here is a man who has had a successful career in institutional terms but who sees himself as an adjutant and never as 'his own man'. How can his colleagues deal with him especially when he becomes an irritation—as all assistant principles do at some time or another? What strategies are developed to cope with a man who fills every job he is given with statistical probabilities and then is unable to make decisions because he has come to see decisions as too complex? Politically everyone else knows where he stands ultimately but he is totally confused in his role which he sees as requiring 'objectivity' yet objectively determined by total loyalty to one man (the principal) in the organization. One device he uses is to hide behind administrative procedures which with him become byzantine in their complexity and apocalyptic in their duration. Getting a decision out of him is like consulting the Delphic oracle and the Sibyl of Cumae at the same time. The principal uses him to obscure issues rather than to clarify them and a matter passed for his consideration can be relied on to disappear until it is no longer of any importance. He throws himself into every venture with equal hyperactive enthusiasm and squeezes the energy out of his working colleagues. As a consequence he is puzzled when no-one continues the project they have begun with him. Not surprisingly he never feels himself to be adequately appreciated yet he is always seeking personal confirmation. His telephone conversations are long monologues of self-appreciation but one always feels he is asking for help (though, of course, that is he one thing he will never be able to do). Always on the edge of a nervous breakdown, hyperactive, and overly self-conscious he is becoming increasingly separated from his colleagues though he tries with increasing vigour to be seen as a good companion—only to spoil it all with consciousness of his status and the retailing of his achievements.

To place this person in his organizational context is to begin to understand how political behaviour has developed around him—people using him and avoiding him because of *who* he is rather than *what* he is. By his very energy he personalizes the position of deputy principal in an alarming way and in so doing helps to destroy the very organizational objectivity he claims to be perpetuating.

Other Personal Cases

Although they tell more of me that of the people I am writing about, I give four more examples of how educational politics centre on individuals. The examples are not intended to be parodies but perhaps political behaviour is itself a parody of deeper underlying conflicts.

The Dean of the Faculty of Education in one college was a person of excessively high self-regard. He was largely contemptuous of his colleagues, often reminding them that he had taught in a university while they had not. His personal pretensions were such that he identified with the office of Dean to such an extent that he became disassociated from it—he once referred to the Dean of Education and forgot that that was himself! (Was the office of 'Dean' greater to him than the significance of his personal self?) Having such a high opinion of himself he created fantasies around what Deans do and began to recreate a C. P. Snow-type world of academe around himself. His behaviour was characterized by extreme egocentricity by which he placed himself at the centre of a network of power and began to play out personal fantasies in the institution where he saw himself as a successful man of intrigue and influence. Other people found difficulty in coping with this fantasy world—since they did not share his imagination and withdrew from contact, the isolating effect of which was to reinforce his sense of importance and power. In an educational institution this man could be left to his own world because as time went by ways of ignoring him would be found and developed. In the long run there was no function which could be performed only by him alone and others would gradually take over jobs from him. In political terms, power was increasingly a correlate of others' perceptions of the Dean rather than a function of his actual behaviour.

In another college, the principal was originally a party political appointment and he was expected to inaugurate a reforming regime. This he did with considerable enthusiasm and effect but in his own terms, related to his concepts of 'education' and not in terms of his patrons who were after a 'political' (that is party political) objective. The tensions between the governors, who were also politically divided, and the principal were considerable and increased as he pursued educational ends which conflicted with local political expediency. Inevitably his success was absorbed into the natural development of the institution and the novelty impact of his early days became a continual irritation as he embraced new cause after new cause. Eventually, there came the need to amalgamate the college with another and this presented the governors with an opportunity to readvertise the new principalship and not to appoint him to the new premier post.

On the surface this is a typical, abbreviated, study in institutional politics. If we adopt a subjective perspective we may look for a psychological analysis. How could a man who was clearly so able as to be sought after for the initial appointment put himself so much at risk that he could eventually be dismissed by the very people who appoint him (albeit in a changed external political situation)? One answer lies in the personality of the man and the consequent way he viewed the organization. A psychological interpretation posits that the way an individual thinks about himself (his self-image) determines the way he perceives his experiences (structures his world). This principal created a college which was essentially a fulfilment of himself, which served his personal organizational needs. The need for the college to fulfil his personal needs was so over-riding that no alternative could be permitted. Such a creation would occur even if the principal were entirely realistic because in normal circumstances we each create a consistent and persistent picture of our organization, otherwise we would never be able to relate properly to it. In this case, one of the principal's personal needs was to challenge others to the point of rejection—part of his way of justifying himself to himself, of rewarding and punishing himself. All around him, others in the organization had to accommodate their own behaviour to the principal's and there is no doubt that he remained the most powerful person right up to his eventual resignation. But the exercise of power was a consequence of the fantasies that the principal lived out rather than the material exigencies of the circumstances. Power was not allocated and reallocated according to the rules of a game; there was only one player and his dice had to have six sixes.

In yet another case, the head of a secondary school became increasingly at odds with his colleagues and felt himself more and more under pressure from an unco-operative staff. Eventually he received notice from the Chief Education Officer that staff had complained about him and his frequent absenses from school. This was the last straw and he tendered his resignation, only to have his request for early retirement refused. This head had a picture of himself as a skilled manager. He frequently lectured on the management of schools up and down the country and had published many articles. He genuinely tried to put his theories into practice as he understood them. For example, every teacher had a full job description and it was because he felt the management of the school was so well sewn up that he believed he could visit so many other places to tell people about how to run a good school. There had been warning signals from his deputy but these were dismissed as the responses of an unimaginative and inexperienced but ambitious colleague. To discover that one or more of his colleagues had 'reported' him came as a devasting shock and the head took a few weeks off school on doctor's orders before taking a breakdown pension.

The politics here are a little different from the other examples. While the head believed his power was intact and even impregnable, his staff saw simply an absentee and a man out of touch with daily reality. The head's need to believe himself a good head was so great that he was impatient of the process of actually becoming one. He took short cuts which meant he never built up the response from his colleagues that he wanted. Yet he genuinely believed he had designed and implemented a good management system. In fact, he never really had power, the notional power that good will bestows in the early days of a person's holding a new post does not last forever and by free grace. He should have worked to earn power but by imagining it and never testing if it were really there, he lost it. When it did appear, it surfaced unexpectedly elsewhere at one of the weak points in the system. The ones who complained were chancing their luck but everyone was colluding with the head in imagining that power was 'at the top' when it no longer was.

The problem of dealing with power is the problem of detecting reality. In each of these examples, the 'manager' believed something to be the case that was not but how could he have tested for reality? (Presumably, if one has a fatal flaw of perception the consequent failure is inexorable.) Reality testing is conditional upon a realistic self-concept so that information is not distorted by ego needs. Successful leaders/managers learn to hear what is said to them in its own terms and not by trying to make it fit what they want to hear. Perhaps the only way to cure an unreceptive listener is by personal therapy. Yet this skill of counselling, and of being able to be counselled, is the one most markedly absent from management.

A fourth example may help to illustrate the point. The principal of a college had become increasingly at odds with his governors and the employing local educational authority. Events moved to such a stage that the LEA commenced legal action against the principal but such is the ponderous nature of local government that matters just eventually petered out. Obviously there is something seriously wrong in a situation when a local education authority and a senior employee have recourse to law against each other. To understand what was the cause of the problem—although there were, of course, other causes and other problems in the same nexus—one needs to understand the personality of the principal. He was a man with considerable ego needs; he needed support and approval and a good deal of emotional confirmation. Indeed, he needed an intensity of affection that his position denied him. Consequently the more he played the principal, the fewer affective strokes he received; the fewer strokes he received the more he demanded them. His need for affection on the one hand and his rejecting people on the other spiralled until he could not get back into a good relationship except as a consequence of a real threat to his job, when he simply climbed down and modified his behaviour. But he became a bad listener and would spend most of his time with colleagues repeating his achievements tirelessly. People began to discount him more and more, he became distanced from all his colleagues and was only fortunate that no one resorted to high-energy political activity to bring about his downfall.

In all these examples the political energy of the organization was dedicated to dealing with difficult or impossible individuals. Because they exercised power to bolster up their own ego states, organizational decision-making became distorted. All their colleagues used their energy to keep their superiors at bay rather than to engage in a collaborative relationship. Bargaining ceased to be realistically related to a variety of legitimately competing needs but was used instead to fend off the intrusion of the senior person into areas of concern to others. All of these cases suggest that psychotherapy was essential for the personal as well as the organizational health of the individual. Could the top man be restored to emotional health the problems surrounding him would disappear or at least be sufficiently modified to enable his colleagues to deal with him more effectively, with less organization disruption. But organizational balance may be a hypothetical state: it may well be that organizations distort personal behaviour and distorted personal behaviour in turn throws up greater organizational stresses. Perhaps the mere fact of institutionalization puts at risk the delicate balance of personality that allows most of us to survive and thrive at the intimate level of personal friendships. Be that as it may, whatever the balance in personality an individual may have, once he becomes inextricably involved in formal organizations that balance is at risk.

My thesis is that the problems of the individual help to distort the functioning of the organization because the problems of the individual have a direct correspondence in the problems of organization. It is a widely held and conventional view that the head of an institution who feels himself to be under personal threat may project his paranoia on to the organization; his personal enemies became enemies of the institution. Likewise, over-confident principals often find themselves presiding over institutions that exude a sense of over-confidence in many of their collective manifestations. It is quite reasonable that this should be so since as institutional rewards emanate from the boss, most members will attempt to accommodate to his expectations and this will result in a reflection of his modes of working in the behaviour of his colleagues.

In many institutions this 'reflective' culture is quite remarkable. Staff model their whole working style on the principal and what they imagine to be his preferred behaviour. The management process relentlessly reflects the value system and behaviour patterns of the top man with the result that members who do not share this organizational culture find themselves quite unable to communicate because nothing they say can be heard. Power struggles are bad enough when all sides know what they are about but where there is no comprehension they are absurd. The mechanism to filter out alternative viewpoints and criticisms is a means of defending the ego and when it is a collective ego that has to be defended the organization has reached a state that leaves it almost beyond help, short of removing the key person. When the key person is at the top, or in a senior position as head of a unit, it is often impossible to break the impasse.

Are Politics Unhealthy?

The examples I have given illustrate the dysfunctional aspects of personality in organizations. Political interest does seem to be in the seamier side of organizational life but since political behaviour is concerned with the redistribution of power, it is inevitable that discontent will be associated with it. I am by no means certain that disappointment and disenchantment can be avoided and in some measure someone will always be hurt. The difference between helpful and unhealthy politics, however, depends on the basic sharing of values—both personal and organizational—for if political behaviour be directed towards what is generally (within the organization) accepted as good, the personal changes involved for individuals will be acceptable. Furthermore, in organizations characterized by commonality of interests and values the need for managers to initiate action is lessened. Where members are psychologically in tune with one another, political behaviour is comparatively unimportant because open discussion and sharing of values, ideas, and needs supplants coercion. Examples of such a supportive climate can be given but in the general view are not easily perceived as the acceptable side of political behaviour.

Is Personality Enough?

Is it enough to explain the politics of educational institutions simply in terms of individual psychology? Clearly, this is only one direction of political explanation but it seems especially relevant to education because education is much more of an individual activity than most jobs in firms. The job of a teacher is essentially an expression of himself while the job of, say, an accountant is an expression of a set of operations. But there is a complication in educational careers in that promotion takes the teacher away from the line function (the professional one) to the staff function (the administrative one) without there being a clear institutional acknowledgement that the function has changed. Professors who become vice-chancellors are still expected to produce academic work even if it only be editing collections of papers. This requirement to continue a line function is not made in other organizations (in hospitals doctors do not generally become hospital administrators). A consequence is that academics who become administrators often expect (and are expected) to be active on two fronts and to compete in two spheres. Feeling inadequate on the academic front they compensate on the administrative. Feeling vulnerable as administrators they compensate by increased academic activity. This is true too in schools where heads are expected to be good and active teachers as well as perfect managers. Perhaps this duality of competition is one reason why school politics are both low-key and largely ineffectual, since individuals can slip from one to the other. In practice, a good deal of conflict can be avoided by simply not attending staff meetings.

Perhaps all politics are an exercise in imagination. But because education as a process is so personal and so intangible, it is an engrossing puzzle why there is such a wide failure to accept and understand just how educational institutions are politically organized. Is all the energy used to exert administrative influence just a way of dealing with the unpalatable reality that the higher one's position in the institution, the less one is a part of the basic function of education—teaching? If the rewards really went for teaching, the politics would certainly take a different turn. Perhaps the seeking after promotion is not only ambition and a search for greater personal recognition but also a means of avoiding the frustration that is inevitable by being a teacher in an institution, since by definition institutions are administrative systems. If it were more widely recognized that the function of education is to provide individuals with personal freedom (the ability to exercise greater and better choices) the whole thrust of administrative activity would be away from system reinforcement towards greater openness. Perhaps that would not do away with politics in education but it would very much change its nature.

REFERENCES

Bacharach, Samuel, B. and Lawler, Edward J. (1980). *Power and Politics in Organisations*, Jossey-Bass, San Francisco.
De Board, Robert (1978). *The Psycho-Analysis of Organisations*, London: Tavistock.
Gray, H. L. (1976). Exchange and conflict in the school, in Houghton V. *et al.*, *Management in Education* (Reader I). London: Ward Lock Educational/Open University.
Gray, H. L. (1980). Organisations as subjectivities in Gray H. L., *Management in Education*, Driffield: Nafferton Books.
Hodgkinson, Christopher (1978). *Towards a Philosophy of Administration*, Oxford University Press. Blackwell.
Homans, George (1961). *Social Behaviour*, London: Routledge and Kegan Paul.
Mangham, I. L. (1979). *The Politics of Organisational Change*, Westport: Greenwood.
Pratt, Simon (1982). The micropolitics of educational improvement, *Educational Management and Administration*, **10**, No. 2, June.

PART II

Applications, Cases, Tales, and Myths

PART II.

Applications to Area, Time, and Weight

Power, Politics, and Organizations: A Behavioural Science View
Edited by Andrew Kakabadse and Christopher Parker
© 1984 John Wiley & Sons Ltd

Chapter 7

Managing the Socio-political Context in Planned Change Efforts. Elements of a Framework for Practitioners

JOEL R. DELUCA

INTRODUCTION

The importance of the socio-political context (SPC) in understanding planned organizational change is discussed. Three separate but interconnected elements of strategy development are presented as follows: (1) strategic orientation levels which fundamentally affect practitioners' response to the SPC are described; (2) a methodology for mapping the SPC is outlined; and (3) strategy levers which serve as tools for shaping practitioners' actions are identified. These three elements can assist practitioners in determining the range, focus, and shape of strategies for dealing with the socio-political context.

Managers and consultants alike have long been interested in changing organizations to improve their effectiveness. Recently, change agents employing behavioural science principles have systematically engaged in planned organizational change. Many of these professional change practitioners belong to a growing field known as Organizational Development (OD). OD is basically an educational strategy (Bennis, 1969) seeking to improve the organization's current and long-run problem-solving processes (French and Bell, 1973). OD practitioners generally use participative methods to create self-directed change to which organizational members can be committed (Beer, 1980).

These OD practitioners frequently operate from a humanistic value system which impacts the types of change strategies they consider (Alderfer, 1977; Kahn, 1974). One area in particular which has often been under-emphasized is organizational politics. Avoiding addressing the political nature of organizations can result in naive and impractical intervention strategies (Harrison,

127

1973; Porter, 1976). The importance of viewing organizations as essentially political systems consisting of shifting coalitions has aptly been portrayed by several organizational researchers (Allison, 1969; Kaufman, 1964; March, 1964; Zaleznik, 1970).

This chapter takes the view that organizational politics, or more accurately the socio-political context, is a major component in any large-scale change effort. While the chapter addresses the socio-political context as it relates to planned organizational change, many of the issues discussed are relevant to anyone who manages a discrete programme in an organizational setting.

The term socio-political context (SPC) refers to the power, political activity, and informal social network among actors in an organizational setting. All organizational development activities occur within such a context. Elements of a practitioner framework for systematically understanding and dealing with the socio-political context of planned organizational change are now presented.

A SOCIO-POLITICAL CONTEXT VIEW OF ORGANIZATIONAL CHANGE

There are many calls for stricter evaluation of planned change efforts. These calls are frequently based on what can be labelled the $X \rightarrow Y$ model of organizational change. This model assumes there is a defined change goal labelled Y and a defined methodology labelled X to attain that goal. To learn more about organizational change the proponents of stricter evaluation research believe more valid information is needed on whether X causes Y. Some of these proponents accuse practitioners of not subjecting change efforts to strict evaluation in order to prevent exposure of incompetency. It is true that rejecting formal evaluation can shield practitioners' egos. However, the scarcity of formal evaluations may result more from the inadequacy of the $X \rightarrow Y$ model of organizational change than from practitioner evaluation error.

The socio-political context (SPC) is a major reason why the $X \rightarrow Y$ model is frequently inappropriate for studying organizational change. The SPC view of organizational change assumes the SPC significantly impacts the actual conduct of most planned change efforts. The goal (Y) of a change effort represents outcomes defined by the SPC. The methodology (X) represents an approach acceptable to the SPC for reaching Y. In other words, it is the SPC which defines both Y and X.

The SPC is also dynamic, not static. An examination of an SPC at one point in time provides only a snapshot of changing actors, interests, and power. Promotions, firings, transfers, retirements, reorganization, etc., alter the number, kinds and relationships of actors. Changes in sales or economic conditions can alter actors' interests and affect their willingness to employ their power. As a result, the SPC not only defines Y and X at the start of a change effort, it also redefines them constantly throughout the effort.

Operating within dynamic SPCs, practitioners often face a series of delicate balancing acts. Support of the change effort's sponsors must be maintained. Detractors must be placated. Acceptance of the target participants needs to be gained and maintained, and those neutral to the effort must be won over or at least monitored. A favourable balance among these shifting organizational actors must be kept if organizational development is to proceed. In the $X \rightarrow Y$ model of organizational change practitioners would attempt to hold the SPC constant in order to employ X to attain Y. Yet it is changes in the SPC and how they are adapted to and managed (how Xs and Ys are changed into Qs and Zs) that are key aspects of organizational change. In many instances they are more important in understanding organizational change than the particular interventions (Xs) themselves. The socio-political view of organizational change assumes that responding to shifts in the SPC is a central aspect inherent in planned organizational change.

STRATEGIC ORIENTATION LEVELS

Many change practitioners recognize the importance of the SPC. However, this recognition generally exists at an intuitive or 'gut' level. As a result, practitioners seldom question the orientations they adopt towards an SPC. Without a conscious awareness of their SPC orientations, practitioners lack the information necessary to determine the level best suited to their particular setting. Four such strategic orientation levels toward the SPC are now postulated.

Strategic Orientation Level I: Reacting. Practitioners operating with this orientation recognize the importance of the socio-political context, but assume it is something to be lived with like the weather. The change effort and the SPC are seen as separate and distinct. Practitioners view their role as to plan and conduct change efforts while responding to whatever happens in the socio-political context. They believe that since they have little or no control over shifts in the socio-political context, their task is primarily to react competently when shifts occur.

Strategic Orientation Level II: Forecast-reacting At this level practitioners also view the change effort and the socio-political context as distinct entities. But if they cannot change the socio-political weather they can try to forecast it. Practitioners with this orientation try to anticipate shifts in the socio-political context. Change efforts are then designed to incorporate possible SPC shifts.

With this strategic orientation, practitioners also pay explicit attention to environmental factors affecting the organization. These factors include general economic conditions, new legislation, market and technology changes, etc. Even though far removed from practitioners, these factors are potentially relevant in predicting shifts in the SPC. A downturn in the economy can make developmental efforts appear as ripe places for cutting back. Anticipating such a downturn, practitioners could be prepared to ensure the merits of the effort get a fair hearing. Practitioners at the forecast-reacting level systematically assess the socio-political weather and develop plans accordingly.

Strategic Orientation Level III: Forecast-proacting. At this level, practitioners do *not* draw sharp distinctions between the change effort and the SPC. They see the SPC as an inherent part of any organizational change attempt and design interventions appropriately. They not only forecast, they attempt to influence the SPC.

Influencing could take such forms as information seeding and issue control. An example of seeding is providing relevant organizational actors with information on the potential impact an SPC change may have upon the change effort. This seeding would be an attempt to influence decisions which may affect the effort. An example of issue control is attempting to raise or lower the organization's attention to issues relevant to the change effort. Practitioners frequently have access to many organizational levels. They can use their interaction with various levels to heat up or cool down certain issues which if brought into the open could help or hinder the change effort.*

*A word on manipulation. Many change practitioners have a value system which prohibits conscious manipulation on their part. The foregoing discussion on influencing the SPC may sound suspiciously like manipulating the SPC. One guide to distinguishing manipulation from other types of influence attempts is to apply the following condition: if the objects of the influence attempt knew the true motivations for it, they would not let it happen. If this condition is true, the influence attempt probably involves manipulation. A practitioner desiring to avoid manipulation charges would influence the SPC openly. The reasons behind an influence attempt would be stated clearly to the parties involved. This openness can occur if the practitioner believes the change effort is in the best interests of the organization.

The danger of manipulation increases as one moves from Strategic Orientation Level I to Strategic Orientation Level II and from Strategic Orientation II to Strategic Orientation III. At Orientation Level II, the change effort could be manipulated in response to shifts in the SPC. At Orientation Level III, both the change effort and the SPC itself could be manipulated.

Practitioners might operate at lower orientation levels because they fear engaging in manipulation and thus acting contrary to personal values. Operating with Level II or III orientations without engaging in manipulation is difficult. Other organizational members do not have self-imposed openness code and thus possess a tactical advantage. While it is riskier to state explicitly the purposes of influence attempts, the potential long-run benefits of that type of modelling can outweigh the risks. The main alternatives are to engage in manipulation and raise value issues or to operate at a lower orientation level and reduce the probability of a successful change effort.

Strategic Orientation Level IV: Steering. This strategic orientation level represents a more radical view of organizational change efforts than the previous three levels. At Strategic Orientation Level IV, the SPC is seen not only as an important part of an organizational change effort as in Strategic Orientation Level III, but addition, it is viewed as *the* primary component of the organizational change effort. Rather than interventions occurring within the SPC, the interventions have the SPC as their ultimate target. At this orientation level, the SPC is both context and object of the change effort.

Normally, with interventions such as job redesign or socio-technical analysis, the primary focus of the change practitioner is on the intervention methodology itself. The SPC is dealt with in ways to allow the intervention to proceed. At the Level IV orientation level these types of intervention methodologies are of only secondary focus. The purpose is not to redesign jobs but to alter the values of the organization in a desired direction.

In the first three orientation levels the change process is important in order to ensure good *results*. At Strategic Orientation Level IV, the reverse is true. Good results are important only in order to ensure continuation of the change *process*. Level IV can describe an organization in which a value war is occurring. The battles seem to be about the merits of various interventions. In actuality, the skirmishes are over the question of 'how should we be doing business as an organization?' Since these battles are frequently fought underground *versus* out in the open, the question of manipulation is more difficult here than at any other level. Very little knowledge is available about practitioner processes which occur at this strategic orientation level.

The strategic orientation level a practitioner adopts fundamentally affects the way he views and responds to the SPC. Each level represents a different set of assumptions regarding the value of planning and influence. The higher the level the greater the range of activities a practitioner is willing to consider. Conscious selection of a strategic orientation is the first move toward systematic management of the socio-political context.

Awareness of the various orientation levels, credibility and power in the organization, and possession of relevant tools each increase the practitioner's ability to operate at a higher level should the situation warrant it. One such tool, the SPC map, is discussed in the next section. A summary of the four strategic orientation levels is provided in Figure 1.

MAPPING THE SOCIO-POLITICAL CONTEXT

At Strategic Orientation Levels II–IV, some way of systematically mapping the socio-political context is necessary. SPC mapping allows for forecasting SPC shifts and can serve as a basis from which strategies for adapting to and influencing the SPC can be developed.

Strategic orientation Level I: Reacting	1. SPC seen as *separate* from change effort 2. Intervention methodologies seen as *prime* component of change attempt 3. Practitioner seen as having *no control* over shift in SPC 4. Role of practitioner is to respond competently to shifts in SPC 5. Change process important to ensure good *products*

Strategic orientation Level II:
Forecast-reacting
	1. SPC seen as *separate* from change effort
	2. Intervention methodologies seen as *prime* component of change attempt
	3. Practitioner seen having *no control* over shifts in SPC
	4. Role of practitioner is to
	    (a) *collect* information on SPC
	    (b) *forecast* potential shifts in SPC
	    (c) shape change effort to take into account potential SPC shifts
	5. Change process important to ensure good *products*

Strategic orientation Level III:
Forecast-proacting
	1. SPC seen as *significant component* of change effort
	2. Intervention methodologies seen as *prime* component of change attempt
	3. Practitioner seen as being *able to influence* the nature of and shifts in SPC
	4. Role of practitioner is to
	    (a) *collect* information on SPC
	    (b) *forecast* potential shifts in SPC
	    (c) *influence* SPC openly to benefit change effort
	    (d) shape change effort to blend with nature of SPC and its shifts
	5. Change process important to ensure good *products*

Strategic orientation Level IV: Steering	1. SPC seen as the *prime component* of change effort 2. Intervention methodology seen as *secondary* component of change effort 3. Practitioner seen as being *able to influence* SPC 4. Role of practitioner is to co-ordinate and direct various SPC forces in order to incorporate a new *value system* into organization 5. Good products important to ensure continuation of change *process*

Figure 1 Elements of practitioners' strategic orientations toward the SPC

An SPC could be mapped in many ways. One could use an extensive method such as Beckhard's (1977) which helps to identify power groups and the forces to which they are likely to respond, or a simple listing of the significant power groups might be sufficient. The basic criterion of any useful SPC mapping approach should be that it focuses practitioner attention on strategy-relevant aspects of an SPC. The mapping technique presented below has its roots in Lewin's (1951) force field analysis and is particularly useful in graphically summarizing several key aspects of an SPC on a single form. Components of this SPC mapping technique include actors and their power characteristics, the form of the map, and methods for constructing the map.

Actors in the SPC

Four categories of organizational actors relevant to a change effort can be distinguished: Controllers or the power elite, Targets, Interventionists, and Others.

Controllers:	the set of actors with the power to sanction or terminate change efforts.
Targets:	the set of actors in which change is desired.
Interventionists:	the set of actors employed to bring about change in the targets.
Others:	the set of actors relevant to the change effort but not belonging to the above defined sets.

The controller set would include the president, vice-president, division chiefs, staff heads, or any members of the organization's power elite who can directly influence the presence or absence of planned change efforts. Targets may be assembly line or clerical workers whose jobs are being enriched, members of an entire department which is being restructured, or the controllers themselves in a team-building effort. The set of interventionists include any internal and external consultants engaged in conducting the change effort. The set of 'others' represents all individuals who, although not directly involved in the change effort, can potentially affect its outcome. They include staff members who influence information flows within the organization and those who control resources relevant to the change effort.

Actor Characteristics

Four actor characteristics are useful in developing a map of the SPC: potential power, applied power, stability of applied power, and relationships to other actors.

Potential power:	amount of influence available to an actor to affect the change effort.
Applied power:	amount of influence actually employed by an actor to affect the change effort.
Applied power volatility:	the degree to which an actor is likely to change the amount of influence applied.

Actor relationships: the number of type of involvements with
                              other actors.

The first three actor characteristics are indicators of the power aspects of
the SPC. Potential power and applied power are frequently different. A
division chief may have the potential power to stop a planned change effort
but may not *apply* any of it until the first results of the effort become known.
Every actor in the SPC is likely to vary the amount of potential power
applied as the change effort progresses and more information becomes available. The likelihood of actors changing the amount of their applied power
is the volatility of their applied power. A staff head may know little about
the change effort initially. Therefore, he or she may apply little power at
first. As more is learned about the effort, however, the staff head may be
predicted to commit heavily one way or the other. If this were the case the
staff head would be initially labelled as low in applied power but highly
volatile.

The fourth actor characteristic is an indicator of the socio aspects of the
SPC. Informal relationships among various actors can be dramatically different from their official organizational relationships. Designating the existence and type of informal relationships among actors begins to provide a
picture of the coalitions and interpersonal barriers woven into the SPC.

Form of an SPC Map

Once actors and their characteristics have been identified, a mapping of the
SPC relevant to the change effort can be constructed. The map provides a
visual summary of the SPC at a given point in time. The basic form of the
map is shown in Figure 2.

Map axes

(1) The vertical height corresponds to the *potential* power of an actor
    to affect the change effort.
(2) The horizontal axis corresponds to the *applied* power of the actor.

Map zones

There are two vertical zones. Certain actors have 'absolute' potential power,
These actors such as the president and selected vice-presidents can single-
handedly terminate the change effort. Actors with this type of potential
power are placed about the 'absolute' potential power line in the SPC map.
Actors without this potential power are placed in the region below this line.

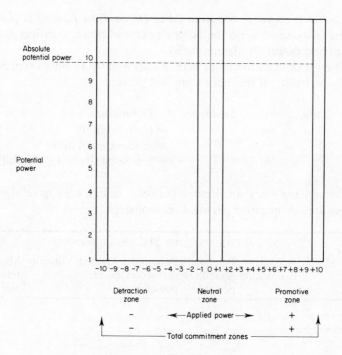

Figure 2 An SPC map form

There are four horizontal regions or zones in Figure 2. To the immediate right and left of the vertical axis is the *neutral* zone. Actors in this zone have potential power to affect the change effort but are currently adopting a 'wait and see' attitude. To the left of the neutral zone is the *detraction* zone. Actors in this zone are using at least some of their potential power to resist or block the change effort. They may feel that the change effort will not benefit the organization or that it requires too many organizational resources. To the right of the neutral zone is the *promotive* zone. Actors in this region of the map are employing at least some of their potential power to assist the progress of the change effort. At the two extremes of the horizontal axis are the *total commitment* zones. Actors in these zones are devoting all their potential power either to resist or assist the change effort. The ratio of applied power to potential power equals one in these zones.

Constructing an SPC Map

The data indicated in th SPC information collection sheet shown in Figure 3 are gathered for each person in the SPC. The following steps are then completed:

(1) Each actor's set designation letter (C_i or T_i or I_i, etc.) is placed on the map based upon the actor's potential power (vertical axis) and applied power (horizontal axis).

(2) The set designation letter is then enclosed by a symbol representing the volatility of the actor's applied power.

Scale Rating		Symbol	Definition
3	=	▽	= high volatility
2	=	○	= moderate volatility
1	=	□	= low volatility = high stability

(3) Connecting lines are drawn between actors who have significant positive or negative personal relationships.

SPC ACTORS AND THEIR SPC CHARACTERISTICS

Name	Actor set designation	Potential promotive power	Potential detraction power	Applied power	Volatility	Major relationships and type sign
1. _____						
2. _____						
3. _____						
4. _____						
5. _____						
6. _____						
7. _____						
8. _____						
9. _____						
10. _____						
11. _____						
12. _____						
13. _____						
14. _____						
15. _____						
16. _____						
17. _____						
18. _____						
19. _____						
20. _____						

Actor set designations: C_i = Controller T_u = Target I_i = Interventionist I_i = Other

Potential promotive power: 0 to +10 scale   *Potential detraction power*: 0 to −10 scale   *Applied power*: 0 to 10 scale

Volatility: 1 to 3 scale   *Major relationships and type sign:* set designations of actors with which actor has strong + or − personal relationships

Figure 3 SPC information collection sheet

(4) A dashed line is drawn around any two or more actors who possess absolute power as a coalition, but not as individuals

Figures 4 and 5 represent hypothetical examples of a completed SPC information collection sheet and the resulting SPC map. The SPC map illustrated in Figure 5 assumes the change effort already exists. Therefore, only the potential detraction power (power to terminate the effort) is shown. For efforts which are planned but not yet started, another map using the

SPC ACTORS AND THEIR SPC CHARACTERISTICS						
Name	Actor set designation	Potential* promotive power	Potential detraction power	Applied power	Volatility	Major relationships and type sign
1. B. Johnson	C_1		-10	+4	2	$C_3^{\ddagger}, T^{\dagger}$
2. J. Adams	C_2		-10	-4	2	$O^{\dagger}$
3. H. Clayton	C_3		-10	+2	3	$C^{\dagger}$
4. R. Anson	C_4		-8	+1	3	$C_5^{-}, C_7^{\ddagger}, C_8^{\ddagger}$
5. C. Brewer	C_5		-8	-7	2	$C_4^{-}, C_6^{\ddagger}$
6. S. Samdin	C_6		-7	-10	1	$C_5^{\ddagger}$
7. J. Alexander	C_7		-7	+2	3	$C_4^{\ddagger}, C_8^{\ddagger}, O^{\dagger}$
8. A. Bell	C_8		-6	+1	2	$C_4^{\ddagger}, C_7^{\dagger}, I^{\dagger}$
9. R. Koontz	T_1		-10	+5	1	$C^{\dagger}, I_2$
10. Mktg. Dept.	(T_2-T_{16})	-2 (individually) -10 (as a group)		+5	2	$I_3^{\ddagger}$
11. J. Lane	I_1		-5	+7	2	$I_3^{\ddagger}, C_8^{\ddagger}$
12. R. Shannon	I_2		-6	+8	2	$T_1, I_3^{\ddagger}$
13. K. Askon	I_3		-5	+10	3	$I^{\dagger}, I_2^{\ddagger},$ $(T_2-T_{16})^{+}$
14. P. Saunders	O_1		-8	+5	2	$C_2^{\ddagger}, C_7^{\dagger}$
15. Miscellaneous staff members	(O_2-O_{10})		-4	-1	2	
16. _____						
17. _____						
18. _____						
19. _____						
20. _____						

Actor set designations: C_i = Controller T_i = Target I_i = Interventionist 0_i = Other

Potential promotive power: 0 to +10 scale *Potential detraction power:* 0 to -10 scale *Applied power:* 0 to 10 scale

Volatility: 1 to 3 scale

Major relationships and type sign: set designations of actors with which actor has strong + or − personal relationships.

* not necessary in conducting figure 5, change effort already exists.

Figure 4 SPC information collection sheet (hypothetical example)

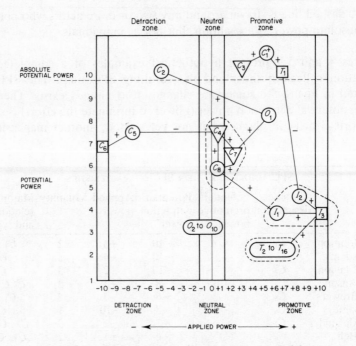

Figure 5 An SPC map form (example constructed from
data on example SPC information collection sheet shown in
Figure 4)

potential promotive power (power to get the effort started) would be
constructed.

Value of SPC Mapping

Mapping an SPC can provide several benefits for practitioners. A few of
these are now discussed.

Practitioner consensus. Practitioners frequently engage in SPC discussions *assuming* they agree on the potential, applied, and volatility of power
associated with various actors. Often strategy differences stem from these
differing views. The mere act of collecting the information necessary to
construct an SPC map makes explicit many of a practitioner's assumptions
about the SPC. Wide variances between practitioners can thus be pinpointed
and these variances indicate where discussions need to take place if practitioners are to act from a common base of knowledge.

Information summary. The number and types of variables comprising an
SPC are immense. Due to natural cognitive limitations it is unlikely that a
practitioner could mentally hold a significant number of relevant SPC aspects.

Mapping the SPC provides a systematic way for summarizing many of its key aspects. It also serves as a baseline to track changes in the SPC over time.

Identification of action subsets. Earlier, actors were segmented into controller, target, interventionist, and 'other' sets. These sets represent demographic or static characteristics of actors. The SPC map with its various zones divides these sets into action subsets. Action subsets represent dynamic characteristics of actors, those potentially amenable to practitioner influence. Each way of subdividing the actors in the SPC provides a different type of information. The SPC map allows the actors to be subdivided in a variety of ways depending upon the needs and purposes of the practitioner. Some of these action subsets are as follows:

(1) *Promoters*: by glancing at the right side of the SPC map in Figure 5, one isolates those actors who are actively supporting the change effort.
(2) *Detractors*: the left side of the SPC map shows those actors actively opposing the change effort.
(3) *Neutrals*: the centre of the SPC map locates those actors who have power to affect the effort but who have not yet decided how much power to apply or in what direction to apply it.
(4) *Total Committers*: the right and left extremes of the map point out the number and kind of actors employing all their power to affect the change effort.
(5) *Absolutists*: the top of the map isolates actors of critical importance, who single-handedly could terminate the change effort if they decided to employ all their potential power to do so.
(6) *Volatiles*: the number of map triangles indicates the likely changeability of the SPC over time.

Attention priority. The SPC map also indicates which actors deserve priority. The attention priority given an actor by a practitioner increases as the actor's potential power, applied power and volatility increase. In other words, the more power an actor has and uses, and the more volatile the use of that power, the more attention the actor warrants from practitioners. An actor with the potential power to terminate the change effort who is applying much of that power and could quickly change to applying full power would be highest on the attention priority list. This actor would appear on an SPC map as a triangle in the upper left corner.

SPC activity. If most actors are located towards the centre of the SPC map it indicates that the SPC has low activity. There may be high potential power but at present most actors are not applying it. As actors apply their potential power their locations shift away from the centre. An SPC map where most actors are located away from the centre indicates an SPC where high activity is occurring. Practitioners will generally be affected more by high-activity SPCs than by low-activity SPCs. SPCs with high activity and many triangles (highly volatile members) require more practitioner planning than other types of SPCs.

It can also be useful to look at the activity (distance from the centre) of specific sets of actors. If detractors have generally high activity while promoters have generally low activity, it may indicate where the practitioners should address the SPC. If the controllers have very little activity as a set, it may indicate little involvement on their part in the conduct of the change effort.

Coalition levers. The relationship lines in an SPC map provide the foundation for identifying coalitions of actors. Often when one member of a coalition changes position, other members of the coalition follow. Identifying key members of various coalitions helps to narrow the number of actors requiring critical attention by practitioners. The key member of a coalition acts as a lever by which several actors can be influenced.

The relationship lines in an SPC map also indicate potential consequences to the entire SPC of a change in an actor's position. Actors with negative personal relationships are more likely to influence each other in opposite ways than actors with positive personal relationships. In a highly connected SPC (one with many relationship lines) a change in a small set of actor's positions is more likely to cause change in the entire SPC than in an unconnected SPC.

Aid to external consultants. Just as internal practitioners can be so close to the SPC that they cannot see it, external consultants can be so far removed from the SPC that they do not adequately take it into consideration. Constructing a map of the SPC can not only bring out internal practitioners' views and assumptions about the SPC, it can also serve as an efficient way to bring external consultants 'up to speed' on the SPC. A great deal of information is summarized in an SPC map. Such information can be valuable to external consultants as they attempt to select interventions of potential benefit to the organization.

STRATEGY LEVERS

No single strategy or set of strategies is appropriate for all SPCs. Each SPC is unique—an evolving collage of actors, interests, and power. It is more useful to identify basic elements from which strategies can be developed. Strategy levers are elements available to practitioners that can be used in a variety of ways to shape practitioner strategic activity. The SPC map assists in focusing practitioner activity. Strategy levers help shape that activity. Three SPC strategy levers are briefly discussed: inclusion level, actor permeability and SPC feedback characteristics.

Inclusion Level

Practitioners frequently have several ways to include actors in a change effort. Basically, inclusion level deals with information management. By selecting an inclusion level, practitioners control amounts and forms of information to which actors are exposed. Different inclusion levels can be expected to have differential impacts on actor's reactions towards a change effort. A list of inclusion levels is presented in Figure 6.

Increasing an actor's inclusion level increases the chances that the actor will more accurately perceive the change effort. Many change efforts suffer from misunderstanding on the part of various actors in the SPC. By increasing these actors' inclusion level, this misunderstanding can be reduced and some of the actors' resistance to the effort may decrease.

However, inclusion is a double-edged sword. Two-way feedback channels allow both information *and* influence to be exchanged. Included actors generally have more accurate information on the change effort but also tend to want to influence the effort more. Allowing detracting actors 'in', practitioners risk activation of their potential detraction power to alter the effort in undesirable ways. The task for practitioners is to choose inclusion levels for various actors which enhance a clear understanding of the effort while maintaining the change effort's integrity. Figure 6 illustrates that as the inclusion

Inclusion	*Interaction*	*Ownership*
Very Low		
1. No information	none	none
2. Placed on reports/correspondence distribution list		
(a) information only	none	low
(b) feedback/recommendations requested	low	low to moderate
3. Special reports tailored to actor		
(a) information only	none	none to low
(b) feedback/recommendation requests	low to moderate	low to moderate
4. Oral presentations		
(a) formal	moderate	low to moderate
(b) informal	moderate to high	moderate to high
5. Observer	low to moderate	
6. Consultant	high	high
7. Participant	very high	very high
Very high		

Figure 6 Action inclusion levels

level increases, interaction and ownership are also likely to increase. Inclusion levels start at zero interaction, move to one-way written communication, then to two-way written communication, then to two-way oral communication away from the actual operation of the change effort, and finally to two-way oral communication 'face to face' with those directly involved in the change effort. As communication becomes two-way and 'face to face' its richness increases. Placing Promoters in high inclusion levels can be part of one strategy for maintaining their support.

An inclusion level not only indicates the amount of information SPC actors are likely to receive about the change effort, it also indicates the amount of information practitioners are likely to receive about the actors. Two-way interaction provides valuable data about an actor's current attitudes towards the change effort. The higher the inclusion level the more practitioners are likely to learn about an actors shifting position in the SPC.

By selective use of inclusion levels, practitioners can more effectively influence and learn about the SPC. Inclusion levels can be altered throughout the life of the effort. Gradually increasing or decreasing actors' inclusion levels is a way of phasing them in or out of the change effort. Inclusion levels can thus be a very flexible strategy element available to practitioners.

Actor Permeability

This strategy lever is concerned with the ways SPC actors accept information and influence attempts. Individuals have different information acceptance styles, source credibility criteria, and data validity criteria. Each of these factors affects the degree to which individuals will accept information produced by the change effort.

Information acceptance styles refer to ways in which individuals prefer to receive information. While one person with a highly cognitive style may obtain a feel for the change effort by reading a report and asking questions, another may have to experience it more directly to arrive at a similar level of understanding. Some people prefer to see results before being told about processes. Others want to know costs before they pay attention to anything else. Unfortunately, practitioners sometimes relate uniformly to actors in the SPC by providing identical reports or briefings to everyone. By diagnosing information acceptance styles of key actors, practitioners can develop more effective approaches for transferring desired information.

Source credibility criteria determine who an actor listens to. No matter how reliable and valid certain information is, if it comes from certain individuals, an actor may not accept it. For example, in some research and development organizations, some actors will not believe certain information unless it comes from a person with engineering experience. Practitioners often find that they themselves have no credibility with certain actors. When this is the case, practitioners can determine who in the organization does have credibility with a given actor. Practitioners might then develop their strategies around communicating indirectly to the actor by transferring information to those who have a relationship with and are credible sources for the actor.

Data validity criteria refer to the level of proof information must have before it is believed by an actor. Some actors require rigorous levels of proof, such as research reports and statistical analysis. Others may require only anecdotal evidence. Generally, the more an actor has personally experienced a phenomenon, the less rigour is required for acceptance of the information relating to that phenomenon providing it coincides with the actor's experience. Actors in high inclusion levels frequently need less proof to accept change effort results than actors in low inclusion levels.

Information acceptance style, source credibility criteria, and data validity criteria are overlapping factors. They characterize the ways in which actors will be permeable to information. By taking an actors' permeability into account, practitioners can choose more appropriate inclusion levels and channels of communication within these levels.

SPC Feedback Characteristics

Another important strategy lever is the type of feedback environment which characterizes a particular SPC. Understanding an SPC's feedback characteristics allows practitioners to decide on approaches for developing and testing their strategies. Two central attributes of feedback environments are their *richness* and their *benevolence*.

In feedback-rich environments, practitioners receive extensive feedback from the SPC. In feedback-poor environments, practitioners may not learn for a long time the effects various activities had on SPC actors. For example, a briefing presented in a feedback-rich environment would quickly produce feedback on the actual reactions of the attending SPC actors. In a feedback-poor environment, practitioners might not hear for months, if ever, the true reactions of attendees.

A second attribute of feedback environments is their benevolence. The more benevolent a feedback environment is the less a mistake will cost. Should practitioners choose an inappropriate strategy in a malevolent feedback environment the costs could be drastic. Deciding to prohibit union participation in the initial stage of an organization-wide change effort could be a strategy that in a malevolent environment would topple the change effort should the strategy turn out to be inappropriate.

Combining the two attributes of richness and benevolence provides a general guide for the degree of strategy development. This guide is presented in Figure 7. The guide assumes practitioners have already established an overall change effort strategy.

In feedback-poor malevolent environments, practitioners are not likely to receive accurate feedback and the costs of mistakes are high. In such environments, the practitioner is advised to spend much time developing a complete and thorough strategy before initiating any change effort activity. Practitioners will not have reliable information from the SPC to guide strategy alterations. They had better be right the first time. Extensive long-term planning is essential in such feedback environments.

In feedback-rich benevolent environments, extensive detailed planning is not required. In fact, such planning would be a misuse of practitioner time. Only a basic outline of a change strategy is necessary. As soon as the practitioners act they will receive feedback, and mistakes are not costly. In this type of environment, practitioners are advised to act first, then plan efforts according to the information received from the SPC.

In feedback-rich malevolent environments, a small-step approach is recommended. Feedback abounds but mistakes can be costly. It is not necessary to plan in great detail all aspects of a change effort. Such an approach is unrealistic since practitioners will gain much information from their initial steps from which to revise and improve their efforts. However, since mistakes can be costly, in-depth planning for the first few steps is critical. In feedback-rich malevolent environments, change efforts evolve in a plan-a-little, act-a-little fashion.

Lastly, in feedback-poor benevolent environments, there are no strong imperatives for prioritizing planning versus acting. While feedback is not

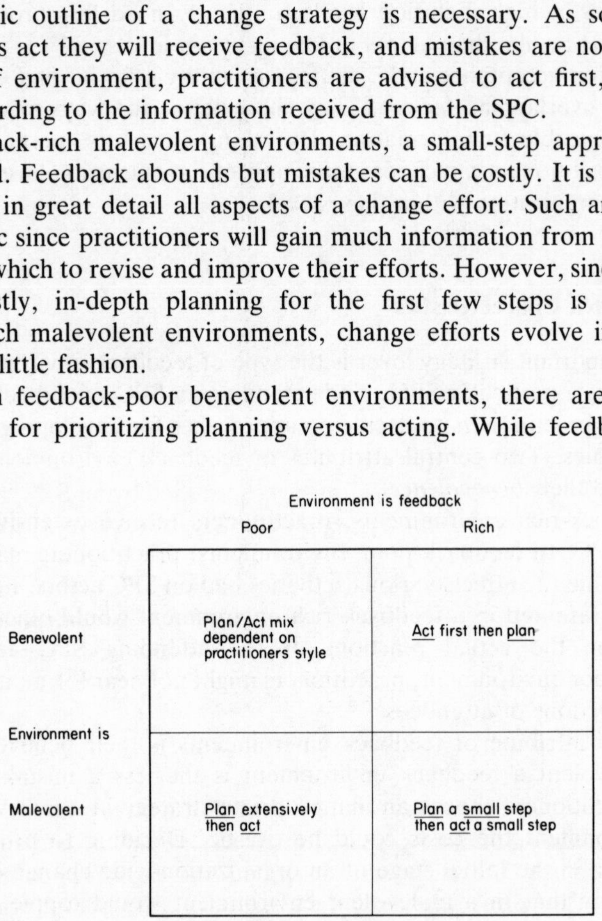

	Environment is feedback	
	Poor	Rich
Benevolent	Plan/Act mix dependent on practitioners style	Act first then plan
Malevolent	Plan extensively then act	Plan a small step then act a small step

(row label at left: Environment is)

Figure 7 Practitioner planning/acting mix for various
types of feedback environment conditions

abundant, mistakes are not costly. Once a general change approach has been established, the appropriate planning/acting mix in this type of environment depends more on practitioner style than on other factors.

SPC feedback environments frequently cannot be cast easily into one of the four pure types presented in Figure 7. Normally an SPC is some mixture of these four types. SPC segments and even different SPC actors may each differ along richness and benevolence attributes. The relevant point for practitioners is that they consider adjusting their planning/acting mix contingent upon feedback attributes of the situation.

SUMMARY

An important part of planned organizational change is how change agents relate to the relevant socio-political context (SPC). Four strategic orientation levels were discussed. The levels vary to the extent they assume the SPC can and should be influenced. At the lowest level the SPC is viewed as separate from the change effort, not amenable to practitioner influence. At the highest level the SPC is seen as the basic object of change efforts and practitioner influence is viewed as possible and desirable. The strategic orientation level a practitioner adopts fundamentally shapes the nature of his or her relationship to the SPC.

A useful basis for developing strategies for dealing with an SPC is the SPC map. By collecting information on various actors in an SPC, such as their potential power, applied power, and relationships to other actors, a summary of the SPC can be constructed. Mapping the SPC in this way allows key aspects of the SPC to be identified.

In developing strategies for SPC aspects identified by an SPC map, certain strategy levers are available to practitioners. Inclusion level is the degree to which actors are involved in the information flow of the change effort. Actor permeability indicates ways in which various actors can most easily accept the information they are provided. SPC feedback attributes indicate the appropriate practitioner planning/acting mix for various types of feedback environments.

Conclusion

Strategic orientation levels, SPC mapping, and strategy levers are merely first steps in helping practitioners systematically to understand and deal with the socio-political contexts of their change efforts. The socio-political context is a major variable in understanding the process of planned organizational change. This variable has received too little attention in the past and is sometimes completely ignored in theoretical discussions of organizational change. Significant advances in understanding planned organizational change are not likely to occur until the role and dynamics of the SPC are more fully explored.

REFERENCES

Alderfer, C. P. (1977). Organization development, *Annual Review of Psychology*, **28**, 197–223.

Allison, G. T. (1969). Conceptual models and the Cuban missile crisis, *American Political Science Review*, **63** (3), 689–718.

Beckhard, R. (1977). *Organizational Transitions*, Reading Mass: Addison Wesley.

Bennis, W. G. (1969). *Organization Development*: Its Nature, Origins and Prospects, Reading, Mass: Addison Wesley.

Beer, M. (1980). *Organization Change and Development: A Systems View*, Santa Monica, California: Goodyear, p. 10.

French, W. L. and Bell, C. H. (1973). *Organization Development*, Englewood Cliffs, NJ: Prentice-Hall, p. 15.

Harrison, R. (1973). Role negotiation: A tough-minded approach to team development, in W. G. Bennis, D. E. Berlew, E. H. Schein, and F. I. Steele (eds), *Interpersonal Dynamics* (3rd ed.), Homewood, ill: Dorsey Press.

Kahn, R. L. (1974). Organization development: Social problems and proposals, *Journal of Applied Behavioural Science*, **10** 485–502.

Kaufman, H. (1964). Organizational theory and political theory, *The American Political Scientist Review*, **58** (1), 5–14.

Lewin, K. (1951). Field Theory in Social Science, New York: Harper and Row.

March, J. G. (1964). The business firm as a political coalition, *Journal of Politics*, **58** (1), 662–678.

Porter, L. L. (1976). Organizations as political animals. Presidential Address: Division of Industrial-Organizational Psychology, 84th Annual Meeting of American Psychological Association. (Speaker's manuscript)

Zaleznik, A. (1970). Power and politics in organizational life, *Harvard Business Review*, **48** (3), 47–60.

Power, Politics, and Organizations: A Behavioural Science View
Edited by Andrew Kakabadse and Christopher Parker
© 1984 John Wiley & Sons Ltd

Chapter 8

Myths, Magic, and Gobbledegook. A-rational Aspects of the Consultant's Role

ADRIAN MCLEAN

Since being stung into action by well-founded criticisms of political naivety, writers on organizational change have been much concerned to assuage their critics by directly addressing the question of politics in organizations generally and the political aspects of the consultant's activities in particular.

Much of this writing has addressed itself to ways in which power is acquired and sustained inside organizations, examining and identifying the bases of power, ways of gaining access to such bases, modes of influence, and so on. This chapter presents an alternative approach to the question of change agent power. Its preoccupation is less with the acquisition and strategic use of power than with an examination of the potential forms of power inherent in the role of consultant, but particularly with the power which inheres within the relationship between a consultant and his client. Such a definition is based on the notion that a particular form of power emerges as a consequence of a relationship.

Power is, of course, a relational concept, and many writers have explored the intricacies of the ways in which one individual has power over another individual. The focus of this paper has less to do with some of the ways in which one individual acquires the means by which to influence another— although we fully accept the validity of such a view of power—than with the power which is an emergent property of a relationship, such that as a consequence of such a relationship new possibilities for acting and being are now open to both parties.

We begin with an examination of the notion of power so as to establish the senses in which we are and are not using the term and proceed to present and describe four forms of power: collusive power, intuitive power, paradoxical power, and analogic power.

There is considerable discussion and debate regarding the precise concep-

147

tualization of power. Some theorists add layer upon layer of complexity and refinements to the concept, whilst others point to the futility of trying to over-refine what is essentially a 'primitive' term (Bacharach and Lawler, 1980). Certain underlying assumptions seem to provide an unquestioned basis for subsequent elaboration. James (1977) suggests one of them:

> The concepts of power, influence and authority may be related to the concept of control (or compliance or obedience). Power in an organization will normally be used to secure control, that is control is the ends and power the means.

A possible explanation for this may be found in the frequent observation that 'most conceptions of power are based on Weber's (1947) classic definition that power is the probability that a person can carry out his or her own will despite resistance' (Bacharach and Lawler, 1980). This leads the same authors to the observation that: 'Power is inherently coercive and implies involuntary submission, whereas influence is persuasive and implies voluntary submission'. The notions of control and coercion are contained either explicitly or implicitly in most definitions of power.

A second assumption is that of intentionality, that the property of power arises as a result of conscious efforts to acquire and exercise it over others. Thus people develop a variety of strategic and tactical ploys. Tannenbaum (1968), for example, regarding power, control and influence as synonymous, argues that:

> [Control refers] to any process in which a person or group of persons determines, that is, *intentionally* affects, the behaviour of another person, group or organization.

Walter Buckley (1967) defines power as 'control over or influence over the actions of others to *promote* one's goals without their consent, against their will or without their knowledge or understanding (for example by control of the physical, psychological or some cultural environment within which others must act)'.

Bacharach and Lawler (1980) summarize the view of politics held by social psychologists:

> For social psychologists politics is a series of competitive tactical encounters. These encounters entail an assessment of a situation (that is an assessment of one's power vis à vis that of significant competitors) and a selection of counter-tactics by which to thwart the competitor's tactics. Parallel encounters occur in organizational settings.

Abell, (1975) of describes power as: 'the ability of an actor to *get his way* when opposed by others with competing objectives.

The central suggestion of this paper is that such definitions are founded on underlying assumptions which constitute an epistemological limitation for our understanding of power and proposes another formulation of the concept based on an alternative epistemology. The limitations of space are such that we will confine our exposition of the alternative epistemology to a summary of its main characteristics, referring interested readers to more painstaking descriptions elsewhere. Our main interest, in the present context, is in the implications of formulating an understanding of power from an alternative paradigm.

For convenience, we begin by suggesting that the alternative basis for conceptualizing power derives from an ecology of influences and developments. Prominent within such an ecology are the ideas of Bateson, those of the new Paradigm research group, the feminist movement, some psychotherapists and Bakan.

We will begin with the ideas of Bakan (1966) who postulates two basic tendencies of human existence, which he terms the agentic and the communal. The agentic are characterized by separation (of subject and object), repression (of feelings), conquest, mastery, and control (of others and/or nature), contracted (relationships), ordering, quantifying, and masculine traits. He contrasts these with communion tendencies which are those of fusion, expression, acceptance, uncontracted co-operation, non-linear patterning and feminine traits. Reinhartz (1982) suggests that such distinctions 'closely parallel' two research models, the one which she attributes to mainstream sociology and which corresponds to agentic tendencies, and the other that she terms an alternative or feminist model, corresponding to the notion of communion.

Thus the latter modes of research are less concerned to value objectivity, hypothesis testing, and value-free approaches to inquiry using methods where there is a sharp distinction between researcher and subject. They are more concerned with encouraging the emergence of ideas and insights from an intimate experiential familiarity with the subject matter where the nature of the relationship between researcher and subject is more collaborative, and which takes account of the ambitions of both parties to the venture. It is a model of discovery which holds that understanding emerges from a fusion of effort and experience on the part of what are traditionally termed researcher and subject, such that both parties occupy both roles and that allows for these roles to be reversed as well as the possibility of both parties simultaneously occupying first one role and then the other. In Bateson's terms (1973) such a model allows for symmetrical relationships as well as the complementary relationships characterized by more traditional models of research. These ideas also resemble what has been termed the 'new paradigm model of research' (Reason and Rowan, 1981) which embraces a humanistic approach to research together with what at times amounts to an evangelical fervour for collaborative, non-alienating methodologies. The psychotherapeutic links are to be found with the importance placed by some therapists on right-brain processes of intuition, empathy, and insight, emotionality, and the significance of metaphor and artistic expression. We will invoke some of those ideas particularly when examining one aspect of the power relationship between consultants and their clients.

Our proposition is that if we formulate our understanding of power according to this alternative epistemology we begin with an assumption that is radically different from the control (and agentic) notions that underpin current conceptualizations of power, instead we have a view of power which does not represent a struggle of one person to gain control over another but where, as a consequence of their interacting, power is *created* which is *liberating* for both parties, that as a consequence of their relationship new possibilities for acting and being emerge for both of them. Power in this sense is a product of the interaction, is embedded within the relationship and emanates from the relationship. Whereas current definitions of power discuss sanctions and pressure both potential and actual that can be brought to bear in order to enforce the wishes of one of the parties, that is, calling on resources that may be external to the relationship, this alternative conceptualization, that we will term immanent power, derives its potency from the relationship itself, it is a form of inspirational power. Whereas one might grossly simplify existing discussions of power as concerning power over, we are proposing a view of the topic in terms of power with and power from. This reformulation renders meaningless notions of winners and losers, of being one up, and so on.

Traditional writing places much emphasis on the acquisition of power, and ways of gaining access to power bases; this paradigm emphasizes more the creation or realization of power that emanates from within an individual or a relationship.

Adopting formulations of power that are based in this alternative epistemology allows us to understand some aspects of the relationship between consultants and their clients that complement more traditional discussions of the relationship. In the remainder of the chapter we present four manifestations of immanent power. they are collusive power, intuitive power, paradoxical power, and analogic power. But first to summarize the characteristics of immanent power.

Immanent power arises as a consequence of the *relationship* between consultant and client. It is a liberating form of power that opens up new possibilities for acting and being in a way that does not necessarily constrain others and is not necessarily at the expense of others—in this sense it is a creative form of power. It cannot satisfactorily be attributed to either party but emerges for both actors as a consequence of their interaction. It is different from more conventional formulations in that it does not imply a specific set of behaviours for either party but increases rather than decreases their autonomy. Such forms of power are different from influence in that they do not imply an objective or a desired direction or form of action. We influence someone *to do something*, or act in a *particular way* or to adopt a particular attitude or point of view. Immanent power is characterized by the fact that it allows others to recognize the boundaries of their self-imposed constraints and to relinquish them without necessarily replacing them with something created by the consultant.

COLLUSIVE POWER

Collusion may be described as the mutual acceptance of a deception. Laing describes some of the essential features of what he describes as a game.

> . . . collusion is necessarily a two-or-more person game. Each plays the other's game, though he may not necessarily be fully aware of doing so. An essential feature of the game is not admitting that it is a game . . . Desire for confirmation from each (party) is present in both but each is caught between trust and mistrust, confidence and despair, and both settle for counterfeit acts of confirmation on the basis of pretence.

Laing's discussion is heavily seasoned with references to the negative connotations and consequences of collusion:

> Collusion is always clinched when self finds in other that other who will confirm self in the false self that it is trying to make real and vice versa. The ground is then set for prolonged mutual evasion of truth and true fulfilment. Each has found another to endorse his own false notion of himself and to give this appearance a semblance of reality.

There is some evidence to suggest that collusions occur from time to time between organizational consultants and their clients. We have described elsewhere (McLean *et al.*, 1982) the phenomenon whereby an eminent consultant is revered by some members of the client organization. Consultants are sometimes described as gurus by their clients. Margulies (1978) describes five 'magical' aspects of the consultant-client interaction two of which are discussed in this section. The first is the 'placebo' whereby,

> If the client believes organizational development procedures can bring about change, the important changes will occur regardless of the scientific validity of the procedures.

The second 'magical' aspect of Organizational Development that he recognizes is the notion of Doctrinal Compliance which he describes as:

> the implicit desire on the part of the client to act in terms of the OB doctrine prescribed by the consultant. Even if the changes made are surface ones, *potentially real organizational change is now possible.**

The collusion that exists between consultant and client may then be summarized as follows.

The client organization wishing to bring about internal changes (and not all clients do) appoints a prestigious outsider as consultant. The consultant's track record of other assignments, together with the fact that he may have authored several influential publications, coupled with a personal charisma, combine to impress the client that here, indeed, is someone with the knowledge and skill to guide them safely through the traumas of organizational change. The consultant, by his presence, engenders an excitement in the client organization that real change is possible and he can be the focus of much speculation, with extraordinary powers attributed to him. Thus, for example, members of the organization may believe that the consultant has the ability to anticipate, predict, and even stage manage events in a way that no-one else can. They may also believe that he has an over-riding understanding of events, perhaps with a capacity to predict individual behaviour and reactions. This apparently strong desire on the part of some organizational clients to cast the consultant in the role of guru, mystic, or shaman is accepted by some consultants as an opportunity such that they are prepared to collude with these expectations for a limited period in order to allow the client to experiment with new ideas and activities that might otherwise appear to be excessively disturbing or risky.

A similar phenomenon in psychotherapy is known as 'holding the transference' (Hawkins, 1982). It is in this sense that the client is empowered to act, by relinquishing familiar patterns and routines and, in the process, letting go of self-imposed constraints while simultaneously developing and improvising new patterns of responding. The dependency on the consultant can be used creatively to engender a faith in the possibility for change and a heightened preparedness to take the risks essential for change to occur. Collusive power may be used by consultants in accordance with conventional definitions of power, by exploiting their clients' dependence to lead them in directions that the consultant chooses or considers to be appropriate. It is our contention however that such a use of collusive power is not inevitable and that some consultants can and do harness this power to allow their clients to take the risks of embarking on change without imposing the consultants' specific ambitions or ideas for new direction/habits.

*Our emphasis.

INTUITIVE POWER

In a much quoted book, Ornstein (1977) described the differences between the way information is dealt with by the left hemisphere of the brain and how it is processed by the right:

> The left hemisphere of the cortex which subtends language and mathematics seems to process information primarily in a linear, sequential manner, appropriate to its specialities. The right side of the cortex processes its input more as a 'patterned whole', that is in a more simultaneous manner, than does the left. This simultaneous processing is advantageous for the integration of diffuse inputs, such as for orienting oneself in space when motor, kinaesthetic and visual input must be quickly integrated. This mode of information processing, too, would seem to underlie an 'intuitive' rather than an 'intellectual' integration of complex entities.

Others have observed that the traditions of Western science and thought are founded on the processes of the left hemisphere, of reason, logic, of lineal sequencing, of cause and effect, and rationality, whereas Eastern philosophies emphasize more the qualities of the right hemisphere. Close parallels would appear to exist between the two research models that Reinhartz describes and the two hemispheres of the brain, with the left hemisphere corresponding to what she describes as mainstream sociology and the right hemisphere modes of processing information equating with what she terms feminist models of research.

It is our contention that some consultants may empower their client organizations through means which can best be understood in terms of the modes of information processing dominant in the right hemisphere of the brain. We would suggest that such power is termed intuitive power.

Intuitive power, then, refers to the consequences of non-rational exchanges between individuals and as such is founded in the right hemisphere of the brain. It is in contrast to the power of logic and rationality and reason of the left hemisphere. Psychotherapists have long pointed to the value of accessing the right brain as a means of effecting therapeutic change. Watzlawick (1978), for example, suggests that;

> . . . the language of dreams, fairy tales and myths, of hypnosis, delusions and other similar manifestations (the language of the right hemisphere that, consequently, offers itself to those areas of the mind in which alone therapeutic change can take place) has always been known to be particularly condensed and charged with meaning.

Indeed Watzlawick argues that the key to therapeutic change lies not in rational approaches that rely heavily on reason and logic, attributes of the left brain, but instead he claims that the therapist is more likely to succeed by 'learning the patient's right-hemisphere language and using it as the royal route to therapeutic change'.

We wish to suggest that it may also be the case that some organizational consultants either wittingly or unwittingly have a similar effect on their clients to that described by Watzlawick. We do not wish to suggest that there is hard evidence to prove such a connection but we believe that there are sufficient grounds to enquire further into the possibility of such a link.

It is possible to recognize similarities between the role of some psychotherapeutic techniques and the activities of some organizational consultants. Certainly both are intervening into complex social systems with a view to effecting some sort of change in those systems. Both resort to a set of techniques that guide their activities, but both also report the difficulty of pinning down precisely what it is that they do that makes a difference. Yalom (1980) makes the point for psychotherapists:

> Formal texts, journal articles, and lectures portray therapy as precise and systematic, with carefully delineated stages, strategic technical interventions, . . . and a careful, rational program of insight-offering interpretations. Yet I believe deeply that (like the master chef) when no-one is looking, the therapist throws in the 'real' thing.

Elsewhere (McLean *et al.*, 1982) we have noted the caution of some OD consultants in applying rational labels or clear-cut concepts to their activities, some actively resisting this option.

A third similarity pertains to the significance of what Watzlawick (1980) described as 'right hemispheric language'. Our observations and comments here are based on data from a research project which analysed accounts by OD consultants of their involvement in what at the time were current OD projects (McLean *et al.*, 1980). Two of our findings seem to be particularly significant in the present context.

We have already made the observation that some of these consultants were resistant to imposing rational explanations and logical accounts on to some of their actions. On occasions consultants suggested that they acted intuitively, in one case exclusively so:

> When I said that, I said it because I do all things intuitively. My post rationalization is that really what we're about in that department is ownership throughout the whole structure. Trying to get an ownership of change, not just this top management box.

Another consultant commented:

'It's not a level of thought that I work at. Perhaps we do it intuitively, without worrying about it'.

Such a discovery is not in itself particularly remarkable. It would seem reasonable to assume that most if not all people act in accordance with their intuitions from time to time. What is more interesting is the fact that these consultants are explicit about the importance of intuition in guiding some of their professional practice, they are in effect confirming their faith in the value of right-brain modes of processing information. This leads us to our second point; both the consultants' own accounts and the accounts given by the clients of these consultants suggests that, for some exchanges with their clients in conversations or presentations, consultants draw heavily on imagery and metaphors as a way of communicating ideas, and rely far less on the use of abstract concepts. Imagery and metaphors, or drawing pictures with words, is much closer to right-brain modes of processing and representing information than to those of the left brain. Some have suggested that whereas the left brain processes information digitally, the right brain does so analogically (Palazzoli *et al.*,). We wish to emphasize that our evidence does not suggest that all consultants operate in this way, and indeed no single consultant resorted exclusively to metaphors and imagery in the descriptions of their activities. However, one example that we encountered illustrates the phenomenon nicely. Here an external consultant is describing his relationship with his internal counterpart in the client organization:

So it's a personal level, helping confidence to *grow*, confidence and practical experience and knowing himself. The interpersonal level between him and his clients, him and his *umbrella* in his personnel subsystem, him and his *dotted line troops* out in the mere sub-systems. Them, and him with his *tatty umbrella* with externals that have been *shooting up* by doing the wrong thing at the wrong time or the right things at the wrong moment and the wrong way, or any mix that you like to . . . *unscrewing his credibility* . . . and it would be his fault. So I would try to be his *tail lights*. All in twelve days a year!

Two things strike us as interesting about this description: its rich, varied, and at times vivid imagery, and secondly the fact that it does not flow in a logical or systematic fashion, sentences are left unfinished and new images superimposed on existing ones in a way that combines to create a bombardment of metaphors.

As researchers we were struck by a curious contradiction. The experience of tape-recording the interview with this consultant had been highly stimulating and exciting in terms of ideas. Later, while analysing the tape-recording, and particularly the transcript of the recording with our colleagues on the research project, we were surprised to find that not only did those of our colleagues who had not been present at the interviews fail to share our excitement, but they found the transcript disjointed and confusing. We wondered whether the consultant left his clients feeling equally confused. What we could not deny was that this particular consultant has an impressive track record, runs a highly successful consultancy and has established a good reputation among his professional colleagues. We were further intrigued to hear that clients of this consultant did indeed have the same experience as our own:

> . . . it felt impressive while you are there but when you sit down and think about it (with the MD), and he said, 'Well, what the hell was that all about?'

In our efforts to reconcile these discrepancies the most plausible explanation that the research group could offer was that the consultant, whether wittingly or unwittingly, bombarded the client with a variety of imagery or metaphors in such a way that a number of them matched up with the images or metaphors held by the client or that there was a form of compatibility between them. We formulated an explanation in terms of sound frequencies suggesting that the excitement felt occurred when there was a resonance between the signaller and the receiver and that the signaller evoked sympathetic echoes in the receiver. In this way the consultant established a rapport between himself and the client which furnished him with valuable information about his client while simultaneously causing some excitement in the client. We suspect that such sympathetic 'tuning in' could equally stimulate distress in the client as much as excitement. The imagery of the consultant may have acquired an added potency because of the confusing context in which it was set; the illogicality of the overall account. Confusion as a device for blocking the logic and reasoning capacity of the left brain is a technique deliberately used by some hypnotherapists. In the midst of a rambling, confusing and illogical monologue the therapist inserts suggestions in the form of vivid imagery. Watzlawick (1978) makes the point in reference to Erickson;

> Into this stream of inanities and obscurities the actual suggestions are then either interspersed . . . . and thus made inaccessible to intellectualizations, or they are given suddenly and clearly in the midst of this intellectual fog as the only concrete piece of meaning which is, therefore, grasped and held onto with particular tenacity.

In short we are suggesting that the specific illustration that we have presented contains many of the hallmarks of right-brain ways of processing information; it is analogic, drawing heavily on images and metaphors, it does not cohere logically into a reasoned framework, sentences are left unfinished, and it evokes both confusion and stimulation in the listener. Our thesis is that this particular mode of expression, with its heavy use of metaphors and imagery, engenders a form of excitement, optimism, and enthusiasm in clients by using essentially non-rational, right-brain ways that escape the logical defences and objections raised by the reasoning left brain. As a consequence the client may envisage possible activities, projects, and processes that might otherwise have fallen victim to his body of logic and reason. In short we are suggesting that intuitive power is more likely to lead clients' systems to creative and novel ways of construing events such that they are more likely to identify new opportunities and possibilities. This form of power may also carry risks. We see the main risk as not following through on the energy and excitement engendered but becoming stuck at a stage of chaotic creativity. If this form of power is a way of creatively opening up possibilities and accessing hitherto latent sources of energy it also requires a careful management or harnessing of that power if it is not simply to dissipate and possibly lead to a sense of depression following an unprecedented 'high'. It is during this period, the stage of follow-up, when more conventional political activities are likely to figure.

PARADOXICAL POWER

At a conference in Holland on consultant-client relations, one of the participants had been invited in order to give 'the insider's view' of an intervention into his company by a major consulting organization. Apparently, on discovering this, the consulting firm withdrew from the conference. We were given an explanation for their withdrawal when the 'insider' graphically described what was seen as a disastrous intervention which left the client in such a state of chaos, confusion, and turmoil that the client organization had no choice but to sort it out for themselves. Out of this crisis emerged a new found sense of commonality, many creative suggestions, and ultimately an organizational structure that was generally agreed to be a significant improvement on the situation before the consultant had arrived. One suspects that were more attention paid to clients' accounts of interventions many similar stories would be unearthed. The irony, indeed the paradox, is that in dealing with the disturbance created by the consultant the client organization had taken charge of its own affairs in a way that led not only to an overall improvement in functioning but which may have enhanced levels of skill and confidence within the organization in its ability to manage its internal affairs better in future. It would be stretching the limits of credibility beyond reasonable bounds to suggest that this had been the intention of the consulting company. However, it illustrates, albeit in an extreme way, a form of potency that can emerge from the interaction between the consultant and the client system. The significance of paradoxical power is that it enables change to occur not because of what either the consultants or the clients may have done directly in terms of the techniques of intervention, but because of what happens at one level removed, the meta-dynamics of client consultant interaction. We will now explicate these ideas in more detail before illustrating them with a further case example.

The essential conservatism of social systems is a characteristic that has been observed by many writers in the fields both of organizational behaviour and of psychotherapy. Schon (1971), for example, referred to the dynamic conservatism of systems which he described as 'a tendency to fight to remain the same'. In the context of family therapy a group of Italian therapists (Palazzoli *et al.*, 1978) describe the ingenuity of their client systems in devising ways of neutralizing the threat posed by the therapists to their internal (albeit pathological) stability or what the therapists termed the 'family game':

> Our own learning through trials and errors with these families has led us to conclude that even real and concrete changes, whether introduced from the outside or from the inside, are absorbed in the ongoing family game. They thus become further threats to the continuation of the game and thereby pragmatically strengthen it.

In as much as we can assume that some organizational consultants are seen to pose a threat to the conservatism of the system (and we fully recognize that not all of them do) it would seem reasonable to expect to find signs of attempts by client systems either to neutralize the threat or to expel it altogether. On the basis of our own experience and the evidence of some recent case-studies it is possible to speculate on some of the ploys adopted by organizational members to counter the threat posed by external consultants.

(1) *Cosmetic involvement and commitment.* This is the practice of following what is seen to be a senior management fad or fashion because it is known to be politically acceptable, but inwardly remaining sceptical and uncommitted, with the consequence that there is not sufficient diffusion of commitment throughout the organization over a long enough period of time to sustain any real change. Gradually, and perhaps imperceptibly, over time the status quo reasserts itself. The recent reappraisal of the Shell experiment may be an example of this. (See Blackler and Brown, 1980).

(2) *The consultant as Aunt Sally.* Perhaps one of the crudest and most obvious ploys is to invite the consultant to give an 'expert's opinion' or to make expert recommendations for 'solving a problem', ideally in the form of a report. This then leaves the organization members

maximum scope for disconfirming both his analysis and the appropriateness or workability of his solutions, based on their far more intimate familiarity with the complexity of the situation. This approach might also be termed the 'yes-but' approach. Furthermore if the consultant commits his recommendations to paper this opens up another set of possibilities; nit-picking points of detail, and introducing it into the endless bureaucratic machinery of committees and subcommittees until it has been sufficiently diluted or discredited so as to no longer pose a threat.

(3) *Political embarrassment.* This tactic involves declaring information which undermines the consultant's position either by offering contradictory facts or assumptions to those that he is using or by revealing new and unflattering information in public arenas. It also includes damning with faint praise.

(4) *Gratitude at problems solved or progress made.* This is perhaps one of the more seductive ways of neutralizing the threat posed by the outsider. Quite simply it is to express deep gratitude for help given and problems solved together with warm praise for the consultant's perceptiveness and skill and an open invitation to keep in touch (with no promise of further work however).

(5) *Cultural entrapment.* This occurs when the outsider is unwittingly drawn into conforming to the culture in terms of norms of behaviour and values and, while he may be attempting to effect change through what he says, he is in fact reinforcing the cultural status quo by how he acts and the way in which he says things. In short he is no longer an observer of the game or an interventionist in it but has in fact himself become a player. Miner (1982) gives a cautionary account of how the consultant was disabled by inadvertently being drawn into the role of arbiter in the complicated entanglements of a family firm.

Each of these 'ploys' suggests ways in which members of organizations act to reduce or eliminate the likelihood of the consultant disturbing the status quo. The irony is that these efforts, in reacting to the consultant, can in themselves paradoxically lead to change. Exactly how and why change ensues from such situations is open to speculation, although two possible explanations commend themselves. The first is the notion of the therapeutic *double-bind*, that the organization is faced with two possible courses of action, both of which require the organization to change, either by acceding to the requirements of the consultant or by mobilizing support to reject them and/or their proposals. The second is related to the first and is the notion of *making the covert overt*, bringing or forcing out into the open hidden opposition and also perhaps hidden support for proposals such that it is possible to engage actively with an issue as opposed to undermining it covertly by using some of the ploys described above. To use a military analogy, it is akin to locating enemy positions by drawing their fire through the use of a vulnerable decoy. These ideas seem to fit as an explanation in the following example.

A team of OD consultants had been working for three years with little sign of progress in a family-owned manufacturing company. A variety of OD interventions had been undertaken, most notably a series of survey-feedback activities had been completed in various strategically important parts of the company. These seemed to have identified several key issues in the company. However, despite these the consultants had experienced the use of many ploys to discredit, undermine, and generally wreck the possibility of any changes occurring as a result of the intervention.

The consultants came to liken their work with this company to dipping a finger into a bowl of rice pudding. While there was no difficulty in introducing one's finger into the rice pudding, neither was there any discernible sign of it ever having been there after withdrawing it. This image has much in common with a comment by an informed member of the organization who some years later commented that the consulting team were effectively 'punching sponges'. By this he explained that the members of his organization would never actively fight or oppose the consultants, but simply wear them down by absorbing their energy and not fighting back. Certainly, the consulting team was growing noticeably more tired and exhausted by their work in this company, and their enthusiasm waned markedly. Realizing the limited fruits of their efforts the consultants decided to experiment with a different approach. They chose to abandon the classic OD stance of seeking to facilitate the process of identifying issues of importance to the organization and took a more traditional expert role. This was a conscious choice designed to test their belief that there was powerful but covert opposition from some members of the organization. The new strategy was to submit a report on a substantive issue which represented an area of expertise in the consulting team together with recommendations for change.* The intention was to force a response from the company, with the belief that this response would be predominantly critical and unsupportive, but that even this would prove beneficial to the consulting team in assessing their willingness to continue.

Events confirmed the consultants' view. The report was disseminated and became the focus of sharp comment and criticism. At presentations of the report to middle and senior managers the findings were questioned on the basis of technicalities, sample sizes, apparent inconsistencies between paragraphs in different sections, points of detail were challenged and factual

---

* The report was an appraisal of the implications for the introduction of machinery of industrial democracy containing three options open to the company and which allowed for them to undertake a cautious, moderate, or radical approach.

errors claimed and denied but, significantly, there was no serious discussion of the main issues and principles contained within the report.

Shortly following this the consultants, one by one, gradually withdrew from active involvement in the company except for one or two isolated projects. The general air of relief among the exhausted consultants was tinged with disappointment, frustration, and a sense of failure. Some three to four years following this withdrawal the consultants learned, to their surprise, that the recommendations contained within their report had been completely implemented, including some of the more radical suggestions.

An account by a senior manager of the internal processes within the organization, subsequent to the consultants' departure, indicated that the change occurred paradoxically. As a consequence of individuals discrediting the report it became much clearer where people stood on the issue generally, such that those who supported the principles were able to discover who was opposed to it, and the consultants generally, since their opposition was now no longer hidden but clearly apparent. Because of this it then became possible to debate the issues more openly, as well as allowing supporters to become more effective politically now that the opposition had shown itself. Once the opposition to the ideas was apparent it meant that the supporters could more readily and confidently identify genuine support also. As it happened this support was considerable, hence the adoption of the recommendations. But as long as the opposition was covert it remained impossible to engage with it in open debate and difficult to gauge the quality of support that was being expressed, albeit cautiously.

Without fully realizing it, the intervention had succeeded in disturbing a ground rule, or a facet of the culture which effectively was blocking the possibility for change.

ANALOGIC POWER

First we must define these two terms. Watzlawick, Beavin, and Jackson (1967) give us a clue when attempting to answer the question: What is analogic communication?

> The answer is relatively simple: it is virtually all nonverbal communication. This term, however, is deceptive, because it is often restricted to body movement only, to the behaviour known as kenesics. We hold that the term must comprise posture, gesture, facial expression, voice inflection, the sequence, rhythm, and cadence of the words themselves, and any other nonverbal manifestation of which the organism is capable, as well as the communicational clues unfailingly present in any *context* in which an interaction takes place. (p. 62)

Analogic communication refers to the way in which meaning is transmitted other than through the use of language, either in the form of the spoken or written word. A crucial difference is that when language is the medium for the transmission of meaning, an intermediate process occurs whereby the information is translated into symbolic form, words which do not directly represent the event, activity, or idea. Analogic communication occurs in contrast when there is a more direct communication, when the meaning is contained in the situation or behaviour. Thus we may describe ourselves as being 'happy' while our general demeanour, appearance, and behaviour (our analogic communication) would indicate that we are 'sad'. Analogic communication occurs simultaneously with verbal communication, sometimes supplementing it (congruent communication), sometimes defining an overall context of meaning in which a verbal statement is to be set (nudge, nudge, wink, wink!) and sometimes contradicting it as in the example above (incongruent communication).

As Watzlawick, Beavin and Jackson indicate, analogic communication is more than that which is inferred from body movement, facial expressions, and so on. It also refers to other forms in which meaning is expressed such as context, the juxtaposition of events, the flow of actions or statements, whether fluent or halting. In the following quote from a consultant we can see that the communications that he holds to be significant in his dealings with a client are, on this occasion, the analogic messages: here the consultant has been asked about how he recognizes 'readiness' in a client;

> The nonverbals would change to begin with, the look in their eyes will start changing . . . the amount of time they take over saying that will tell me . . . the speed with which they leave those sorts of statements will tell me that . . . there will be that sort of stuff which will tell me that its beginning to crack . . . like they're going to say 'Well we're coming towards the end of a meeting, we've got one in a month's time, but I rather think we ought to get together rather more quickly on this, can you make something like tomorrow?' And then I would normally say, 'Well, what do you want to get together that fast for?' and they'll say, 'Well, really I think we ought to get on with this, don't you?' instead of 'We've got a meeting in a month, why not let's swap agendas before we meet . . . which means it's their stuff they're working on, they're in control of the pace, the direction of the event, and it isn't something they're trying to get up and do. Those sorts of things will tell me first that they're ready.

Essentially this consultant is most influenced by the analogic messages . . . 'the look in their eyes . . . the speed with which they leave those sorts of statements' . . . the priority that the activity is assigned among other activities, together with the urgency which he senses in their behaviour. It is to such things that consultants are referring when they talk about attending to the music not the words.

Linking the concept of analogic communication to that of power enables us to recognize that both conventional definitions of power and definitions based on viewing power as an immanent property of a relationship can be understood in analogic terms.

Analogic expressions of conventional forms of power are ubiquitous and range in grandeur. The graphic representation of hierarchy is still to be found in feudal towns and cities whereby the largest, grandest, most central and highest building is the castle or dwelling place occupied by the lord. Modern parallels have been drawn with business organizations, the executive suites often to be found at the top of the office blocks. Steele (1973) describes how visitors to Hitler's winter palace would be required to walk through several huge, vaulted, and echoing rooms before entering the reception room, even then still being kept at some distance from Hitler's large desk as a further expression of the individual's insignificance.

Conventional power is also expressed in less dramatic ways that form the commonplace of much organizational life. To a stranger visiting an organization the analogic communications give a clue as to key power figures. To whom do people direct their comments, whose approval or sanction is sought, whose interruptions are left unchallenged, from which individuals do others take their cues? At a seemingly petty level it may be possible to infer a good deal about an individual's conventional power by such indicators as which car park he/she uses, or indeed, if extremely powerful or extremely foolish, whether they feel able to disregard car-parking regulations altogether.

In the context of consultant-client relations we believe the analogic power can also be considered as a form of immanent power whereby, as a consequence of joint involvement in an event or activity, both parties envisage new possibilities and feel more free to engage to new activities or to respond differently in familiar situations. In this sense analogic power serves to encourage people to question those things that they have come to regard as unquestionable, as fixed or inevitable. To some extent it might be said that it addresses issues of organizational culture; the pervasive collection of habits, attitudes, values, the taken-for-grantedness of organizational life that can come to be regarded as concrete constraints on action.

Analogic power in an immanent sense occurs when the consultant demontrates through his behaviour that what were taken to be absolute constraints or facts of life are not quite as immutable as was believed, and that such constraints may be challenged or ignored without invoking the catastrophic consequences imagined. The example of analogic power that follows may seem trivial or insignificant to the reader. However, we would suggest that its significance can be considered at two levels, the immediate, overt significance of the event itself and the meta-significance, or what might be termed the principle that the example is denoting.

The example is set in an organization where the culture places much emphasis on the value of individuals being active, and conspicuously so. Needless to say managers are expected not only to endorse such a value but also to epitomize it. Hence one of the first things one learns on meeting a director of the company is that he is 'always in the office before 7.15 a.m.' even though the factory does not start up until 8.15 a.m. and office staff are not formally required to begin work until 8.45 a.m. Later in the conversation it emerges that the same director 'rarely leaves work before 8 p.m.' Individuals are concerned to be seen to be 'busy' with the consequence that middle managers and supervisors have learned an elaborate set of techniques for 'making work'. Such things as report writing, conducting surveys, devising complex procedural manuals and writing, circulating and reading lengthy memos.

This emphasis on constantly being active and busy is reflected in the management development programmes, with course participants being required to achieve a working day which starts at 9.00 a.m. and often does not finish until 10.00 p.m. Even then, they have private assignments which they are expected to complete in their 'spare time'. Moreover the attitude towards training and development generally reflected the culture of the organization which had been likened to a power culture (see Reason 1978, now Chapter 10, this volume) with a characteristic concentration of power and supposed expertise at the top, and the dominant flow of decisions and information being from the top downwards. Course tutors were encouraged to be didactic, to impart their wisdom to course members via a tightly timetabled series of lectures, case-studies, and discussion groups and to supplement them with extensive handouts. Major punctuations to the day were the meal-times which were to be strictly observed and around which the timing of all other activities was geared.

Into this culture the outside trainers were asked to run a session which encouraged the course participants to examine the culture, in order to be more aware of it, and to question the appropriateness of various aspects of the culture to the circumstances that the company faced.

The manner in which the day-long session was conducted was analogically counter to the requirements of the culture in several key respects. First of all there was little specific content or input from the trainers. Contrary to the cultural requirements of being led by an 'expert' and having the situation analysed and explained, the session was designed to encourage course participants to generate their own views of the culture and to work with the trainers to identify themes and generalizations. The formally timetabled agenda was revised several times to take account of the value being gained from the activities and even the most fixed constraints of all, the canteen ladies, were discovered to be amenable to negotiated changes in meal-times. Far from filling the day with activities, lectures, exercises, and handouts the participants were encouraged to take their time to reflect on issues of importance such that, for much of the time, people appeared to be 'doing' very little.

The course members' response to this was at first to feel uncomfortable but gradually to express increasing excitement and insight, indicating that they could not only discuss aspects of the culture in abstract terms, but they began to point out the effect of the culture on their immediate behaviour. They expressed excitement about the possibilities for experimenting with constraints and problems that they had hitherto considered to be absolute, and indeed discovered to their delight that there were some aspects of the course that they could change so as to make them more satisfactory, and did so successfully. They identified, as a central feature of the culture, their habit of defining themselves as passive, dependent, helpless, and predominantly reactive. By the end of the session there were signs that they were beginning to become more assertive, both individually and collectively, and had started to take initiatives to such an extent that they were actively managing the trainers.

The trainers had spent the most part of the day in roles that were (in terms of the organizational culture) unconventional. When they were not involved in briefings or group discussions they spent much time strolling through the extremely pleasant grounds of the training centre. Ironically the trainers reported themselves* as experiencing insights into the organizational culture during the day.

Follow-up interviews with course members, together with reports from them, indicated that for some of them things had significantly changed. Indeed some of their bosses were reported as having seen such a change in their behaviour as a result of the course that they were anxious to send all of their subordinates.

To summarize, it is suggested that here is an example of analogic power contributing to organizational change. The trainers drew attention to the culture analogically (through their behaviour) as well as digitally (through their statements) in a way which enabled course members first of all to recognize those things which they had taken to constitute concrete constraints, and secondly to recognize the possibility of redefining such constraints in a way that opened up new alternatives for both thinking and acting. We would suggest that analogically the training had demonstrated the negotiability around such constraints and the possibility of acting in ways which were not completely prescribed by cultural requirements. In effect it is suggested that the trainers demonstrated the possibility that the culture is

* See McLean and Marshall (1982)

not fixed and immutable but that there is the possibility of influencing it and, perhaps, changing it.

CONCLUSION

In this chapter we have sought to demonstrate that the phenomenon of power can be usefully studied by using an alternative epistemology from that which underpins existing discussions and debates of the concept. We have sought to show that individuals, groups and possibly organizations can become empowered to act in new ways as a result of the client-consultant relationship but that this empowering differs from traditional notions in two key respects. Firstly, immanent power cannot be attributed to either party but emerges as a consequence of the relationship, and secondly, the notion of intentionality, a concept that is considered by some to be a key defining feature of more traditional formulations of power, is less appropriate in the context of this alternative formulation.

REFERENCES

Abell, P. (Ed.) (1975). *Organizations as Bargaining and Influence Systems*, London: Heinemann.

Bacharach, S. B. and Lawler, E. J. (1980). *Power and Politics in Organizations*, London: Jossey-Bass.

Bakan, P. (1966). *The Duality of Existence*, Chicago, Ill: Rand McNally.

Bateson, G. (1973). *Steps to an Ecology of Mind*, St Albans: Granada.

Blackler, F. H. M. and Brown, C. A. (1980). *Whatever Happened to Shell's New Philosophy of Management? Lessons for the 1980s from a Major Socio-Technical Intervention of the 1960s*, Farnborough: Saxon House.

Buckley, W. (1967). *Sociology and Modern Systems Theory*, Englewood Cliffs, NJ: Prentice-Hall.

Hawkins, P. (1982). Personal Communication.

James, L. E. (1977). *The Analysis of Power in Organizations*, University of Aston Management Centre Working Paper.

McLean, A. J., Hyder, S., Mangham, I. L., Sims, D., and Tuffield, D. (1980). *Implications of Interventions in Organizations*, Chemical and Allied Product Industry Board, Staines, Research Paper.

McLean, A. J. and Marshall, J. (1982). *Working through Cultures—The Initiation of the Sorcerer's Apprentice*, Paper presented to Ideas in Development Conference, Centre for the Study of Management Learning, University of Lancaster, September.

McLean, A. J., Sims, D. B. P., Mangham, I. L., and Tuffield, D. (1982). *Organization Development in Transition: Evidence of an Evolving Profession*, Chichester: John Wiley.

Margulies, N. (1978). The myth and magic in organization development, in French, W. L., Bell, C. H., and Zawacki, R. A. (eds) (1978). *Organization Development: Theory, Practice and Research*, Homewood: Business Publications.

Miner, R. (1982). *Replacing a Chief Executive: A Case Study Analysis*, Paper presented to 'Qualitative Approaches to Organizations' Conference, University of Bath, April.

Ornstein, R. E. (1977). *The Psychology of Consciousness* (2nd edn), New York: Harcourt Brace.

Palazzoli, M. S., Cecchin, G., Prata, G., and Boscolo, L. (1978). *Paradox and Counterparadox. A New Model in the Therapy of the Family in Schizophrenic Transaction*, New York: Aronson.

Reason, P. W. (1978). *Is OD Possible in a Power Culture?* Working Paper, Centre for the Study of Organizational Change and Development, University of Bath. (Now Chapter 10, in this volume.)

Reason, P. W. and Rowan, J. (eds) (1981). *Human Enquiry: A Sourcebook of New Paradigm Research*. Chichester: John Wiley.

Reinhartz, S. (1982). Experiential analysis: a contribution to feminist research methodology, in Bowles G. and Duelli-Klein, R. (eds), *Theories of Women's Studies*, Vol II, California: Berkeley.

Schon, D. (1971). *Beyond the Stable State*, london: Temple Smith.

Steele, F. I. (1973). *Physical Settings and Organization Development*, Reading, Mass.: Addison Wesley.

Tannenbaum, A. (ed.) (1968). *Control in Organizations*, London: McGraw-Hill.

Watzlawick, P. (1978). *The Language of Change: Elements of Therapeutic Communication*, New York: Basic Books.

Watzlawick, P., Beavin, J. H., and Jackson, D. D. (1967). *Pragmatics of Human Communication*, New York: Norton.

Yalom, I. D. (1980). *Existential Psychotherapy*, New York: Basic Books.

Power, Politics, and Organizations: A Behavioural Science View
Edited by Andrew Kakabadse and Christopher Parker
© 1984 John Wiley & Sons Ltd

Chapter 9

Politics of a Process Consultant*

ANDREW KAKABADSE

In this chapter, the experiences and views of a process-oriented consultant (one who works with a client on his problems rather than trying to impose predetermined solutions) are explored. In particular, the consultant's model of change is examined. His actions in an intervention he recently conducted into a large public service organization are discussed. It is indicated that the consultant considered himself as having no option but to act 'politically' in the circumstances of this particular case. The intervention is still currently active and whether the consultant will eventually be 'successful' is open to conjecture.

It is concluded that perceived political interactions are a natural everyday experience for most people is any organization setting. There is no positive or negative side to life; just life itself.

DIFFERENTIATING CHANGE

In a previous paper (Kakabadse, 1982), it was argued that theories of change emanating from a management or organization development (MD and OD) base, when practised tend to maintain rather than change traditions and systems in organizations. The argument centres on the assumption that attempts at change involve three components:

(1) the intentions of the change agent;
(2) the processes of change;
(3) the predicted and unexpected outcomes of change.

The hypothesis offered in the paper (Kakabadse, 1982) is that most theories of change in MD and OD are naive and practically unrealistic. The reason for this is that most theories are considered to concentrate only on particular

*This chapter was presented as a paper at the Quantitative Approaches to Organizations Conference at Bath University, UK, 19–21 April, 1982.

processes or outcomes. Some of the earlier theorists such as Lewin (1951) and Rogers (1951) examined ways of improving interpersonal processes; whilst others (Jacques 1952; Burns and Stalker, 1961; Woodward, 1965) identified ideal organizational forms (outcomes).

The change practitioner literature emerging from the USA in the 1960s was mostly descriptive, identifying processes of change and at times quite prescriptive in indicating what ideal outcomes of change to achieve. In this category can be found such names as McGregor (1960); Schein (1969) and Beckhard (1969). In fact, Argyris (1970) argues that only under certain conditions could effective change be introduced. He identifies the three primary tasks necessary for successful change:

(1) the generation of valid information;
(2) a climate which allows people to make free and informed choices about alternatives;
(3) internal commitment on the part of those involved to make the changes work.

Argyris (1970) summarizes the position adopted by so many of the writers on change—for effective change to take place, sufficient freedom for the generation of valid information and choice must be present in the situation.

Such a hypothesis in no way takes account of the intentions and particular interests of the individuals in the organizations who wish to control the outcomes of change. Further, the views and values of external change agents are not considered in terms of the outcomes that they would wish to pursue. Interventions are not a value-free, but very much a value-laden experience.

From the writer's practical experience, meaningful change does not take place until all interested parties are involved. The parties are likely to hold divergent views, which makes the processes of sharing and open debate a virtual impossibility. In essence, ideal change is not an open forum situation, but more of a closed, small-group, vested interest, a power struggle amongst people who sincerely hold quite different values as to their ideal world.

Dissatisfaction with the values base of the present theories of change stimulated the process consultant to develop his own model of change. The model is based on examining the intentions of internal and external change agents. Having identified intents, it is proposed that different types of intents will require alternate strategies of change. Similarly to other writers (Golembiewski, Billingsley, and Yeager 1975; Alderfer, 1972), three separate classes of change are identified.

Maintenance Change

Attempting maintenance change involves the change agent in accepting the constraints, values, and power dependencies of the total organization. The intentions of the change agent would be to work with particular groups to strengthen their existing beliefs and values concerning personal interaction and appropriate behaviours at work. In fact, maintenance change is aimed at maintaining the status quo.

The dominant beliefs and values in the group that determine a stereotypic group identity are achieved through control of group membership. Control is applied at the initial entry stage to the group by assessing the individuals's worth in terms of task skills. During the period of membership of the group, norms and values are maintained by paying special attention to interpersonal interactions. Individuals who are identified as actively supporting group norms are rewarded by other group members and even actively dissuaded from leaving the group. Those who are identified as deviating from group norms are slowly excluded from the group.

For the third-party interventionist invited to operate at the group level, certain factors must be taken into account if the intervention is to be a success. Gaining the trust of group members is vital and must be achieved before entering into any substantial activities. Gaining and maintaining trust can only be achieved by an exhibition of acceptance of group values. Once trust has been established, a conscious effort to maintain existing norms and behaviours is vital if the intervention is to develop meaningfully.

Kakabadse (1982) argued that so-called OD interventions attempt maintence change. The values of acceptance, trust, working together, and sharing indicate nothing more other than an acceptance of the predominant group values. Openness and trust can only be achieved if those involved in the situation see and feel about the same things in the same way. Therefore, what impetus to change? Other writers (Brimm, 1972; Pettigrew, 1975; Porter, Allen, and Angle 1981) seem to have reached a similar conclusion that OD interventionists are 'systems maintainers' who make little attempt to address the fundamental processes in organizations.

Subsystems Change

Attempting subsystems change will involve the change agent in accepting the values of the total organization, but questioning the constraints and power dependencies within the subsystems—divisions, departments, or units.

Introducing change at the subsystems level will involve interacting with individuals who do not hold similar norms and values about work, work goals, departmental and organizational structures and objectives. Under such circumstances, it is necessary to recognize that participative decision-making is unlikely to be a strong, shared value. However, people appreciate that they cannot progress without involving other parties or groups. In this way decisions made between the parties involved may not be to the advantage of all concerned. The decisions agreed for action are merely those decisions that each party can tolerate, bearing in mind their constraints and those of others involved in the situation.

The key actors in the decision-making process would be organization unit or subunit heads and the issues stimulating interaction would include short- to medium-term future planning; coordination of tasks; control of outputs between organizational units, subunits, and bodies outside the organization; the allocation of additional marginal resources which have to be negotiated but not necessarily fully agreed to by the interacting parties.

The skills required effectively to operate subsystems change are interpersonal skills and a cognitive appreciation of the subsystems in the organization. For the interventionist, it is important that he can utilize behaviours that are acceptable to the various actors in the various situations, but further can rationally argue about the current and future roles of units and subunits within the total system. Discussing the behaviour of units and subunits within the system requires the interventionist to develop a rationale for the existing and future behaviour between and within units and departments in the organization. Working on a model of subsystems relations involves an ability to deduce what systems information is required, how it can be acquired, how that information can be collated and utilized, and what further information is needed.

Visionary Change

Attempts at implementing visionary change will involve change agents in not accepting the existing values, beliefs, tasks, role and power dependencies within the organization. The successful operationalization of visionary change not only involves questioning and debating existing dominant beliefs, but further exhibiting an ability to disengage from the previous beliefs and identities held by the marjority in the organization and aim towards developing, if necessary, new organizational forms.

Individuals who are effective at introducing visionary change operate at a higher order level both by being able to conceptualize and identify dominant beliefs and values and by being able to alter the existing pattern of values and beliefs (or introduce new patterns of beliefs) by introducing new patterns of work systems. In order to implement new work systems, the change agent must be able to identify and isolate long-term trends in the external environment, develop strategy plans, work in conjunction with others towards implementing the strategy plans and conceive of the operational units which will reduce strategy into a series of activities and co-related tasks and subtasks. Such abilities, Vickers (1973) terms systemic wisdom, for an appreciation of the existing values within the organization, a general preparedness to change and the skills to determine whatever changes are required, are the components of systemic wisdom.

Individuals who adopt a visionary change approach are likely to be entre-preneurs who develop new organizations, key organizational personnel who feel confident to handle all-embracing change in the organization, and influ-ential third parties who stimulate major changes of policy within the existing organization.

It is likely that visionary change agents operate in isolation from other organizational personnel. The development of new beliefs, work philosophies and strategies is dependent on a well-identified but personal philosophy concerning the future. However, substantial interactions with others will take place during the many phases of implementation.

The reason sharing at the values development stage is virtually impossible, is that it is difficult to co-operate with someone who has the ability to develop equally well-formed ideas that are different or even similar but stem from different personal values. In-fighting amongst senior management can be the result of such fundamental differences of opinion. Unless one person leaves, the rest of the organization may suffer. It is the individual's ability to interpret current events, predict future trends and generate an alternative identity that makes his view of the world unique. Basically, it is a matter of two into one will not go.

However, it is to the advantage of the change agent to share with others the way in which fundamental strategies, once decided, should be imple-mented. The involvement of others not only ensures that strategies are put into practice, but through doing so, allows others to identify with the new norms and values.

The visionary-oriented change agent must be able to appreciate how the total system operates. The capacity to rationalize in whole organizational terms and identify fundamental, realistic and acceptable (acceptable to other organizational members) strategies, and then work towards developing a series of interrelated task groupings that match the original strategy, involves the ability to think independently of the current dominant philosophies. Such independence does not necessarily involve revolutionary change. The process of change could be evolutionary as it could revolutionary. Whether the change of dominant organizational values is a sudden or more lengthy process depends on the view of the change agent in the situation in which he operates.

THE CASE

A major public service organization in the UK has recently faced substantial criticism for its handling of various community problems. In response, the organization has attempted to examine how and why certain problems have arisen.

As part of the examination process, the director of the organization de-cided to initiate a study of career development and motivation within his organization. The brief to undertake the study was passed down to his director of personnel who decided to call a meeting of the various interested parties in the organization. After a limited number of meetings, the interested parties decided to form themselves into a steering committee. They recognized that they shared neither the expertise nor the insight to conduct a study of motivation and career development in their organization. They obtained the assistance of a consultant (John) but he could offer only a limited amount of time as he was fully employed as an internal consultant by a large multi-national company. John and the steering committee met on a number of occasions for a period of a year but made only limited progress. Eventually, John suggested that a project team should be formed to carry out an in-depth study of career development. The steering committee agreed and formed a project team consisting of three senior managers, two middle managers and one junior manager who acted as the secretary/administrator to the team. The steering committee decided that a second consultant should be hired to act as adviser to the project team. A second consultant (David) was eventually hired. The intervention described below is centred on the activities of the second consultant—David.

The Intervention

A number of individuals were approached to see whether they would be interested in acting as consultant to the project team. A favourite candidate was eventually identified. He was an academic who had been used as a visiting speaker at the organizations own training college. He had already established a reputation as a good lecturer on their senior management programme and his experience as a researcher and consultant made him attractive to the organization. In addition, both the manager of the training college, who was shortly to be promoted to a top management position in the organization, and the senior management programme tutor favoured the individual and argued for his acceptance.

The chairman of the steering committee, a senior manager in the organization and an exceptionally influential individual, invited the academic (David) to act as second consultant to the project team. David agreed, if the fee was right. The directorate of the organization found David's fee acceptable but did not have the authority to issue payment. Only a central servicing unit could authorize payment. They stated that they would have to be convinced that the money was to be spent wisely. This proved embarrassing for the client. Both the client and David recognized that the central servicing unit were unlikely to make a quick decision. In addition, the director of the organization was demanding results and had already indicated a deadline for the project team one year ahead. The central servicing unit could well have delayed the proceedings for up to six months. David indicated that he would do the job on the understanding that he most likely would eventually receive his fee. The chairman gratefully agreed, thanked David for taking the risk and organized separate meetings of the steering committee and project team in order to introduce the consultant to the parties involved.

At David's first meeting with the project team, the atmosphere was tense. David gave a brief resume of his past work experience and indicated that he looked forward to working with the team. The most senior man on the team welcomed David but stated that the team did not expect as many problems as they faced when they first agreed to take part in the project. As the conversation developed, it became clear that the project team had had no real guidance, nor had they any real experience of working on people- and manpower-orientated problems. The members of the team shared an additional anxiety. Recognizing their lack of knowledge and experience in the area, they questioned whether they could produce any meaningful results and if that happened, would that be to the detriment of their careers? David listened and agreed with the team that at this early stage, a number of meetings would have to be held to identify what direction the team should take.

A number of meetings were held between David and the project team. David stated that he would not wish to work with the team if they established any processes of formality such as an agenda. Protests were pushed aside by David, who stated that he was taking over the running of the team and anyone who felt he could not continue would always be free to leave. David knew that no-one dare leave because of career implications. The meetings quickly became brain-storming sessions, exactly as he desired.

The team, influenced by David's view, decided that simply examining career development systems in operation in other public service and private organizations was insufficient. A study would have to be conducted examining the existing career development system in the organization. Some members of the project team were against the idea, stating that the study could uncover views held by members of the organization that would be highly critical of senior management. How could the project team feed that information back? David advised them not to concern themselves with the results of the study before they had even planned its structure.

The chairman of the steering committee approached David enquiring as to progress made. He indicated that the other members of the steering committee would wish to meet David and even if it was early days, be given a brief report of developments to date. David readily agreed, stating that he would wish to meet John (the first consultant) before the steering committee meeting. The two consultants arranged to meet.

The meeting was polite but tense. David concluded that John would probably be in favour of a study. It also became clear that John had not really identified the direction the intervention should take. If John could be given some role in the study, then he would argue in favour of the study at the steering committee meeting. By probing John, David concluded that various members of the steering committee were anxious about the results of the whole intervention. The senior managers on the steering committee also felt their careers to be potentially in jeopardy if the eventual results produced were considered unsatisfactory. The two consultants agreed to support each other at the steering committee meeting.

Before the steering committee meeting, David decided that the intervention was concerned with subsystems change. David also recognized that he had begun to behave in ways that could be considered, if not unethical, at least on the border line. The values of working with your client at his pace in his territory, being open, and sharing information were unrealistic in the situation.

The only clear policy the consultant could identify, was to pursue the diagnostic study of career development in the organization whether the client wanted it or not. If change was needed at the *subsystems level*, then some form of data base was required.

David's first meeting with the steering committee was uneasy. The consultant was introduced by the chairman of the committee who then asked David to address the members. David offered his view of his role in the intervention and went on to explain the various ways of examining career development in any organization. He indicated that the various approaches had been fully debated by the project team and that the only sensible direction to take would be to pursue a study of career development in the organization. It would not make sense to develop policies for the future without understanding how people felt about their jobs, their level of work satisfaction, their views on promotions and methods of appraisal. At this point, both David and the chairman sensed that the other members of the committee seemed restless and anxious. The chairman confronted the group by stating that if others were perturbed about what was said or just wished to ask questions, they should feel free to do so. David agreed, stating that he preferred this to be an open honest meeting and that the members should feel free to ask any questions.

Certain minor questions were asked concerning how such a study could be conducted. After half an hour's discussion, one member stood up stating that he was not in favour of such a study. What use would such information be to the organization? David responded by asking what alternative approach could be undertaken, bearing in mind the organization director's demand for results. The member (a senior and influential manager) stated he did not know but there must be some other way. However, he could not remain to discuss the matter as he had other meetings to attend. He added that this one seemed to be a waste of time. David thanked him for his valuable input and when he had left the room, the consultant asked the others whether they could offer any alternative suggestions to examining career development.

Another member stated that David was right. The only way to begin to examine career development would be to analyse peoples' views about their jobs, work, promotion prospects, and the management styles adopted by their superiors. With the one member leaving the meeting and the other seemingly in favour of some sort of study, the remainder seemed visibly to relax. David capitalized on the pro-study contribution by asking the others for their suggestions on how they would go about organizing such a study. Numerous contributions were made and even the most nonsensical was warmly praised by the consultant. After one hour's discussion, David felt confident that he had managed to turn the mood of the meeting in his favour. He dramatically stopped the conversation and turned to John (who had remained silent throughout) and asked him to give his expert opinion on whether a study on career development should be undertaken. John stated that he could see no alternative. David, dramatically turning to the other members, asked whether anyone was in favour of the one dissenting voice that had left the room. No-one was and in fact they all considered his objections to be destructive. The meeting unanimously concluded that the study be carried out.

Reflecting on the meeting, David decided to take the following steps:

(1) to reduce the level of anxiety amongst the members of the steering committee and project team;
(2) to isolate and reduce the level of influence of the steering committee members who objected to the study;
(3) to develop a warm and positive relationship with each senior and influential manager in the organization.

David became more pro-active with the project team. He paid less attention to their needs and issues and more to the mechanics of conducting a study. The consultant organized a series of workshops on research methodology and interviewing techniques. In addition, more brain-storming sessions were held, exploring how to conduct the proposed research. During this time, one of the members of the project team was identified by David and the other members of the team as being unsuitable. David approached the chairman of the steering committee to discuss the unsuitability of this one project team member to the study. To the approval of all (including the project team member concerned) the individual was transferred. David wanted him replaced by the senior management tutor currently at the training college. After a number of 'phone calls and informal one-to-one discussions with influential senior managers, the senior tutor was appointed to the project team. David agreed that once the senior tutor was in the post, he would spend substantial time coaching him into the project at no extra cost.

David, together with the senior tutor, agreed that a pilot study was necessary. This pilot study should be conducted as a series of semi-structured interviews. A sample was identified and members of the project team were each given particular sample populations to interview. David stated that only he would interview senior management as he would be seen as least threatening.

David used the opportunity to develop friendly relations with the senior managers that he could arrange to see. Some of the managers sat on the steering committee. Not only did they offer information about their jobs, task activities, and motivations, but they were encouraged by the consultant to discuss the project at length. Fears and anxieties that individual senior managers held were reduced through discussion with David. The one member of the steering committee who objected to the study refused to be interviewed. His superior also refused to take part in the study. In discussions with the chairman of the steering committee and his superior, David emphasized the co-operation he had received from most members of the organization except from the one who objected and his superior. Slowly the word got around that only one group in the total organization were difficult and unco-operative in a project that was now recognized as important to the future of the organization.

Throughout this time, the members of the project team met to discuss the data being gathered in the pilot study. In the opinion of all, the data was more valuable than originally expected. A steering committee meeting was held to discuss progress to date, which both the consultants and project team members attended. It was agreed at the meeting that the pilot study results were valuable and that the main study should be started. The individual who had originally objected to the study was not present, nor had he attended the last few meetings. David, at the end of the meeting, invited the steering committee members and the members of the project team to his university for lunch to celebrate the successful completion of stage 1 of the study. Most of those invited attended the lunch, which turned out to be a success. By now David was viewed as acceptable to the organization.

IDENTIFYING THE POLITICAL STRATEGIES

The project team are ready to embark on the main study. The actual results of their studies so far, or even what they intend to do, are irrelevant as far as this paper is concerned. What is of importance is to identify and examine the strategies adopted by David in the intervention.

The Strategies

1. Identify the stakeholders

It is imperative in any intervention to identify those individuals who have an interest or stakeholding in the situation. Whether their interests are compatible or incompatible with those of the individual, all the stakeholders have to be approached so as to identify their intentions in the situation. In the case above, David identified all potential stakeholders, and with any whose views were not acceptable, attempts were made to isolate them from their colleagues and hence reduce their capacity to influence others.

2. Work on the comfort zones

In order to influence anyone effectively, work on the other person's comfort zone unless it is absolutely necessary to do otherwise.

An individuals's comfort zone consists of those behaviours, values, attitudes, drives, and ideas that the person in question can accept, tolerate, manage. The reason the comfort zones are emphasized is that every individual has developed a range of values and behaviours which he/she finds acceptable and wishes to put into practice. The range of values and behaviours is his identity. The person concerned may call it his personality. Something unique that is him.

Hence, people will pay attention to the concerns of others as long as their own are not threatened. Once an interaction with another concentrates on the issues important to one party only and is threatening to the other party, that interaction is likely to be terminated. And why not? People meaningfully interact only when they have sufficient interest in a situation.

People hold two interests in any situation:

(1) the final objective, that is, what is in it for them;
(2) the manner in which the final objective is achieved, that is, the process.

People are equally concerned with both processes and outcomes. By handling the interactions so that the process feels comfortable to the receiving party, outcomes can be managed so as to satisfy most parties.

David used this strategy more than any other. At this stage, he is generally recognized as being a friend to most of the stakeholders.

3. Network

Organizations are a mixture of various cultures and group identities. The group identities may or may not coincide with the hierarchical structure or overt objectives of the organization. In terms of what really does and does not get done, the network may often be a more powerful force than superior/subordinate relations. For any outsider entering a situation that he wishes to influence, it is necessary to identify the networks that exist and the individuals who are generally recognized as upholding the values of the network. These individuals are then influenced by working on their comfort zone. David identified a number of networks and gained access to most. He plans to utilize his access to the key stakeholders in the networks in stage 2 of the study.

4. Make deals

Making a deal with other individuals or groups is common practice in most large organizations. Whether resources are limited or not, different individuals or groups may agree to support each other to achieve a common purpose as long as there are benefits for them. It is realistic to expect individuals and groups in the organization to wish to promote their own goals, which may be at the expense of others. Consequently, coming to some sort of agreement about common policies, or at least not disturbing each other's aims, may be necessary.

Two deals were made by David. First to continue on the project without fully agreeing the financial side to the contract. For his own career ends, David wanted the contract and was therefore willing to take a risk of doing work which may have gone unpaid. By making such a deal with the chairman of the steering committee, it was hoped that the chairman would argue forcefully to have David's financial terms accepted.

The second deal was to coach the senior tutor who was a latecomer to the project team, for no extra payment. Apart from the fact that the tutor and consultant were personal friends, the tutor also possessed substantial knowledge and experience in the 'people management' type subjects which made him the most important member of the project team.

5. Withhold and withdraw

It is impossible to satisfy the needs of all parties in any large, diverse organization. One way of ensuring that certain groups do not over-react to issues which they recognize as important, is to withhold information. By preventing certain information from becoming common knowledge, the manager is able to achieve whatever objectives he has identified without facing opposition that could destroy his plan. In such circumstances, the manager should be fairly convinced that his plan is valuable—but that others cannot or will not recognize its worth. However, to constantly withhold information is not recommended, for such behaviour is indicative of a manager who cannot confront certain problems. Continuously withholding information is a means of protecting the manager and not the policy.

Withdrawing from a situation is at times necessary. There are times when the presence of a manager in a dispute or negotiation is of no help. To withdraw and allow the different factions to negotiate their own terms, or for management to withdraw an unpopular policy and shelve it for the time being, are common practices. The larger and more diverse an organization becomes, the more important is the timing of actions. When to introduce or withdraw plans and information are important considerations for policy implementation.

David used the strategy of withholding information and withdrawing from potentially difficult situations, on numerous occasions. Criticisms of particular individuals or of the organization which the consultant felt would be unacceptable to the project team or members of the steering committee were withheld. In fact, the project team had no knowledge of the data David gathered in his interviews with senior management.

Throughout the intervention, David was consistently not presenting the full picture to the senior managers he met. Each was told a slightly different story from the other as to the objectives and expected outcomes of the study, according to what David considered would be acceptable. In addition, if a slightly unpleasant situation required attention, David would approach one of the senior managers, offer him information and advice on how to handle the situation and then withdraw so that he would not be implicated in the outcomes of the interaction.

6. If all else fails

The practice of any one or more of the above strategies will not guarantee success. It is necessary to identify some fall-back strategy if all else fails. Each person concerned would have to identify his own fall-back strategy according to the demands of the situation and what he could personally handle. In this intervention, David identified two fall-back strategies.

First, if this particular intervention failed or if David were not chosen to work with the project team, then at least the consultant had negotiated warm and friendly relations with important people in the organization who could call him in at a later date on other projects or refer him to other organizations where he could get work.

Second, David had only just begun to work on the comfort zone of the boss of the chairman of the steering committee. This person was the former manager of the training centre and now promoted to a senior position in the organization. It was predicted that he would be the next director but one. Whether these rumours turn out to be true in the future is unimportant. The fact that he was currently considered as important and influential was sufficient reason to nurture his favour. He could provide substantial consultancy in the future.

CONCLUSION

When individuals interact with others for any length of time, then personal and vested interests (not in themselves bad) determine the direction of the interaction. Consequently, all people who interact with each other require guidance on how both to protect themselves and still attain their objectives, in part or wholly. The aim is to help all people in organizations improve on their attempts at influencing others.

As a consequence, the current dominant philosophies arising from management and organization development on the theme of change are rejected.

The data feedback theorists, such as Bennis (1966) and Nadler (1977) who seem to assume the existence of the one fundamental, rational truth—data are merely the vehicle by which people will jointly recognize the truth—or the sharing, caring, participation philosophies, as epitomized by Argyris (1970), not only were and are unrealistic, but further are irresponsible. Change is not about one truth or an open sharing of views. Change is about renegotiating certain dominant values and attitudes in the organization in order to introduce new systems and subsystems. Under such circumstances, visions and values are not likely to be shared, with the likely result being a clash of wills. Successful change involves one person or group influencing the organization according to their values. Under such circumstances, change is a painful experience for those involved. The element of irresponsibility in the philosophies of prominent behavioural scientists is that the painful processes of change can turn into a guilt-ridden experience, since the 'experts' set standards that never were attainable.

REFERENCES

Alderfer, C. P. (1972). *Existence, Relatedness and Growth*, West Drayton: Collier Macmillan.
Argyris, C. (1970). *Intervention Theory and Method*, Reading, Mass.: Addison Wesley.
Beckhard, R. (1969). *Strategies of Organisation Development*, Reading, Mass.: Addison Wesley.
Bennis, W. (1966). *Changing Organisations*, New York: McGraw-Hill.
Brimm, M. (1972), When is change not a change? *Journal of Applied Behavioural Science*, **8** No. 1 102–106.
Burns, T. and Stalker, G. M. (1961). *The Management of Innovation*, London: Tavistock.
Golembiewski, R. T., Billingsley, K., and Yeager, S. (1975). Measuring change and persistence in human affairs: types of change generated by OD designs, *Journal of Applied Behavioural Science*, **12**, No. 2, 133–157.

Jacques, E. (1951). *The Changing Culture of a Factory*, London: Tavistock.

Kakabadse, A. P. (1982). Politics in organisations: re-examining OD, *Leadership and Organization Development Journal*, **3** No. 2, Monograph.

Lewin, K. (1951). *Field Theory in Social Science*, New York: Harper and Row.

McGregor, D. (1960). *The Human Side of Enterprise*. New York: McGraw-Hill.

Nadler, D. (1977). *Feedback and Organisation Development: Using Data-Based Methods*, Reading, Mass.: Addison Wesley.

Pettigrew, A. M. (1975). Towards a political theory of organizational intervention, *Human Relations*, **28** No. 3, 191–208.

Porter, L. W., Allen, R. W., and Angle, H. L. (1981). The politics of upward influence, in Staw B. and Cummings, L. (eds), *Research in organisational Behaviour*, vol. 3, Greenwich: JAI Press.

Rogers, C. (1951). *Client-Centred Therapy*, Boston, Mass.: Houghton-Mifflin.

Schein, E. (1969). *Process Consultation: Its Role in Organisation Development*, Reading, Mass.: Addison Wesley.

Vickers, G. (1973). *Making Institutions Work*, New York: Halsted Press.

Woodward, J, (1965). *Industrial Organisation: Theory and Practice*, Oxford University Press.

Power, Politics, and Organizations: A Behavioural Science View
Edited by Andrew Kakabadse and Christopher Parker
© 1984 John Wiley & Sons Ltd

Chapter 10

Is Organization Development Possible in Power Cultures?

PETER REASON

INTRODUCTION

Variety is said to be the spice of life, and much attention is paid these days to contingency theories and other attempts to describe the various forms and processes which take place in organizations (Friedlander, 1971; Galbraith, 1973). In one attempt to describe organizational variety Harrison (1972), whose ideas were taken up by Handy (1976, 1979), developed a typology of four organizational *ideologies* or *cultures*: the *power* culture, the *role* culture, the *task* culture, and the *person* culture. It is from this that I take the concept of a power culture.

To describe variety as the *spice* of life may be a bit misleading, since a spice is something one appreciates and savours. The variety of organizational cultures is certainly a fascinating phenomenon, which behavioural scientists as *observers* may savour, but as *actors* we need to be able to *manage* if we are to be competent to intervene in a range of organizational situations. *Power* is an aspect of organizational life—one of the essential spices—that OB and OD are often accused of ignoring (Friedlander and Brown, 1974; Srivastva, 1975). Srivastva and Brown (1974) have asserted that 'power corrupts, powerlessness corrupts absolutely': this chapter is written as the author emerges, reeling slightly, from an encounter with a power culture, in which his only power was the very significant one of being able to leave the field. This paper describes an attempted OD project in this culture, and asks whether OD theory is sufficient to encompass interventions in such power cultures. First, however, the nature of power, culture, and OD requires further consideration.

POWER

While the reality of power appears self-evident when we come across it in

185

everyday life—especially from a position of relative powerlessness—power seems to be an elusive concept to define theoretically. Lukes (1974) has borrowed the phrase 'essentially contested concept' to describe it, and traces three steps towards an encompassing view of power.

First, there is a view of power solely in terms of which party gets its way when disagreements arise: a 'one-dimensional' view of power, which involves a 'focus on *behaviour* in the making of *decisions* on *issues* over which there is overt *conflict* of (subjective) *interests*' (Lukes, 1974, p. 15; original emphasis). That this view is inadequate is pointed out by Bachrach and Baratz (1970), since it is evident that power is frequently exercised through 'non-decisions' to *prevent* issues coming to the public forum for consideration, and to limit the scope of debate to issues innocuous to those in power. This is a 'two-dimensional' view of power, since it 'allows for consideration of the ways in which *decisions* are prevented from being taken on *potential issues* over which there is observable *conflict* of (subjective) interests' (Lukes, 1974, p. 20; original emphasis). Lukes argues that this two-dimensional view of power is inadequate on three counts. First, power is not only manifest through decision-making (or non-decision-making), but also through the overall bias of the social and political system towards consideration of certain issues and exclusion of others. Second, power is not only associated with observable conflict, but may also be used to shape desires and stop conflict from arising. Third, power is not present only when there are grievances, since:

> is not the supreme and most insidious exercise of power to prevent people, to whatever degree, from having grievances by shaping their perceptions, cognitions and preferences in such a way that they accept their role in the existing order of things, either because they see or imagine no alternative to it, or because they see it as natural and unchangeable, or because they value it because it is divinely ordained and beneficial? To assume that the absence of grievance equals genuine consensus is simply to rule out the possibility of false or manipulated consensus. . . .
>
> (Lukes, 1974, p. 24)

Thus a 'three-dimensional' view of power is close to the view that 'Power in society includes the power to determine decisive socialisation processes, and, therefore, the power to *produce* reality' (Berger and Luckman, 1966, p. 137; original emphasis).

Huckabay (1975) has argued in connection with the Women's Movement that the most important tool for maintaining any particular social form or relationship is this power to define reality; a power which is developed and maintained through control over reality-defining processes and institutions. Thus power, as used in this paper, refers to this capacity to impose definitions of reality on others: to prescribe what is and what is not, what may or may not be considered and discussed, what behaviour is appropriate—and indeed ultimately the power to define the personal identity of other individuals and classes within the social system.

ORGANIZATION DEVELOPMENT

Organization Development is an approach to organization life which involves a 'change in the organization's culture from one which avoids an examination of social processes . . . to one which legitimises and institutionalises this examination' (Burke and Hornstein, 1972, p. xi); it usually involves a variety of action-research methods to generate 'valid information' about organization processes from which change can take place based on 'free choice' and 'internal commitment' (Argyris, 1970). Thus OD may be seen as a straight-forward approach of using third-party interventions to mobilize information and energy about organizational processes which would not otherwise be available for system improvement. It is thus a very rational, common-sense strategy (Fordyce and Weil, 1971); a bit personally threatening for some people maybe, but all in a good cause.

If, however, we take a second look at OD processes we may see that some aspects of the OD strategy strike directly at the reality-defining processes of the organization: in other words, activities aimed at system improvement also involve basic processes of system creation. Mangham (1975) has described OD as 'negotiating reality'; but how much reality are we negotiating? Very often it is impossible to generate 'valid information'—such an innocent-sounding phrase—without finding that we are questioning the basis from which that information arises and the fundamental assumptions of organization members. Sometimes, when we start asking questions, there seems to be no limit to the questions we *could* ask; and when we start to define the social issues around which OD work is indicated, we may begin to renegotiate the very reality which holds the organization together.

CULTURES

A culture involves the 'sets of values and norms and beliefs—reflected in different structures and systems' which pervade the organization (Handy, 1976, p. 176). The culture is the real world as constructed through organizational processes, and at the same time the means by which that reality is defined and redefined. As Harrison points out, 'Among people in organizations, ideas of "what is" and "what ought to be" merge into one another and are—or are made to appear—consistent' (1972, p. 120). In this chapter I am primarily concerned with power cultures and with role cultures.

Handy likens the *power culture* to a web, depending on a:

> central power source, with rays of power and influence spreading out from that central figure. . . . Control is exercised by the centre largely through the selection of key individuals, by occasional forays from the centre or summonses to the centre.
>
> (1976, p. 178)

Harrison argues that:

> An organization that is power-oriented attempts to dominate its environment and vanquish all opposition. It is unwilling to be the subject to any external law or power. And within the organization those who are powerful strive to maintain absolute control over subordinates.
>
> (Harrison, 1972, p. 121)

Power cultures are proud and strong, able to move fast and react to threat or danger; they support 'power-oriented, politically minded, risk-taking' individuals (Handy, p. 179); they are competitive, jealous of territory, and self-serving (Harrison, p. 121).

In a power culture, some people are power*ful*, some are power*less*; relationships nearly always have a vertical (one-up, one-down) character: even colleague (i.e. presumably equal and collaborative) relationships are often arenas for competitive striving and gamesmanship. The power to define reality and to define relationships lies in the hands of a very small number of people at the centre, and the ability of other members of the organization to raise and define issues is drastically curtailed.

In contrast the *role culture* is like a Greek Temple to the god Apollo:

> this culture works by logic and rationality. The role organization rests on the strength of its pillars, its functions or specialities. These pillars are strong in their own right. . . .
>
> (Handy, 1976, pp. 179–80)

The role culture is predictable, stable, respectable; correct, rather than effective. 'Procedures for change tend to be cumbersome; therefore the system is slow to adapt to change' (Harrison, 1972, p. 122). The role or job description is often more important than the individual who fills it; rules and procedures are the most important methods of influence.

An organization that is role-oriented aspires to be as rational and orderly as possible. In contrast to the wilful autocracy of the power-oriented organization, there is a preoccupation with legality, legitimacy, and responsibility. . . . Competition and conflict . . . are regulated and replaced by agreements, rules and procedures. Rights and privileges are carefully defined and adhered to. While there is a strong emphasis on hierarchy and status, it is moderated by the commitment to legitimacy and legality.

(Harrison, 1972, pp. 121–122)

Power in role cultures is much more evenly spread than in power cultures. There is of course a greater accumulation of power towards the top, but this power is tempered by the conservative power of the *system*, a conservation that Schon (1971) has tellingly labelled *dynamic*—'a tendency to fight to remain the same' (p. 32). The potential power to define reality and to define relationships lies widely in the hands of organization members, although most people do not experience themselves as possessing such power, since they feel impotent in the face of 'the system', usually personified as Them. Thus it is the experience of impotence rather than of power which is widely shared.

ORGANIZATION DEVELOPMENT AND ROLE CULTURES

I have defined culture, power, and organization development as being ultimately concerned with the construction and reconstruction of reality, the taken-for-granted backcloth against which all transactions and interactions are seen by organization members. OD, if it is to make any significant contribution to organization life, intervenes directly into the reality-defining processes of the organization; since these processes will be characteristically different in different cultures, we may hypothesize that similar OD interventions will have different outcomes in different cultures. My assumption is that OD grew up as a response to role cultures, and that the theory and practice of OD is primarily relevant to role cultures and to their movement towards being more appropriately task-oriented. OD expresses a concern for the entrapment of the individual in impersonal processes and for the loss of task effectiveness in the red-tape of bureaucracy, rather than the political manoeuvring and naked power plays of the power culture. Role cultures aim to be 'as rational and orderly as possible': OD offers a meta-rationality of 'planned change' in which even emotions can be rationally taken into account. Further, I suggest that OD professionals tend to be liberal rather than radical, in that they are oriented to rational, negotiated change processes within an accepted cultural framework: fundamentally, they accept the role-based Western culture and their involvement in it, and they take for granted the basic distribution of power within that culture.

In role cultures the reality-defining processes may be seen as out of control—taken over by 'the system'. OD, in helping people better to understand and take action in their situation, enables them once again to take charge of their organization and of their lives. In this sense, the amount of total power in the organization is increased, and with it the possibility of increased mutual influence. Everybody 'wins', so collaboration and consensus are possible.

In power culture, this cannot be true; if a small group of people hold a position from which they can impose their definitions of reality, any move to explore the reality of the organization and any suggestion of a renegotiation must be seen by them as a threat. It is to a detailed consideration of one such power culture that I now turn.

THE POWER CULTURE AT 'CORMORANT'

Cormorant is an engineering factory, part of a very large international group, which manufactures in quantity specialized engineering components. Its history over the past few years has been chequered and as a result of this the factory was a few years ago in a sorry state, with low morale, hostile attitudes to the parent company management, run-down plant, and an outdated product.

In response to this situation the parent company collected together a large and strong management team under a super-strong General Manager to 'turn the place around'. The measure of their success is that in a few years the factory has reorganized and introduced new management information systems, made major investments in new plant and equipment, developed an important new product, and in addition to all this appears to be moving steadily into a profitable situation.

Larry Campbell, the General Manager, is a large, bouncy, talkative, tremendously energetic man. He is enormously possessive of Cormorant, very careful to protect it from outside interference and from interventions from Head Office Departments. He has been known to order outsiders off the site, and Cormorant is often referred to as 'Chateau Campbell'.

Larry has an enormous capacity to memorize detail. He introduced information and control systems which provide him with enormous amounts of detailed information about every area and function in the factory. He often appears to manage 'by detail' apparently knowing more about a particular subject than the manager responsible.

He is not, however, simply a detail man: he is also one of the most charismatic leaders I have ever observed. At the management lunch table he is absolutely central, cracking jokes, laughing loudly and infectiously, producing ideas and excitement such that no-one can, or would want to, compete. He is the prime task *and* socio-emotional leader, lavish in both praise and rebuke, expecting and inspiring a high standard of performance, and usually getting it.

Some comments about Larry from interviews with members of his management team may give some flavour.

I'd go through hell fire for Larry—he understands my problems, makes demands that are hard to meet, but just attainable. A first class guy to work for.

Campbell—my kind of guy, a pusher, a goer, I can react to him.

Larry—the guy we needed, but a bit unpredictable, a bit controlling. I admire the drive, the energy, the memory.

Larry presents his management team with excitement, challenge, the need to manage tremendous amounts of detail, and an enormous workload; on the face of it, the team is very tightly bonded. For example, on the telephone most of them would speak sharply and abusively to subordinate members of the factory, shouting into a loudspeaker attachment so that anyone else around could hear the performance; however, if a management team colleague were to call, they would immediately lift the handset and speak more reasonably—almost fraternally, calling each other 'mate'; and if it were Larry on the 'phone (and when Larry calls, the 'phone is arranged to ring continuously until answered), the tone of the conversation shifts again slightly but perceptibly towards the subservient, always starting with a smart 'Yes, Larry. . . .'

While on first impressions the management team appears tightly bonded—and this is *certainly* the impression that they work hard to create and present to outsiders—it is not difficult to get an impression of some strains. Members commented to me that lateral communication was not good; that there were splits—for example between the 'thinkers' and the 'doers', between the inner cabinet and the rest; that some members were quite ruthless and 'ran over' the rest. Certainly in meetings, Larry is the centre of communication, defines the issues, and adjudicates. He may cut through a discussion with, 'Can we just get this clear . . .', summarizing and instructing out of the general confusion. He does this to such an extent that the team relies on his summaries and integration, and team members are free to be undisciplined, to compete for his attention, and to push their own parochial viewpoints.

The most telling point about the team came from an older manager, now slightly on the sidelines:

> The team works well, but . . . they are fragile, there is a rivalry, they don't exactly trust each other. It's a problem: can you be a manager and be pushy, and also be a team member?

The team can probably be best understood in the context of its existence in a difficult and hostile environment: there has been a general threat and hostility from the workforce towards 'management' as a result of the recent difficult times; and the team is faced with the over-riding need to 'turn the place around'. Thus they are pulling together in the face of external threat.

As one moves below the management team a very different picture emerges. While there are one or two 'satellites' surrounding the management team who have an interesting life, one quickly discovers that there is little scope for most people to be other than 'lackeys' to the management team. Many of them are intensely busy, especially middle managers, but rarely involved in any significant decision-making; they are much more likely to be involved in doing work *created* by members of the management team. As one young manager on the edge of the team put it:

> Life is probably pretty dull for the clerks, but there is more excitement as you get near the management group. That is nice for them, but downward communication is not good. There is not much here in the way of participative management. People respond better to rush things if it is explained to them.

Another young manager said more emotionally:

> I'm badgered from pillar to post . . . torn between different loyalties . . . under pressure from a lot of different places. You can't explain things, especially to [Production Manager], but it's right through the management structure. If they needed SS guards to do it they would get them in. . . . Management doesn't realise that you have to *ask* people to do things . . . when the economy picks up there will be a mass exodus.

The activities of the management team—especially their intense involvement in detail—mean that they are constantly impacting on the day-to-day routines of the factory. One prime means of doing this is the Operations Meeting: the aim of this meeting is to review production and sort out bottlenecks, but it is also an opportunity for the Production Manager to exercise his abrasive management style. Each morning, from 9–11, every middle manager in the factory may receive an abusive call on his ever-ringing 'phone. As one of his colleagues on the management team commented:

> What bothers me is the blame and bullshit that his people feed him. The shit hits the fan, and we all catch it unfairly . . . they lie their backteeth off. We get the bollocking, and he gets the kudos—when *he's* the villain.

A more junior manager:

> We tend to get ruled by Production Department, having a strong Production Manager who will run anything. He has an Operations meeting every morning ostensibly to sort out shortages, but it gives him a glorious opportunity for pointing the finger.

And a junior manager working closely for the Production Manager:

> He manages by demand—'I want'—probably a bit too much. He doesn't pay attention to people's problems, they are not helped to think through their problems, they come out of meetings none the wiser. His day to day actions can cause long term problems by cutting through systems; but he always wants it both ways.

The last comment is supported by the Production Manager's own vigorous response to objections: 'I don't care how you do it, but this is what you've got to do. . . .' This strategy of management by demand, the insistence on having one's cake tomorrow *and* eating it today, creates an almost impossible situation for middle managers. Often in order to satisfy their superiors' demands they have to break procedures which the same superiors have instituted and insist are upheld.

Larry and his managers see themselves as working hard and furiously for the survival and success of the Cormorant factory. In my cynical moments I found it easy to turn everything on its head, and see Cormorant and its social relations as really existing only so that a small group of men could have an exciting time playing at being important managers. Much of their behaviour seemed not so much calculated to solve problems as to get one-up on each other or affirm themselves in the eyes of their subordinates. This creates a centrality which precludes the possibility of collaboration between subordinates: divide and rule.

DIAGNOSIS

It must be apparent to the reader that I have strong feelings about the situation at Cormorant. I am sure that I was regarded with considerable suspicion by managers, and it was extremely difficult to feel comfortable there—I found it a very harsh and competitive place, and I felt continually tested and 'put down'. I must therefore be explicit that I regard Cormorant as a place unfit for human beings, a culture where the actualization of any humanistic values must be well nigh impossible.

It is *also* important to stress that Cormorant is an *effective* organization: it has moved from the point of closure to become the success story of the company. Further, one can argue that this success was achieved by competent managers acting with energy and flexibility, and that this is only possible in a power culture. Yet this same power culture causes major problems for the factory and for the people in it, problems which I believe exist independent of my personal value bias.

(1) Since energy, information, and excitement are drawn exclusively to the top of the organization, with the General Manager and his team making all the important decisions, and at the same time making sure that their power remains absolute and unquestioned, then powerlessness, alienation, and misunderstanding are the rule in the rest of the organization.

(2) While the power culture is appropriate for a speedy and decisive response to an unsure environment, it invades those parts of the organization where stability and routine are required for task accomplishment, and where a role-orientation might be more appropriate.

(3) Since power is maintained through a process of divide and rule, the establishment of collaborative task-centred relationships is nearly impossible.

(4) The culture is activist, not given to reflection or introspection: it is not considered at all appropriate to consider alternative approaches to managing the organization.

ATTEMPTS TO DEVELOP AN OD PROJECT AT CORMORANT

I was recruited to help the development of OD work in the parent company, and was offered to Cormorant managers, or maybe imposed on them, as someone who might be able to help them with 'communications' or 'human relations'. I had no clear, explicit contract, and since attempts to develop a relationship as process consultant to the management team were unsuccessful, I decided, with Larry's agreement, to work one level down in the organization, to select a demonstration project to 'show what OD could do'.

Clive, the manager of the Production Engineering Department, and a member of the management team, was interested in my helping him explore problems with his Department, which he presented as twofold. First was the practical problem that his Department was not completing its work programme, which included the ordering of plant and equipment for the expansion and modernization of the factory; second was a more personal problem about his management style, specifically whether he should conform to the tough, harsh, table-thumping style of the Production Manager, or whether more two-way communication and a more participative style were appropriate:

> I need to know whether the way I communicate is right, and no one is telling me this. Should I rant and rave? Are people unclear?

I thought that since the problem was presented first as a work problem and that behavioural issues stemmed from that, it would be seen as useful and legitimate. My notes at the time read: 'This is an opportunity to demonstrate a *process*: i.e. to outline some steps, starting from a "felt need" towards improving a human process.'

This project started well. I met the managers of the Department, discussed the issues, and began to develop collaborative relationships. I was particularly pleased when, after I had suggested a number of ways in which we might proceed with an exploration of the issues, they used my suggestions to design a process of their own to which they were committed and which seemed to suit the circumstances. I was to interview members of the Department in groups by hierarchical level around the question, 'What are the things that happen here that get in the way of effective work and high morale?'; towards the end of each session Clive and his managers were to join the discussion to hear each group's views directly, without of course identifying individuals, and without defending or attacking back.

This design produced a lot of information that was listened to non-defensively. Some of the information was directly and immediately useful for the improvement of Departmental effectiveness, in that it showed specific ways in which time and energy were wasted and misdirected; some of it was more threatening and difficult to grasp since it concerned Clive's style of management, and the impact of the management team as a whole. Clive was described as remote, threatening, blaming and never praising, never admitting mistakes or listening to explanations. The Cormorant management team were seen as inflexible and interfering, not appreciating the work of the 'expert' engineers, overriding their recommendations, and causing unnecessary panics and unnecessary work. Overall, the style was described as 'Victorian'.

At the end of the group interviews I asked Clive if I had done what he wanted and if the process had been useful. His answer was clear, that I had uncovered information that would be useful and which, despite a number of attempts, he had been unable to find out for himself.

Despite this encouraging comment, the project quickly ran into difficulties. It was as if we began tentatively to negotiate a new reality with Clive and his Department, which was followed by a quick move by Clive to reimpose the old reality; I was then closed out of the situation, and finally enough power was mobilized to remove me altogether. All this happened with surprising speed.

Clive and his managers followed up the interviews by taking some immediate measures to improve the working of the Department: they made some changes to the organization of work, and instituted a new structure of meetings at which discussion could continue. Clive seemed keen to pursue and understand the comments about his management style. However, he quickly grew impatient with further discussion, and blamed his subordinates for the problems: he could not conceive that a young and dynamic leader such as himself could possibly be seen as Victorian; his view was that he was seen as threatening only because his subordinates were 'not man enough' to stand up to him; he argued that he had done his bit, and that it was time for his subordinates to respond to the overtures which he had made. His behaviour shifted back from being relatively open and exploratory immediately after the interviews, to being harsh and blaming. This had the effect of closing down the possibility of further discussion of organizational issues within the Department.

From this point on I found myself increasingly isolated and ignored at Cormorant; thus I cannot give a fair account of what happened, I can only guess. I *did* learn that I had been described as working as a shop steward for junior staff; my work was described by one of the management team as 'gaffer bashing'. I suspect that Clive came under considerable pressure from his colleagues to step back into line and prevent me from challenging established definitions of reality.

At this stage, I was instructed by the Head Office OD manager not to visit Cormorant any more while my work there was investigated; it was revealed that I was seen as 'too disturbing'. Eventually, and after considerable difficult discussion, it appeared that it would not be possible to renegotiate a satisfactory arrangement, and I withdrew from my contract with the company.

POSSIBILITIES FOR OD WORK IN POWER CULTURES

In retrospect it is easy to see mistakes; it is also probably easy for the reader of this story to sit back and say, 'I wouldn't have done it *that* way"—but then, what *would* you have done? My own view is that the work I was doing within the Production Engineering Department was a reasonably adequate

OD project which, had we been able to persist with it, would have been successful in improving the local situation. I think however that I was politically rather naive, allowing the project to be naked to outside pressure, and that the project was destroyed because members of the management team saw it as challenging the view of reality espoused by them and imposed on the factory, and also as challenging their sole right to define reality.

I have argued above that the theory and practice of OD was developed mainly in role cultures; and that in such cultures OD may be seen as power-enhancing in that it frees organization members from the constraints of outmoded rules and relationships, and increases the possibility of greater influence all round. A situation such as that at Cormorant is very different: since social reality is defined by a small group at the top and firmly imposed on the rest of the organization, those who define reality experience themselves as powerful, while the suppressed majority are powerless. An intervention which aims to mobilize information about such a situation will encourage the otherwise silent majority to speak and to attempt to define a new reality—which will be seen as a threat by those whose sole power to define reality is thus questioned. Since in a power culture it will be very difficult to establish superordinate goals—almost by definition they are not legitimate—OD under these circumstances is likely to involve a 'win-lose' situation, in that the silent majority can win power to define their world only if the autocratic minority loses such power. Thus *the power dynamics of OD in power cultures are quite different from those in role cultures*, and the theory of OD—as encapsulated in such terms as 'valid information', 'free choice', and 'internal commitment'—is inadequate for dealing with these situations, because this theory assumes the possibility of collaboration and consensus in the service of planned change.

It seems to me that there are three ways of thinking about this in an attempt to understand better the relationship between power and organizational development. The first line of thought might be described as the *top-down* approach, and holds that the major mistake made at Cormorant was the failure to work carefully from the top down through the organization. This is the traditional OD view—indeed a classic definition of OD is that it is a 'planned change effort . . . managed from the top' (Beckhard, 1969, pp. 9–10). From this perspective one would argue that the dynamics of the situation as described above are not in the long-term interests of the management team, and that if they can be helped to see the unintended consequences of their actions they will see the need for change.

Thus the consultant must 'start from where the client is', and work on legitimate issues to gain credibility. His first task is to develop a mutually agreed contract for work, and to establish a ground for collaboration with the client before data gathering. Only so long as he retains the confidence of management can he have any possible base for helping them to 'unfreeze', and he must constantly ask himself the question, 'Who is your client?'

This traditional, top-down approach has been criticized as being naively a-political, relying as it does on openness and trust rather than dealing with the reality of political behaviour in organizations. Recently, theorists of organization intervention have turned their attention to the *politics* of intervention in an attempt to meet this criticism. Pettigrew (1975) identified five potential power resources available to the consultant—expertise, control over information, political access and sensitivity, assessed stature, and group support. Schein (1977) suggests that the 'effective change agent needs to develop his own power-oriented approach', and outlines six possible power strategies: aligning with a powerful other, trade-offs, using the legitimacy of research as cover, using a neutral cover within the organization, limiting communication, and withdrawing from competition. Presumably, this more political approach to OD is particularly suitable in a power culture.

There are, however, three major problems in applying this top-down argument to the Cormorant situation. First, even if you manage to stay alongside the client and gain access to his worlds of meaning without being captured by them, *how* do you accomplish the unfreezing, and *how* do you disengage them from their power orientation? Second, I am sure that if I *had* been able to establish a firm credibility at the top of the organization, this would have closed off many possibilities of access further down, and I would have been unable effectively to gather 'valid information'. Finally, and most important, I believe that to the extent that the top approach *is* successful, it will be only moderating and ameliorating—indeed prolonging the agony of—an essentially untenable and pernicious situation. The very activities described above as necessary for the consultant to survive and have influence in the situation—gaining political access etc.—imply acceptance of those processes, divert attention from major issues, and thus contribute to a continuation of the status quo. Therefore the consultant becomes part of the problem rather than part of a potential solution.

The reader may imagine how self-critical I have been as a result of this experience at Cormorant. That self-criticism has convinced me that had I taken the top-down approach more skilfully, and had I behaved more politically, I would have survived longer in that organization. But I do *not* think I would have been significantly influential.

This leads me to the second line of thought, which is that the OD consultant should *stay away*. This holds that nothing can or should be done about a power culture such as Cormorant; that we should keep out of this kind of situation because we are powerless to act effectively, and may indeed get in the way of 'natural' change processes. One might argue that the organization is not yet 'ripe for change', that the dynamics of the situation will lead to a crisis at which time people within the organization will see more clearly the need for change. Only then will OD be possible. This argument indicates that it is a waste of the consultant's time and skills, and of his precious optimism, to 'work uphill' and that there are likely to be much more fruitful fields for his endeavours elsewhere.

This argument is problematic too. We cannot say for certain that a place like Cormorant will ever be 'ripe for change' without some external intervention: these kinds of oppressive situations are actually quite stable. While the top-down approach assumes the eventual possibility of orderly and planned change, staying away from the situation assumes that nothing constructive can really be done. A third line of thought is a *bottom-up* approach, which is much more revolutionary. It assumes that the basic issue at Cormorant lies in the contradiction between a small group of privileged 'oppressors' and a larger group of the 'oppressed'; and that the primary goal of the oppressors is not so much to run an efficient factory as to maintain their position in power. As I have suggested above, Cormorant may be seen as a stage on which a small group of men act out their parts as dynamic managers, with a large captured supporting cast.

To the extent that this description holds, there is no possibility that, given 'valid information' about the working of the system, the management group will initiate change. As Freire has pointed out, it is the task of the *oppressed* to change the system since:

the oppressors, who oppress, exploit, and rape by virtue of their power, cannot find in this power the strength to liberate either the oppressed or themselves. Only power which springs from weakness will be sufficiently strong to free both. Any attempts to 'soften' the power of the oppressor in deference to the weakness of the oppressed almost always manifests itself in the form of false generosity.

(1970, pp. 28–29)

Similarly Mannheim points out that:

ruling groups can in their thinking become so intensively interest-bound to a situation that they are simply no longer able to see certain facts which would undermine their sense of domination.

(1936, p. 40)

In other words the top-down approach cannot alter the basic dynamics of the situation: it can only be changed through the development of a critical consciousness and action by those lower down in the organization:

[The oppressed] will not gain their liberation by chance but through the praxis of their quest for it, through the recognition of the necessity to fight for it.

· (Freire, 1970, p. 29)

This line of thought suggests that the only successful intervention would be through the oppressed, helping *them* to understand the nature of their situation, to organize and build support groups, and thus find the strength to challenge their oppressors, attempt to establish a dialogue with them, and begin to negotiate a new reality. Freire has suggested that this might be done through a 'pedagogy of the oppressed' through which they might '*emerge* from their submersion and acquire the ability to *intervene* in reality as it is unveiled' (1970, p. 100). Similar ideas for a bottom-up strategy for social change are found in Alinsky's 'rules for radicals' (1972), in the consciousness-raising of the Women's Movement, in the development of an anti-psychiatry (Cooper, 1967), indeed, in many places where the established reality is experienced as oppressive.

This line of thought sounds very revolutionary. One wonders whether the revolution will be bloody, and whether there will be a swing from one dictator to another. One wonders what the impact of all this will be on organizational effectiveness. One wonders what the encounter between the oppressors and the oppressed will look like, since this bottom-up argument focuses on the development of awareness and power for the oppressed, and lacks a theory for a movement to dialogue with the oppressors.

It has been suggested that this bottom-up approach is a political, rather than a managerial, rhetoric, and thus cannot be part of an OD strategy. This may well be true: as we move toward a subversive approach, we step outside the domain of the consultant into the domain of the revolutionary. If, however, we wish to understand power in organizational change, we must realize that there is a well-articulated theory of power which lies outside the scope of OD, and outside the scope of the politicking and manoeuvring which is a normal part of organizational life: this latter is power used basically to preserve the status quo, while the bottom-up approach represents an attempt at a fundamental change in power relations.

The OD profession has always been ambivalent about power, usually ignoring it as an issue although at times castigating itself for this omission. In his review of OD in transition, Burke (1976) holds that OD has yet to come to grips with the politics of change—although he himself devotes remarkably little space to further consideration of the issue. I hope this consideration of OD in power cultures shows how fundamentally uncomfortable are the attempts to add considerations of power to the theory of OD. The work of the 'political' theorists of organizational intervention (Schein, 1977; Pettigrew, 1975) only 'tacks on' political strategies to an OD theory which is basically a-political: they do not get to the roots of the use of power for organizational change.

We must take the comments of our critics seriously: Brimm (1972) describes OD consultants as 'system maintainers' who ignore fundamental variables; Nord (1974) takes a Marxist perspective on the *failure* of applied behavioural science, which he suggests 'encourages exploration of alternative power bases for humanistically oriented change'. If we wish to understand the use of power fully, we must move beyond a consideration of politicking in the service of system-maintenance and explore the radical view indicated above.

I would like to suggest that if there is genuine broad consensus about the existence, nature, and goals of an organization, but the organizational processes have somehow gone astray, then OD as system maintenance and system enhancement may make a contribution. If, however, there is fundamental disagreement or false consensus about the existence, nature, and goals of the organization, so that the organization must be held together by unilateral power, then a more radical view is needed. OD in this latter instance would tend to seek *premature* collaboration and conflict resolution, when polarization of issues, confrontation, and even destruction of organizational forms (Pages, 1974) are essential. We must recognize that there is a major arena in which OD has nothing to offer.

All this reinforces Harrison's point (1972) that much of the business of organizational change is really ideological struggle. If we in OD are going to have a theory of the use of power it must be a radical theory that shows us how to use power in the service of change, rather than how to simply survive in a political environment. But does OD, *should* OD encompass more revolutionary, even subversive interventions? Do we have the skills, the courage, and above all the commitment? Should we work where collaboration and consensus are readily available, or should we move in to participate in a more revolutionary arena? Should we, and do we want to?

REFERENCES

Alinsky, S. D. (1972). *Rules for Radicals*, New York: Random House.
Argyris, C. (1970). *Intervention Theory and Method*, Reading, Mass.: Addison-Wesley.
Bachrach, P., and Baratz, M. S. (1970). *Power and Poverty*, New York: Oxford University Press.
Beckhard, R. (1969). *Strategies of Organization Development*, Reading, Mass.: Addison-Wesley.
Berger, P. L., and Luckman, T. (1966). *The Social Construction of Reality*, Harmondsworth: Penguin Books.
Brimm, M. (1972). When is a change not a change? *Journal of Applied Behavioural Science*, **5**, No. 1.

Burke, W. W. (1976). Organization Development in Transition, *Journal of Applied Behavioural Science*, **12**, No.1.

——and Hornstein, H. A. (1972). *The Social Technology of Organization Development*, Fairfax, Virginia: NTL Learning Resources.

Cooper, D. (1967). *Psychiatry and Anti-Psychiatry*, New York: Ballantine Books.

Freire, P. (1970). *Pedagogy of the Oppressed*, New York: Seabury Press.

Friedlander, F. (1971). Congruence in organization development, *Proc. 31st Annual Meeting of the Academy of Management*.

——and Brown, L. D. (1974). Organization Development, *Annual Review of Psychology*, **25**.

Fordyce, J. K., and Weil, R. (1971). *Managing with People*, Reading, Mass.: Addison-Wesley.

Galbraith, J. (1973). *Designing Complex Organizations*, Reading, Mass.: Addison-Wesley.

Handy, C. B. (1976). *Understanding Organizations*, Harmondsworth: Penguin Books.

Handy, C. B. (1979). The Gods of Management: how they work, and why they fail, London. Pan Books.

Harrison, R. (1972). Understanding your organization's character, *Harvard Business Review*, May–June.

Huckabay, M. A. (1975). *Toward a Theory of Selfhood in Women*, unpublished Qualifying Paper, Department of Organizational Behaviour, Case Western Reserve University.

Lukes, S. (1974). *Power: A Radical View*, London: Macmillan.

Mangham, I. L. (1975). Negotiating Reality: Notes toward a Model of Order and Change within Organizations: *Centre for the Study of Organizational Change and Development*, University of Bath.

Mannheim, K. (1936). *Ideology and Utopia*, New York: Harcourt, Brace and World.

Nord, W. R. (1974). The failure of current applied behavioural science—a Marxian perspective, *Journal of Applied Behavioural Science*, **10**, No. 4.

Pages, M. (1974). An interview with Max Pages, by Noel Tichy, *Journal of Applied Behavioural Science*, **10**, No. 1.

Pettigrew, A. (1975). Toward a political theory of organizational intervention, *Human Relations*, **28**, No. 3.

Schein, V. E. (1977). Political strategies for implementing organizational change, in *Group + Organisation Studies*, **2**, No. 1, March.

Schon, D. (1971). *Beyond the Stable State*, London: Temple Smith.

Srivastva, S. (1975). Some neglected issues in organization development, in W. W. Burke (ed.), *Current Issues and Strategies in Organization Development*, New York: Behavioural Publications.

——and Brown, L. D. (1974). Power Corrupts, Powerlessness Corrupts Absolutely. Address presented at the *OD Network Meeting, Salt Lake City, Utah*, 7–11 October.

Power, Politics, and Organizations: A Behavioural Science View
Edited by Andrew Kakabadse and Christopher Parker
© 1984 John Wiley & Sons Ltd

Chapter 11

Perceptions of Power: A Case-study of a College

MARGARET RYAN

This paper is based on a field study of peoples' perceptions of power in an organizational setting. The starting assumption of the research was that 'What matters is how the individual or group imagines the milieu to be' (Dearlove, 1973)—people behave in accordance with their perceptions of the situation. I wanted to investigate what interpretations organization members were making of processes in which they were themselves directly involved, and to shift the analysis away from the researcher's interpretation of organizational phenomena, and towards that of the organization members themselves.

The research was carried out in an academic setting – the College* – and involved an investigation of decision-making processes, in which financial resources were allocated to various groups and individuals. These processes were researched in 'real time' while they were in train, but were annual events and not so contentious as to make access for the study too difficult.

I was particularly interested to know how people involved in these decision-making processes interpreted them politically, and indeed whether they saw them as 'political' at all. Thus, for example, questions such as who they thought made the decisions, and whether they could themselves influence outcomes, and how, were relevant to the study. But a review of the literature on power shows that what might be perceived as the politics of a milieu is a complex matter, which needs to be considered broadly to include not only interactions between individuals in which one tries to influence the other, although in the end politics boils down to that, but also issues of culture and structure which the perceptual field of those individuals might include. There are also questions of the distinction between power potential and power use, and the non-awareness of political considerations. It was therefore necessary in this research to take into account both what my

*All names, roles, and other nomenclature are fictitious in the interest of confidentiality.

informants and what social scientists might see as 'political'. In order to encompass this possible variety, and to avoid pre-empting what my informants might tell me, I adopted a broad view of the concept of power, being prepared to consider that 'all behaviour at all levels and in all circumstances may be regarded as political' (Mangham, 1979) and that 'power means any chance, (no matter whereon this chance is based) to carry through one's own will (even against resistance)' (Walliman, Rosenbaum, Tatsis and Zito, 1980).

The methodology for the study was qualitative, using a grounded theory approach (Glaser and Strauss, 1967) data being collected by semi-structured interviews, by some participant observation, and by reference to documents. In data collection and analysis I tried to preserve the nuances of differing perceptions, and to maintain the focus of attention on the sense people were making of the events with which they were confronted. I was less interested in such questions as how many people thought a committee powerful, as in the different ways and extent of its being seen as powerful. I also assumed that people had good reasons for the views they held, and tried not to arbitrate as to the 'correctness' of their perceptions.

Because of the nature of this research, it is not possible to cover the whole study in this paper and at the same time do justice to the variety and complexity of what I found in the organization. This will therefore be a general overview, with some findings given more emphasis than others in order to highlight some of the issues which I found of interest. The findings of the research can be conveniently divided into three broad areas—perceptions about structure, about powerful people in the organization, and about culture. This chapter will follow that basic pattern.

PERCEPTIONS OF STRUCTURE

The data about structure related both to its formal and its informal aspects. Much of it concerned the various committees of the College, but there was also a considerable amount about the ways in which people distinguish the existence of groups within the organization, or perceive themselves to be in a group, and the way in which boundaries were drawn between groups and the ease or difficulty with which these could be crossed, issues which will be considered here.

The data showed that peoples' perceptions of structure differed considerably, both as to whether parts of the structure (formal or informal) actually existed, and the extent to which it was seen as having political implications. Some particular examples will illustrate the nature of these differences.

Some informants saw the organization as containing groups of people sharing the same subject discipline and working together in teams. However, many of those in such supposed teams saw themselves as working in isolation from others. Thus one person could talk of 'three or four people working on the same topic area', but another could say, 'There are few, if any, teams', in describing the organization. But not only did people's perceptions differ about the groupings related to tasks or 'division of labour', they also had differing views about the ease and desirability of making informal contacts, and informal groups with other organization members. For example: 'The staff lounge is a good place for meeting and chatting, playing snooker, hearing what other people think of the committee they've been in'. Others, however, pointed out that in the staff lounge people tended only to talk to people in their own departments. 'If you were to go to the wrong group they would drop dead with shock. They would make it so uncomfortable for you that you wouldn't try it again. They wouldn't talk to you' was one of the more extreme views of this barrier to interaction. Not everyone minded about this perceived absence of interaction across departmental or other boundaries, for a variety of reasons. For example, 'I don't mind as long as they leave me alone. I don't get involved in the rest of the College' was the view of someone who wanted to devote all his time to his subject. Even the exchange of ideas at a technical level was not considered of value by some: 'Contributions of other staff . . . would not be useful'. However, there were those who regretted the absence of interaction. As one senior academic said, rather wistfully, 'I tend not to go to the staff lounge—I tend not to know people and therefore I don't talk to them. I have written off that side of things. They are more like amorphous colleagues than people I know'.

It can be said that informal communication channels are an important factor in organizational politics, but it seemed clear that few people in this study saw any political significance in such interaction (or lack of it) across group boundaries. However, there were some examples of politically motivated alliances and groupings of this kind. In one example a department was said to have adopted a deliberate policy of forming good relationships with administrators, seen as a group. 'Admin has always found us cooperative, pleasant and not "anti". This is part of our internal policy.' Some alliances were more opportunist and unstable as when people combined at a committee meeting over particular issues: 'Bill and I gang up against the other group, but sometimes Bill gets a pay-off from advantages they get, so he is not always on my side'.

There were also one or two people who had set out to gather information by informal means to further some interest of their own. For example, one senior academic said: 'You have to assess how the central body is thinking— which way Abbott is thinking.* You do this by getting him talking. I'm not trying to extract information unfairly.' It is interesting to note his reservations about the process—some perceived line between what is proper and what is

* The head of the organization; the name is fictitious.

not, in political behaviour. A junior academic commented: 'The staff lounge is a good place for information. You can arrange to sit next to someone "accidentally", making it look natural, then discuss with them what you want. If you can convince them in fifteen or twenty minutes over lunch or coffee, you have a good chance. Then you put it through the formal system.'

Factors which seemed to work against informal interaction across formal boundaries, apart from the absence of any perceived advantage in it, either technical or political, included the physical distribution of the various departments about the site; the experience some people had had of potential allies 'welshing' on agreements in the past; and norms of behaviour which seemed to inhibit some people from taking the necessary initiatives.

One formal way in which people could cross formal boundaries, was through their membership of different committees. It can be suggested that one reason why some people saw the College as being 'run by a clique' was that a substantial number of senior academics appeared on all the main committees. This raised some questions in my mind about how clear the boundaries of these committees were and which interests were being pursued on what committee. It could also have contributed to the difficulty of deciding which committee was more powerful than which, so that, of two people who might be equally expected to know, one told me that Committee X was more important than Committee Y and controlled it, while the other said that the opposite was the case.

To sum up this section, it can be seen that people in the organization studied held between them a number of different perceptions as to the nature of the structure of their organization both formally and informally, and of its political significance. It can be suggested that, although social scientists might be able to see relatively clear and ordered structures in an organization, this is not necessarily how it appears if the perceptions of organization participants are given equal weight. Nor, of course, are participants necessarily aware of the differences of view between them, but may take it for granted that the structure is to others what it is to them, in so far as they consider the matter at all.

POWERFUL PEOPLE

If you take the view that power is an aspect of the relationship between individuals, and that it is unevenly distributed, it is relevant to consider who is seen as being more powerful than whom in an organization. The research data in this study contained a great many comments concerning the power of individuals, particularly the head of the College, the bursar, and the senior academics. It is not possible to cover all aspects of these perceived relationships here, so I will concentrate on perceptions about the head of College and the senior academics, in order to illustrate their variety, and some of the issues they raised.

If there was one powerful person in the College, one might imagine that Abbott would be that person, as head of the organization, so it was interesting to see what perceptions informants had of him from a political point of view. One feature of these perceptions to emerge was that people related them to the history of the organization as they saw it, and to their experience of other organizations. It should also be said that although the College was not large, some informants had no contact with Abbott, although this did not necessarily prevent their having perceptions of his power.

Among senior academics, perceptions of Abbott were mixed. He was seen as 'having a great influence on' a decision, but also as not being able to get his own way always. On the other hand he was not easy to influence. 'He is easy to talk to but you can't influence him'. He was seen by some as 'very powerful', especially since he could 'wait and do things in the holidays if it is urgent for him to get his way' (when most senior academics would be absent) also as a 'powerful persuader and a strong leader' but 'not putting pressure on people'. He was also seen as a 'fixer' lobbying support for his view before meetings and 'packing' committees. In his relationships with the main academic committee, of which he was chairman, one informant considered that Abbott was 'afraid of' this committee: 'Not that he shivers in his shoes, but he is concerned that the business is carried through. He wants to see that everyone gets a fair crack of the whip, because there is considerable danger of the outcome if they don't.' This suggested that his behaviour was governed by what he thought committee members might do. However, another informant said that Abbott 'manipulates the committee' which suggested that the boot was on the other foot. Another comment which seemed to cast Abbott in the role of manipulator was that 'people who decide academic priorities have power. Especially Abbott, but he has to carry the staff with him. So you single out the opposition and isolate it.' One informant, however, expressed uncertainty about whether or not Abbott was powerful: 'I *think* so, I *assume* so', suggesting that he ought to be powerful, given his role as head of College, but it was by no means certain.

All these comments were from senior members of staff, whether academic or administrative, and most of them had close contacts with Abbott. However, among junior academics, those who had any view at all of Abbott's power and their own ability to influence him, also provided various shades of view: 'He is very accessible, but that doesn't mean he would necessarily listen', 'he is around and you can talk to him. He might discuss things in a general way, but would probably route things back through the head of department'. Another comment raised doubt about Abbott's power more directly: 'I am not sure that Abbott has got a grip on the College yet'—the suggestion being that he would eventually get a grip on it, and indeed *ought* to.

Abbott was not generally seen as a neutral arbiter by either senior or junior staff, but 'he has an agenda of his own', and this could be an advantage or disadvantage to one's own interests. This agenda was to do with policy priorities, such as the encouragement of research, and those people whose interests also lay in that direction were seen as being at an advantage, sometimes to the chagrin of those whose interests were elsewhere. However, he was also seen by some people as partisan on other counts: too close to administrators against a background of dispute over whether the administrators or the academics should run the College; too close to scientific departments, his own academic background being scientific; hostile to the social sciences, and in particular to sociology. However, whether you think any of these suggestions derogatory could depend on your own point of view. As one engineer commented: 'He's a scientist and therefore takes a balanced view of the world'.

As a 'photofit' picture emerging from these comments, it could be said that Abbott was not seen as all-powerful and unlike his predecessor, was not abrasive and threatening; seen to be 'human' and approachable at a personal level, but also able to project his own biases on to the system, and adopting manipulative strategies for getting support for his wishes. His attitudes and priorities were seen as a positive advantage to some people and a threat to others, but these advantages and threats were modified by the perception that Abbott did not fully control events in the organization, although he might influence them, but just how strongly was not clear. It has also to be said that he was seen as having little impact either way on the daily lives of some organization members, which is not to say that there *was* no impact, just that no impact was perceived.

It will be seen that perceptions of the power of Abbott contained considerable variation, and nuances of differing views, and that although a composite picture can be made, this would not necessarily correspond exactly to the perceptions of any one individual organization member. Except in a few instances, the various perceptions of Abbott were not in stark contradiction, but were subtle differences, and should they chance to discuss him with each other, most organization members would not find their view of him discomfirmed. However, it can be assumed that organization members, including Abbott, would not be aware of each other's perceptions, particularly because, as the section on structure has indicated and as the section on culture will further show, many of my informants would be highly unlikely to discuss the head of College, or indeed anything else, with each other.

To turn to the senior academics it can be said that they were generally seen as powerful in the organization, though not without exception, and apart from being individually powerful, were also seen by some people as a powerful group. 'There is a club of senior academics controlling the depart-ments.' Like other academic staff, senior academics could play three different roles: a technical role as specialists in their subjects; a role as head of their subject group or head of department; and a College-wide role, for example, through membership of the major College committees. These options had a bearing on their power in two main ways. One was that if you consider power to be the 'chance to carry through one's will', they had considerable freedom to decide which of these roles they would spend time and energy on, de-pending on their interests. The other was in the impact of this choice on the interests of junior academics. For example, those who chose to concentrate on the techcical role might gain a high reputation outside the College, be able to attract resources, and generally help the careers of junior staff by this means. Some senior academics were clearly seen as patrons in this way. However, if they took on roles as head of department, or College-wide roles, they could be seen as neglecting one of these to the detriment of more junior staff. For example, 'He is always up at the other building because of his contacts with Abbott, and he's always abroad, so we don't get as much attention as one might expect from a head of department', was a comment about a senior academic playing all three roles. External roles as consultants, were also seen by some people to cause neglect of internal roles, to the detriment of junior staff, and to the College as a whole.

Particularly in their roles as Heads of Departments, senior academics were seen, both by themselves and by their juniors, as being able to affect the interests of junior staff in a number of other ways; giving and withholding promotions; arrangement of timetables and allocation to courses; giving or withholding funds, such as payments of conference fees. It was also seen by some people as an advantage to share the same special interests within a subject as your head of department or subject group. Conversely, a head of department with a poor reputation was seen as 'useless', and a block to the progress of more junior staff. Although some formal sanctions were available to senior academics, there was some doubt as to whether these sanctions really applied, some juniors asserting that they did apply, and others being able to cite instances where they had not. The main tendency was to see manipulation and persuasion as the tactics for gaining compliance, rather than the direct use of authority or coercion: '. . . they can't force you to comply, but it's not in your interest to refuse.' But it is also true to say that junior academics seemed more aware of the seniors' direct power in relation to themselves, whereas seniors were more aware of their negotiations with, and power in relation to, each other, rather than over junior staff. Some junior staff also showed signs of adopting manipulative behaviour in relation to senior academics. For example, one informant who had felt it incumbent upon him to apply for a research grant commented: 'I don't expect to get it and would not be overjoyed if I did, because it would mean extra work. My application is a political gesture to demonstrate that the department is doing research, rather than an application as such.'

Although the senior academics were seen as powerful, it should also be noted that senior and junior academics did also very largely share the same interests and values, at least within the same disciplines or groups of similar disciplines. 'Not everything is in dispute' as one junior academic put it, and another described himself as 'a willing horse'. Perhaps for this reason, the limits on the autonomy of junior staff were not always clear—'I don't know what would happen if I did refuse' (a particular duty) was one comment. However, although senior staff were more likely to have the chance to carry through their will, it was also possible for junior staff to have this chance, depending on what their 'will' happened to be.

Some senior academics were clearly aware of being powerful: 'My power position is strong—I could move to another College at any time. They therefore try to keep me happy here'; and 'I don't need this job. Because of my reputation they need me more that I need them.' Who 'they' were in these instances was not clear, but seemed to represent some view of 'College authorities'.

Other senior academics indicated that they were not so powerful; for example, talking of 'muted directives' from higher levels, or complaining that they were not sufficiently consulted or did not have enough authority, 'I'm not in charge'. Nor did they all see themselves as powerful in relation to more junior staff: 'I doubt if I'm seen as powerful. They probably see me more as a clown.' There were also some indications that their power was curbed by possible reactions of more junior staff—'He has to carry the department with him' was one such comment about the role of head of department. However, it also seemed possible for a head of department to adopt a highly coercive role with impunity, regardless of the resistance of junior staff. 'The head of department won't discuss the matter with us. He's a real fascist. He told us we were not important enough to discuss it with, so there is nothing we can do. We are powerless.' In general one could suggest that the political relationship between senior and junior academics was not so much based on formal sanctions as on more subtle issues of values and perceived self-interest, for although 'the fascist' got away with it, he was an exception who demonstrated that although others *could* have used direct authority and coersion they chose not to do so.

It can be seen from these comments that it was not at all clear just who had how much power and why in the organization studied. Although roles could provide opportunities for power, they did not guarantee it; people seen as powerful by others may or may not see themselves that way; and the boundaries of power could remain untested. Some reasons for the ambiguities about the power of individuals are suggested in the next section, on culture.

PERCEPTIONS OF CULTURE

The third broad category of findings of this research concerned the culture of the College—the mixture of norms of behaviour and values of individuals which form the context of the individuals's political behaviour and can be said to provide both opportunities and constraints. As with the other categories, the focus of attention will be on how organization members perceived that culture.

Much of the data showed the organization to be in a process of change, brought about by a combination of a new head of college, the appointment of several new senior academics, and a radical change in policy. The culture at the time of this research, therefore, was seen as exhibiting the tensions between old values and new ones, and the data revealed people's perceptions of, and reactions to, these tensions. The data related to a number of different aspects of the culture: values connected with the new policy; the use of information; competition; the way in which conflict was dealt with; and management style. Of these I shall deal with the use of information and the handling of conflict, in order to illustrate the points I wish to make about perceptions of power. But first, some comments about the background of change.

Some people felt threatened by the change of policy, since it undermined the legitimacy of their activities and interests which had previously been applauded, while others found their position enhanced by it. Some people denied that there was any problem over the new policy, and others thought that, even if there was, nothing could, or even should, be done about it. One senior academic considered that there were dangers in the divisions created by policy change. He felt that people who were favoured by the change '. . . are seen as a privileged group by the disaffected and this has an effect on them. The cost of applying a tough policy . . . is too great'. A tough policy, however, was advocated by another senior staff member. Of the disaffected he said: 'The sooner they leave the better. If they don't like it, hard cheese'. Given the relative autonomy of senior academics, from the viewpoint of junior staff it could matter a great deal which perception of the implications of change your head of department took, and also, one could suggest, the fate of particular individuals might depend on which view prevailed among senior academics when decisions were being made.

In any discussion of people's perceptions of the politics of their situation, the availability of information to them is bound to be an issue. The data in this research raised questions as to whether there were any facts to be known, any information people could count on, what sort of information they had, and how it related to their behaviour.

One piece of information which is important to anyone wanting to influence a decision is the criteria by which those who make the decision will decide. In this study, it was not clear even among the final decision-makers, which of the twenty-five different criteria cited by my informants would be applied. Most people expressed in one way or another a feeling of being 'in the dark' about the decision-making process as a whole, and even some of those who started off with certainty, ended up feeling puzzled when the process was over. The picture was complicated by the existence of both formal and informal criteria. For example, in one decision-making process, one formally stated criterion was 'academic merit' in determining who should have funds. However, people also talked a good deal about the need to give 'fair shares' of the funds available to the various departments and subject groups. This seemed to mean that the money should not all go to one department or group, however excellent their work might be considered. There was also the problem, of course, of determining what academic merit consisted in, and how the relative merits of projects in different disciplines could be compared, which some people perceived the decision-makers as being required to do. It was suggested that the decision-makers contrived to apply both the 'merit' and 'fair shares' criteria simultaneously, as a means of avoiding the unpleasant consequences of infringing either value. Comments along these lines were: 'On the question of prioritizing, in principle we evaluate the projects scientifically, but in practice there has to be equitable sharing—a kind of rough justice'. 'They're prejudiced towards a fair distribution. This is not consciously expressed. It is not done on the basis of numbers of students in each department or anything like that.'

It should not be assumed, however, that the ambiguity about criteria was due to inefficiency or some failure of intelligence on the part of the decision-makers, for there was evidence that it could be serving a political purpose. With a number of possible criteria to choose from, you could pick on those which most favoured your interests and attempt to suppress those that did not, when negotiating with others. For example, one senior academic who was going to make a bid for funds in a committee, admitted that there was a certain weakness in his case in that it did not meet a criterion which might be applied, and commented 'this might become an issue at the meeting if someone chooses to raise it'. Whether someone did attack his case by drawing attention to this criterion might depend on whether they perceived any ill consequences for themselves in doing so—such as having a similar problem in their own case, or there being a possibility of retaliation over some other issue. The chairman of this particular committee described the decision-making process as one in which, 'Six rational people try to make the best decision', but other members referred to 'the fighting' and 'the horse-trading' of the process. It was also described as 'a very private meeting', outsiders having little information about its deliberations and methods of working and some people among the junior staff seemed not even to know of its existence.

There was a good deal of discontent expressed about the outcome of the decision-making process, and it could be suggested that lack of information and ambiguity of criteria both contributed to the discontent among onlookers and those most affected by the outcome of the process. Particularly among those who saw academic merit as being the over-riding criterion, there was discontent or puzzlement as to how the decision could turn out as it did. Because the decision-makers were academics, they were seen as being biased in favour of their own disciplines, and to be explicitly or implicitly 'representing' particular interests (although this was denied by the committee chairman). The more it was claimed that the committee was objective or scientific and assessing 'academic merit', the less comprehensible and legitimate its activities appeared to outsiders. But had the committee openly admitted that it carved up the funds on the basis of equitable sharing between departments, they would have offended those people who saw the existing system as a competitive process in which the cream rose to the top. One could say that people's reactions to the process depended on their political awareness of the pressures which might be involved, what might be happening at an informal level and on their own values, what ought to happen. Acceptance of, or resistance to 'the will' of the decision-makers by those affected, could be said to be conditioned by these factors.

The decisions which were the focus of this research had to be made every year, so that inevitably some people tried to predict the outcome on the basis of what had happened the previous year. Given the ambiguity of criteria and the lack of information from the final decision-making committee in the process just discussed, this proved no easy task, even for committee members. As a consequence some onlookers complained that the rules changed in the middle of the game.

One reason for the failure of prediction seemed to be the model of decision-making adopted by the predictor. For example, one committee member who recognized that the decision-making process was developing from year to year, likened it to doing equations: 'You start with the historic or existing pattern and then adjust it slightly. Like doing equations, you are less likely to make a mistake if you go by small adjustments.' The prediction failed in this instance because other committee members seem to have been playing bridge, not doing equations, and the outcome was not a slight adjustment, but a radical change as compared with previous years.

If people in the organization lack information on which to influence decisions, the question can be asked whether this is due to deliberate attempts by individuals to withhold it. This research showed that although in some instances people *did* deliberately withhold information, either as a bargaining tactic, or to avoid trouble ('It's all so difficult, the less said about it the better') there were also other factors at work. Some people saw no reason to seek information out, because they did not see the issues as of sufficient importance to warrant the effort—'there's no time to fuss about it . . . one would be wasting time'. It can be said too that people who were relatively new in the organization, and relatively junior, did not have access to, or know of the existence of, the possible informal channels of communication. Moreover, communication takes time for the communicator, and people who have information do not necessarily want to spend their time passing it on to others. This may be related to their own priorities, for example being more interested in a role outside the College than with the processes within it—one of the ways in which the interests of senior academics who had information because they were on the committees could be at odds with the interests of junior academics who needed information in order to be able to influence decisions.

The importance of information in political processes has been noted by other researchers (Pettigrew 1973), and the presence of ambiguity in decision-making processes has also been commented on (March and Olsen, 1976). It was suggested by this present research that ambiguity of information might be inherent in the organizational phenomena to which it refers; for example, because decision-makers are dealing with abstract concepts whose meaning cannot be pinned down. Or it may be the result of the limitations on inter-subjectivity—the impossibility of knowing for certain what are another's perceptions, intentions, or even in some cases, actions. There are also the limitations on self-perceptions and self-communication. People are not always certain about what they perceive, intend, or do, and may lack ability to communicate to others, even if prepared to do so. However, ambiguity can also arise for political reasons. For example, there may be perceived self-interest in not giving clarifying information to others, and furthermore, ambiguity may provide a political opportunity, a 'chance to carry through one's own will', because you may be able to persuade others that ambiguous phenomena mean what it best suits your interests that they mean. For example, ambiguity about which criteria will be applied in deciding who should have funds provides an opportunity to persuade others that 'usefulness' should be an over-riding test of any project put forward, and that 'useful' means of immediate applicability in commerce or industry, so that your technological project can have a good chance of being successful. Thus the attachment of particular meanings to ambiguous abstract concepts can be seen as a political process, as it serves the interest of particular individuals and groups, and disadvantages others,

One aspect of the culture which could be seen as related to other perceived characteristics such as the structure, the power of individuals, and to the flow of information already discussed, was the way in which conflicts of interest were dealt with, in the eyes of any informants.

Much of the data revealed two main ways in which people were seen as interacting with their colleagues; the high profile and low profile approaches, or 'the gently, gently' and the 'nasty' as one informant put it. The balance, however, was strongly in favour of the low-key approach, and there seemed considerable reluctance to use a forceful style of interaction. This was re-flected in the kinds of words people used to describe disagreements, or deal with sensitive issues. For example: 'Somewhere in the papers you'll find that Abbott "thinks it unlikely that" these students will get awards—which means they won't. But you don't say that in the College directly.' I was also told that 'People would be surprised if 90 per cent of the awards went to one department'—'surprised,' not 'angry', as they would undoubtedly have been. It was also reported that if a committee had been very critical of the decision of another group, the minutes would record only their 'disappointment' with the group's decision. From a political point of view, it would clearly be important to be aware of the existence and meaning of this local dialect.

My informants, however, did not all agree on who was adopting which style of behaviour. For example, of those who related style of interaction with subject specialisms, one commented: 'Among engineers one is expected to use very direct speech. It is a game. In the arts subjects the tradition of understatement is quite strong. In technology we tend to be blunt. In the Committee my arts colleagues tend to think I'm being bloody-minded.' But a scientist gave a different view of arts people, and spoke of them (with disapproval) as being 'more argumentative and ill-disciplined'.

Reasons given for one style rather than another being used were also varied. It was suggested that the low-profile approach was best so as not to strain relationships in a small community; to avoid the unpleasantness in-volved in contention; because 'nasty' behaviour was counter-productive for getting your way: 'If you put your head down and charge it won't get you anywhere. It is a political situation'. It is interesting to note here that coercive behaviour is not seen as 'political'. Some people deplored the absence of forcefulness in interaction, and some put it down to personality: 'the person-alities at the moment won't push. They like things to be calm. The people on the Committee don't want tensions'. Another person suggested that high-profile behaviour was more effective in getting your own way: 'You have to make yourself heard' and 'theatrical gestures are very useful'. Also, I was told that, because the group was small, far from inhibiting forcefulness, it made it possible: 'We know each other sufficiently well to disagree quite forcefully'. However an interactive style could rather depend on one's own power position and with whom one was dealing. A junior academic com-mented, 'you can blacken your name if you remonstrate with them' referring to more senior staff, so that unless you were sure of winning your point it was better to keep quiet.

The data also showed a number of ways in which the structure of the organization influenced or reinforced the culture in enabling direct conflicts to be avoided. I was told, for example, that the purpose of the hierarchy of committees was to prevent conflicts, not to resolve them. The other side of this coin was shown by an informant who complained that he could not get an issue important to him dealt with because the committee system prevented him from meeting his protagonists personally to argue his case. It was also said that some committees delegated contentious issues to higher levels, so that friendly relationships with their immediate colleagues could be preserved.

It has already been pointed out in the section on powerful people that it could matter what values were held by the head of department and the choice that person made about how to interact with subordinates. In view of that and of the discussion in this section, it might be suggested that the organization had not one culture, but a collection of mini-cultures, some similar and some dissimilar. Any one person's view of 'the culture' would depend on his or her identity with any one mini-culture and extent of interaction with other individuals and groups.

CONCLUSION

I have attempted in this chapter to provide an overview of a research project in which perceptions of power of organization members were investigated during decision-making processes. I hope that I have given some indication of the variety of ways in which people may perceive and think about (if they do) the politics of their situation, both in considering who has how much power, and such politically relevant contextual factors as culture and structure. It can be said that people in this study varied in the level of their awareness of what might be considered 'political' in their situation, and in so far as they appeared to think consciously in political terms, they tended to reserve the concepts of 'power' and 'political' for a rather limited range of phenomena. It could also be suggested that perceived characteristics of the culture and structure of the organization reduced the possibility that differences of perception would be confronted, and hence affected the level of awareness in individuals of political considerations.

The research suggested that when the focus of attention is on the perceptions of organization members, rather than on the perceptions of the researcher (although these can never be entirely excluded), a far from unequivocal picture of the organization emerges, with evidently no right of way of interpreting events or their context. I have come to the conclusion that ambiguity in organizational behaviour deserves further attention, particularly in its role in creating political opportunity—'the chance to carry through one's own will. . .' and in the subtle shifts it can allow people to make in the meaning of events, to serve their pragmatic and/or psychological interests.

REFERENCES

Dearlove, J. (1973). *The Politics of Policy in Local Government*, Cambridge: Cambridge University Press.

Glaser, B. G. and Strauss, A. L. (1967). *The Discovery of Grounded Theory*, New York. Aldine Press; Glaser, B. G. (1978). *Theoretical Sensitivity: Advances in the Methodology of Grounded Theory*, California: Sociology Press.

Mangham, I. (1979). *The Politics of Organizational Change*, London: Associated Business Press.

March, J. G. and Olsen, J. P. (1976). *Ambiguity and Choice in Organizations*, Bergen: Universitetsforlaget.

Pettigrew, A. (1973). *The Politics of Organizational Decision Making*, London: Tavistock.

Walliman, I., Rosenbaum, H., Tatsis, N., and Zito, G. (1980). Misreading Weber: The concept of 'Macht', *Sociology*, **14** (2).

Author Index

219

Subject Index

A–B Model of Power, 22–29
  asymmetry of A's and B's perceptions
    of the event, 24, 25, 26, 27, 28,
    34, 40
  B's acceptance of the context and
    costs to him, 28, 33
  B's motivation and, 28
  B's perception of A's behaviour, 25,
    26, 27, 28, 40
  B's psychological costs of complying
    with A, 27, 28, 35, 36
  distinction between power, control,
    influence and authority, 22, 23,
    24, 25
  in organizational politics, 28
  perception of political activity, 40
  power as a characteristic of A, 26, 27,
    28
  power as relationship between A and
    B, 26, 27, 28, 29
  prerequisites for, 22, 23, 24, 25, 26,
    27, 28, 40
  resistance to the power of A, 34
Abilities vs. power, 31
Acceptance of the power of a powerful
  other, 27, 28, 29, 34, 36, 37, 40
Accountability of multi-national
  corporations concern over, 66
Action sociology of organizations, 78
Actor permeability, strategy lever in
  SPC, 142, 143
Administration, purpose of, 116, 123,
  124
Administrative power, 114, 115, 116,
  117, 123, 124
Agentic tendencies and ecology of
  influences, 149, 150

Altruism, 37, 38
Ambiguity and political behaviour, 94,
  95, 214
Analogic communication, 161, 162, 163
Analogic power, 147, 161–166
  case-study of, 164, 165, 166
Analysis, unit of appropriate to
  organizations, 93
Anthropomorphic view of
  organizations, 73, 74, 80
Applicability of OD, doubts as to the,
  66
Association networks, cognitive, 96
Asymmetry of the power-relationship,
  13, 188
Attribution theory, 41
Authority based on legitimacy, 32, 33,
  34, 35, 40, 41, 49
  based on types of values, traditional,
    legal-rational, and charismatic,
    33
  changes in attitudes towards, 47
  and coercion, 32, 33, 36, 37
  influence and power, related to
    control, 148, 150, 151
  vs. power, 22, 23, 27, 28, 29, 30, 32,
    33, 36, 37, 41
  values and power, 32, 33, 34, 35, 37
Autonomy, valuing of, 36, 37

Behaviour, cognitive-competences and
  perception-enactment model of,
  96–101, 103, 104
  cognitive model of, 88, 96–101, 103,
    104
  critique of determinist accounts, 72,
    73

225

Policy preferences in organizations,
91–92
Political activity and change in
organizations, 82, 87
factors giving rise to, in organizations,
31, 32, 37
Political appreciation of organizational
life, OD's need for, 65, 66, 69, 72,
73, 74, 75, 76, 87, 128
Political behaviour, ambiguity and, 94,
95, 214
cognitive analysis of, 98
at the group level, 89
organizational psychology and the
analysis of, 87
relation of preferred behavioural
strategies to norms and values,
87, 88
Political dimension of organizational
life, consequences of ignoring, 73,
74, 75, 76, 87, 88
Political model of organizations *vs.* self-
actualization model, 69, 70, 72, 73,
74
Political naïvety of writers on
organizational change, 147
Political nature of behaviour, 24, 37, 38,
40
of boundary management, 90, 91
Political processes in organizations,
OD's neglect of, 74, 75, 76, 77, 128
Political structure of organizational and
division of labour, 30, 31
socialization and, 32, 36
Political systems, organizations as, 69,
72, 73, 74
Politics, educational, 115
institutional, 109, 115, 118–122,
203–216
inter-consultant and OD, 78, 79
Politics, of intervention, 78, 90, 92, 101,
171, 172, 198
Politics, membership of an organization
and, 113, 114
micro-, 111, 112
of organizational values, 117, 118,
119–123
perceived, 203
power, 93, 113
vs. power, 95, 113
social psychologists' view of, 148

structures and organizations, 30, 31
trust, 111
Potential power, 27, 147
and roles of consultants, 147, 150
Power, A–B model of, 22–29
acquisition and strategic use of, 147,
150, 151, 166
administrative, 114, 115, 116, 117,
123, 124
analogic, 147, 140, 161–166
analogic, case-study of, 164, 165, 166
asymmetry of dependence and, 26, 33,
35, 37
as an attribute of social actors,
problems with, 75
vs. authority, 22, 23, 27, 28, 29, 30,
32, 35, 36, 37, 41
boundaries to social, 7–8
as a casual construct, 3, 12–15
as a characteristic of the individual, 3,
4–7
vs. coercion, 22, 23, 24, 32
collusive, 147, 150, 151–152
case-study of, 160, 161
commodity, 3, 10–12, 92, 93
community development theorists'
view of, 93
control and, 22, 23, 24, 27, 36, 37
culture and asymmetry of power
relationship, 188
Cormorant case-study, and,
190–196
possibilities in for OD, 185, 186,
188–189, 190–196, 196–201
reality-defining and, 187–188, 189,
190, 197
as defined in the legitimacy cycle, 49,
50
differential distribution of, 25, 29, 33,
34, 35, 36, 37, 92, 93
as an ecology of influences and
dependencies, 149
in educational institutions, case-
studies of, 119–122, 203–216
an emergent property of a
relationship, 147
environmental *vs.* interpersonal
interaction, 5–7
epistemological limitations to an
understanding of, 148, 149
field-study of perceived, 203–216